CORPORATE IMPERIALISM:
CONFLICT
AND EXPROPRIATION

CORPORATE IMPERIALISM: CONFLICT AND EXPROPRIATION

TRANSNATIONAL CORPORATIONS
AND ECONOMIC NATIONALISM
IN THE THIRD WORLD

NORMAN GIRVAN

Routledge
Taylor & Francis Group

LONDON AND NEW YORK

First published 1976 by M.E. Sharpe

Reissued 2018 by Routledge
4 Park Square, Milton Park, Abingdon, Oxon OX14 4RN
605 Third Avenue, New York, NY 10017

First issued in paperback 2022

Routledge is an imprint of the Taylor & Francis Group, an informa business

A Library of Congress record exists under LC control number: 75046112

ISBN 13: 978-1-03-247673-5 (pbk)
ISBN 13: 978-0-87332-073-3 (hbk)
ISBN 13: 978-1-315-17887-5 (ebk)

CONTENTS

ACKNOWLEDGMENTS

These essays are based on research and publications undertaken over the last ten years, and they have therefore benefited from contributions by a considerable number of institutions and individuals. The principal institutions providing time, facilities, and resources have been the Institute of Social and Economic Research of the University of the West Indies, the Institute of International Studies of the University of Chile, the Ford Foundation, the Economic Growth Center of Yale University, and the African Institute of Development and Planning.

It would be difficult to name all the individuals who have stimulated and influenced my thinking on the subject matter of these essays over the years, but special mention should be made of George Beckford, Clive Thomas, Vaughan Lewis, Louis Lindsay, Lloyd Best, Kari Levitt, Osvaldo Sunkel, and Samir Amin. Finally, posthumous acknowledgment should be made to four persons, all of whom, in one way or another, have a stake in these essays: the late Fred Ablin of International Arts and Sciences Press, who needled, cajoled, and finally persuaded me to prepare them in book form; the late Stephen Hymer of the New School for Social Research and Gyorgy Adám of the Hungarian Academy of Sciences, both distinguished thinkers on the transnational corporation; and the late President Salvador Allende of Chile, who died in the cause.

CORPORATE IMPERIALISM: CONFLICT AND EXPROPRIATION

INTRODUCTION

The anticolonial revolution of the 1950s challenged the edifice of political imperialism established by the European powers in the nineteenth century. In the 1970s another revolution appears to be sweeping the Third World, a movement which seeks to challenge the new imperialism of the transnational corporations (TNCs) established in the twentieth century. On the morrow of political independence, it seemed, the underdeveloped countries accepted the role that imperial companies played in their economic life, especially in their natural resource industries. Now this has radically changed. State participation, expropriation, and the activities of OPEC and other associations of primary producing countries have rudely disrupted an international political economy based on the hegemony of the developed capitalist countries and their giant corporations. A state of continual tension and conflict characterizes this area of international economic relations.

These essays, written explicitly from a Third World perspective, suggest that conflict between Third World states and transnational corporations in natural resource industries is an inherent and dialectical result of a system of corporate imperialism. Rather than constituting unfortunate episodes that can be handled by adroit management and "rational" behavior, such conflict should be seen as the manifestation of profound antagonisms among groups within the international capitalist order. These antagonisms are generated by the patterns of domination and exploitation, subordination and dependent underdevelopment, resulting from the strategies pursued and the structures adopted by global companies. The first essay sets out and documents the general thesis, while the second, third, and fourth develop different aspects of it with reference to the experience of the copper industry in Chile and the bauxite industries of Caribbean countries. The last two essays suggest ways

3

of improving the efficacy of Third World action in developing truly indigenous policies for the development of their resource industries, especially from the point of view of the needs of the mass of their people, and in expropriating transnational corporations.

Much of the analysis in the essays is historical, placing contemporary events in the context of the development of company-state relationships since the turn of the nineteenth century. And while the essays record the real progress which Third World states have been making in changing the balance of power, they also indicate many of the limitations. Thus essay 1 suggests that the momentum of nationalization of resource industries by Third World states can be motivated as much by the wish to pursue a model of dependent growth as by a perceived need to supersede it. Moreover, one of the conclusions of essay 3 is that the objective of the Caribbean bauxite offensive of 1974 was not to transform the system of corporate imperialism in the international aluminum industry but rather to redefine the relative status and power of the bauxite-producing states within it. And essays 2 and 4 show how the thrust of nationalization by such states can be blunted — or even reversed — by the formidable battery of economic, political, and military pressures that the transnational companies and their home governments can mobilize.

Notwithstanding these limitations, there is no underestimating the determination of Third World states to change the international economic order, at least insofar as it relates to the role of transnationals in their resource industries, and to exercise sovereignty over their natural resources. The apparent success of OPEC's bid to exercise power in the international crude oil market, the attempts by other groups of primary producing nations to imitate it, the continuing spread of state participation in resource industries, and the rapid development of intergovernmental industrial cooperation projects in the Third World all pose a number of important questions. Is there any place left for the transnationals in the resource industries? Are we in fact witnessing a fundamental shift toward the Third World in the balance of power? How significant are the new developments, in substance as distinct from form?

If the depth of the movement of Third World economic nationalism should not be underestimated, neither should the pace and intensity of the process of concentration and centralization of capital on a global scale in the contemporary age. The significance of the transnational corporation is the emergence of monopoly capital on

4

a world scale: a large and growing share of world output is falling under the control of "a few hundred technically dynamic, massively capitalized and highly organized corporations."[1] By the beginning of the 1970s these "juggernauts"[2] controlled some one-fifth of the capitalist world's GNP; since their rate of growth is about double that of non-TNC output in the capitalist world there is every indication that they will continue to increase their dominance over other forms of business organization and their preeminent role in the world capitalist economy. One apologist of the new system frankly envisages that within a generation some 400 to 500 TNCs will own roughly two-thirds of the fixed assets of the entire globe.[3]

At the same time, it should be noted that the process of internationalization of capital has had a marked sectoral and geographical bias. The rapid spread of transnational corporations has been associated mainly with investment in manufacturing, technology-intensive, and durable-goods industries, and it has been concentrated principally within the developed capitalist economies themselves. Whereas at the outbreak of the First World War the bulk of international investment was found in primary producing activities and associated infrastructure, today that share has fallen to 36 percent, of which oil accounts for the majority share; and some two-thirds of all foreign investment today is within the developed world.[4] On the face of it, the Third World and its resource industries have become less and less important to the operations of international capital; the economic nationalism of the region has emerged too late to make any significant dent in the structure of the world capitalist system and the dynamic of its development.

What then, we may well ask, is all the fuss about? Why has the issue of OPEC behavior and associated questions of the availability of raw materials become so important and controversial in international affairs? Partly because the quantitative data tend to underestimate the qualitative importance of resource materials to the continuing industrial growth of the advanced economies. This importance has been sharply and dramatically manifested in the case of oil in recent years; but the growing fears of long-term shortages of many other strategic materials has brought home to the advanced industrial nations the extent to which their continued growth depends on the utilization of nonrenewable natural resources.[5] Thus, whereas the Third World's resource industries have declined in importance as a direct outlet for the investment capital of the capitalist centers and as a basis for direct incremental profit generation and capital accumulation, their indirect importance to the process of capitalist accumulation remains significant and may even be increasing. To be sure, such developments have stimulated the advanced capitalist countries to accelerate their technological efforts to develop synthetic substitutes for natural materials, such as nuclear energy, and to exploit the seabed — efforts which in the medium to long run may result in a marked structural decline in dependence on the natural resources of the Third World. But in the short to medium run, much of the Third World remains indispensable, through its supplying of natural materials, to the maintenance and growth of economic activity in the capitalist centers.

It is this fact, of course, that has created certain strategic possibilities for the successful assertion of Third World economic nationalism and has given it great significance in terms of the international economic order. But this perverse development — the falling quantitative importance of Third World resource industries coupled with their continuing or rising qualitative importance — also creates opportunities for the cooptation of economic nationalism into the international capitalist order. The difficulty of identifying consistent trends in developments over the last few years, especially since 1973, is due to the bewildering array of crosscurrents generated by the efforts of different actors on the world stage — governments in both the developed and the underdeveloped world as well as corporations — to preserve existing positions of privilege or to define new positions of enhanced power within any new set of arrangements that might emerge from a restructuring of the international order.[6]

Cooptation of economic nationalism involves developing a new and enhanced role for the Third World state in the resource industries. Previously limited to the provision of infrastructure for the benefit of the corporations, which was paid for ultimately by the population, the state's functions can be expanded to embrace formal ownership, provision of capital, and administration of the labor force. State ownership, once viewed with abhorrence by the leading capitalist nations and by the transnationals, can indeed be made to have its advantages. Third World governments may now be made to assume the full risks of fluctuations in primary product markets, especially if the "downstream" facilities such as transport, refining, and marketing, which are necessary to iron out fluctuations, remain in the hands of the companies. The governments become responsible for supplying or raising the considerable amounts of capital required for expansion, an expansion which serves the objective requirements of the center countries. The governments now have an even stronger interest in policing and pacifying the labor force, since it is the direct recipient of the cash flows generated by the industry. Moreover, the transnationals concerned can usually replace the business they lose by ceding partial or complete ownership of the resource industry to the government through signing new and lucrative contracts for the sale of managerial, technical, and marketing services to the nationalized enterprises.

Corresponding to the new role of the state is a new model of dependent industrialization which is represented by the kind of developments that have been taking place in countries such as Iran, Saudi Arabia, and Nigeria since 1973. Large, capital- and technology-intensive projects are initiated in activities such as natural gas liquefaction, petrochemicals, and nuclear power, with the government putting up the capital in partnership with some of the largest transnationals, which supply the technology. Developments of this kind imply that industrialization will be extended to embrace heavy industries of a type from which most underdeveloped countries had previously been excluded. However, they evidently do little to solve the problems of rural underdevelopment and unemployment that form the basis of mass poverty; neither do they contribute to the achievement of a self-centered development model. Indeed, since the technology, capital equipment, and much of the operating inputs are usually imported, these developments imply the emergence of new and stronger linkages with the capitalist centers. But this model of dependent industrialization corresponds to the class interests of the local state bureaucracy, since, in conjunction with state participation in the resource industry, it creates substantial new opportunities for the employment of high-level technical, professional, and administrative cadres.[7]

To become functional, however, cooptation of economic nationalism along these lines requires a new set of political and class alliances to replace those that corresponded to the old international division of labor. It also needs to have a new legitimizing ideology. It is here that the greatest difficulties arise. The demand for a new international economic order,[8] which represents the ideological offensive of the Third World, is viewed with apprehension by those in the developed world who perceive that they stand to lose from the restructuring of international prices and power relations that would be entailed. For it is not only an improvement in the terms of trade between center and periphery that the Third World is seeking: it is a position of greater equality in economic relationships among states. It is this position that the OPEC countries have seized, and that some of them, particularly Algeria, are demanding for the Third World as a whole. Accommodation to these demands implies a reduction in the international economic power of the developed capitalist countries; indeed, such a reduction has already taken place, if only to a limited degree, in relation to the OPEC countries. The process is complicated by the existence of rivalries among the capitalist centers and especially by the decline in U.S. industrial and financial preeminence in relation to Western Europe and Japan. Further complications are provided by the process of U.S.-Soviet détente and Sino-Soviet antagonism. Thus there is naturally little, if any, agreement as to how the demands of the Third World will be dealt with: whether they will be acceded to, if so to what extent, who will pay, and who will lose and by how much. At the level of interstate relations, the fate of the demand for a new international economic order is very much an open question.

At the same time, it is difficult to interpret this demand as an assault on what we have called the system of corporate imperialism. There is no evidence that Third World states as a whole are seeking to reverse the process of concentration of private capital on a world scale, or that they wish to liquidate the role of the transnationals as the principal instruments of the international transfer of capital and technology. They have asserted the principle of permanent sovereignty over natural resources — a demand to which, we have suggested, the corporations can accede without great difficulty. They have also demanded "regulation" of the activities of transnationals.[9] Notwithstanding the loud protests of corporate executives, it is this writer's view that international "regulation" represents no objective, long-term threat to the growth of the world corporate system. Regulation in the developed capitalist countries since the rise of monopolies, and especially since the 1930s depression, has in fact been accompanied by the most extraordinary growth of concentration and corporate power in the history of capitalism. This is partly because regulation is notoriously difficult to police, as the fate of antitrust legislation in the United States eloquently demonstrates.

But the reasons go far beyond that. The fact is that the corporations have largely succeeded in establishing an ideology which identifies the goals of the corporate system with the public interest; anything that might frustrate its growth or presumed efficiency is made to appear as an obstacle to progress. Furthermore, the effectiveness of regulation cannot be divorced from the nature of the political system which gives rise to it. Where private capital has enormous influence and leverage over the governmental apparatus, regulation, if it has any meaning at all, in fact implies regulation of the state's treatment of the corporate sector: the systematization of direct and indirect government subsidies to the corporations and of legislative, administrative, and judicial treatment of them. Such regulation is an enormous asset to the corporations since it gives them the stability that makes it possible for them to plan with certainty. In this context the concept of regulation also has an ideological function: it serves to lull the public into a false sense of complacency that corporate behavior is being regulated in the public interest. Given the extent to which the corporations are regarded as the harbingers of advanced technology by the developed countries, by the Third World, and by many of the socialist countries, it is an open question whether international regulation will result in anything more than a transfer of the experience of national regulation to the international plane.

What is required is not regulation of the system, but rather its subversion. This certainly entails asserting sovereignty over natural resources by depriving the corporations of their property in these industries. It also involves the kind of genuinely revolutionary socialist change that alone can cut off the corporations' bases of politicoeconomic support within Third World countries and reorient economic life in the interests of the mass of the population. Beyond that, it requires an ideological transformation: the development of a consciousness of alternative development models and ways of life within which what the transnationals have to offer is defined as irrelevant, possibly even harmful.

These essays have focused on conflict between the transnational corporations and the nation-state in the Third World because of a recognition that such conflict constitutes one of the most important sources of contradiction in the contemporary world capitalist order. Resolving these contradictions is a necessary step — though only a partial one — toward the changes needed to secure a better life for the wretched of the earth.

Notes

1. J. K. Galbraith, The New Industrial State (New York: Mentor, 1968), p. 21. Galbraith deals with the corporations as a national phenomenon, but many of his

points remain valid when transposed to the international scale.

2. So called by one who has spent much of his life working in senior positions in such companies. See Graham Bannock, The Juggernauts (London: Pelican, 1973).

3. A. Barber, "Emerging New World Power: The World Corporation," War/Peace Report, October 1968, p. 7. For a useful collection of essays on various aspects of the transnational corporation, see H. Radice (ed.), International Firms and Modern Imperialism (London: Penguin, 1975).

4. United Nations, Multinational Corporations in World Development (New York, 1973), pp. 8-12.

5. See, for example, C. Fred Bergsten, "The Threat from the Third World," Foreign Policy, No. 11, Summer 1973: "The Threat Is Real," Foreign Policy, No. 14, Spring 1974.

6. Vaughan Lewis, "World Politics, the Petroleum Crisis and the Underdeveloped World," in Review of the National Savings Committee (Kingston, 1975).

7. Some of these points are developed further in N. Girvan, "Economic Nationalists vs. Multinational Corporations: Revolutionary or Evolutionary Change?" in Multinational Firms in Africa, ed. by S. Amin and C. Widstrand (Uppsala: Scandinavian Institute of African Studies, 1975).

8. See Fourth Conference of Heads of State or Governments of Non-Aligned Countries, Algiers, September 5-9, 1973, Fundamental Texts: Declarations, Resolutions, Action Programme For Economic Cooperation; and United Nations, General Assembly, Programme of Action on the Establishment of a New International Economic Order, 6th spec. sess., May 16, 1974.

9. See United Nations, Economic and Social Council, Commission on Transnational Corporations, Areas of Concern Which Could Be Used as a Basis for Preliminary Work for a Code of Conduct to be Observed by Transnational Corporations, E/C/10/1.2, April 14, 1975; also United Nations, Economic and Social Council, Commission on Transnational Corporations, Report on the First Session (17-28 March 1975), Official Records, 59th sess.

CORPORATE IMPERIALISM IN MINERAL-EXPORT ECONOMIES

1

In mineral-export economies, economic life is structured around the production and export of mineral products. Typically, in such economies the mineral-export industry provides the bulk of foreign exchange receipts and government revenue; and the imports and government expenditures financed by these flows are critical to the maintenance and growth of income and employment. Countries with economies of this kind include the oil-producing states of the Middle East, North and Central Africa, Latin America, and Asia; the copper-exporting nations of Latin America, Africa, and the Pacific; and exporters of bauxite, iron ore, gold, and diamonds in West Africa and the Caribbean. The problem posed is that, in spite of the supposedly favorable conditions for economic development represented by the resource flows from the mineral industry, these economies remain both structurally under-developed and externally dependent. Furthermore, conflict between their governments and the large transnational firms that produce and market the mineral products appears to be continuous and increasing.

Dependence, underdevelopment, and endemic conflict are related to the integration of these economies into a system of corporate imperialism. By corporate imperialism, we mean a system of international capitalism that has two basic characteristics. First, fundamental power in this world system is held by the owners and managers of capital, who exercise this power over other groups and institutions in order to appropriate surpluses and accumulate further capital. These other groups — governmental bureaucracies, workers, peasants, the unemployed — are to a greater or lesser degree dominated, dependent, exploited, and underdeveloped. The second crucial feature is that these relationships are institutionalized within the framework of large, integrated, transnational corporations. The TNCs as a group constitute the institutional base of the system; individually, they are its principal instruments of action. The hierarchy of roles and the network of dominance/dependency relationships within the individual corporation are a microcosm of the roles and relationships within the total system of corporate imperialism; and the corporations' self-proclaimed goals of "profitability and growth" represent the system's objectives of surplus appropriation and capital accumulation. Both the dependency of the mineral-export economy and its persistent structural underdevelopment can be fruitfully analyzed by reference to the economic processes and power relationships within the contemporary transnational corporation.

Within this framework, conflict between the governments of mineral-export economies and the corporations is seen to be structured around three main issues. One is related to the division between company and government of the total surplus generated by the industry, that is, the revenue issue. Another arises at a more sophisticated level, when the government wishes to use the mineral industry as the basis for constructing an authentically national economic system — an objective that conflicts with the existing integration of the industry into the corporate economic system. The third issue is the issue of power itself — that is, it concerns the revolt of the government against its dependent and subordinated role. The power issue normally arises as a result of conflicts generated over the division of the surplus and use of the resource and may in fact be inseparable from these first two issues. The actions of the governments, reactions by the companies, and further responses of the governments form a continuous dialectic that gives rise to modifications in the form, but not necessarily the essence, of the system of corporate imperialism.

The analysis in this essay is based on research on the petroleum, aluminum, and copper industries in the Caribbean, Latin America, and North America. However, we believe that these cases are sufficiently representative to have more general applicability to other industries and areas.

I. TRANSNATIONAL MONOPOLY CAPITALISM

The Emergence of Monopoly Capital

The emergence of monopoly capitalism in the petroleum, copper, and aluminum industries was marked by a number of characteristics common to all three.[1] First, it was associated with rapid technological change in the last quarter of the nineteenth century in the central capitalist countries, particularly in the United States. Such technological change had the effect of establishing these industries on a large scale; they produced essential inputs for the expanding industrial system and enjoyed a high rate of growth. Before this time, while oil, copper, and aluminum were produced, this production took place on a very small scale and at high cost, and was based largely on rich and easily worked deposits of the basic material, such as surface seepages of oil and deposits of high-grade copper ores. Between the 1860s and 1900, however, a revolution in production technology took place which made available supplies that were not only quantitatively greater but qualitatively different. The development of drilling techniques enabled subterranean oil to be brought to the surface; induced changes in the technology of refining and new methods of transport made it possible to move oil over long distances. Ores that contained so little copper that they were once considered worthless were brought into production by changes in the technology of mining and refining. Aluminum metal began to be produced in commercial quantities for the first time.

The changes on the supply side were partly the cause and partly the effect of changes on the demand side, in which technology also played an important part. In oil and aluminum, it was the breakthroughs in the technology of production in the 1850s and 1880s, respectively, that stimulated new uses and the search for new markets; in copper, the rapid growth of demand for wire resulting from the emergence of the electricity industry in the 1880s sparked the drive to mine and treat low-grade ores on a large scale. Subsequently, technical changes on both the demand and the supply side interacted with cumulative effects. Thus, the automobile revolution in the early 1900s created explosive growth in demands for the products of all three industries, and this induced further technical changes on the supply side.

Accompanying these changes was a revolution in economic organization which was no less significant. By the early 1900s, the large number of small, single-stage, local firms in the petroleum and copper industries had been displaced by a small number of large, vertically integrated firms, national in scope and with oligopolistic market control. In aluminum, monopoly of metal production was a feature of the industry from the outset because of Alcoa's acquisition of the patent rights, and the company soon set about integrating itself backward into raw material extraction and forward into fabrication.

It appears that the emergence of the integrated, oligopolistic firm was an inherent and possibly indispensable part of the revolution that took place in the scale of production and demand, in the level of technology, and in the quantity of capital utilized in production. With much more capital committed to production on a much larger scale, firms had to minimize the risks of investment and make sure that their facilities operated at full capacity by acquiring their own raw materials supplies and market outlets. All stages of production and marketing had to be brought as far as possible within the bounds of corporate control. Those firms that got a head start because of strategic control over one stage of the industry or over production technology, because of capitalistic foresight and initiative, or because of a combination of all three, were able, in one way or another, to absorb the weaker and more vulnerable firms. This process continued until a small number of large firms faced one another, each with its own supplies of raw materials and its own market outlets. At that point, they discovered that their competitive struggles could be profitably diluted with collusive market control, that is, cartel arrangements to maintain prices and profits by restraining output. What usually set the limit on the entry of firms or provided the opportunities for new entrants was the scarcity or availability of the natural resources indispensable for profitable production. Thus, the discovery of new copper deposits in Montana in the 1800s provided the basis for the new Anaconda Company to break the control of the Lake Michigan producing pool; the discovery of the Texas oil fields at the turn of the century made it possible for the Texas Company and Gulf Oil to challenge the hegemony of Standard Oil. In contrast, Alcoa's control of bauxite deposits and hydroelectric resources helped effectively to prevent the entry of new companies into the United States industry until after World War II, when Jamaican deposits began to be used by Reynolds and Kaiser.

Another important factor underlying the change in the nature and scope of economic organization was the emergence of national mar-

kets in the central capitalist countries to displace the small, unintegrated local markets that had previously existed. In large
part, this was due to the revolution in transport, especially the
emergence of the railway, in the context of rapidly growing urban
incomes. These changes meant that the typical firm had to attain
national size — in the case of the United States, continental size —
in order to compete. Its marketing outlets had to be established
accordingly. For a similar reason, it had to seek out and acquire
within its home countries as much as possible of the reserves of
the raw materials and ancillary resources needed to produce them.
This was and is necessary not only to ensure long-term supplies
for a firm's refineries and fabricators, but also, and no less importantly, to reduce the actual and potential availability of these
supplies to its competitors. This gave rise to the frequently observed phenomenon of firms' acquiring and holding raw material
reserves far in excess of their prospective needs for decades to
come.

The Transnationalization of Monopoly Capital

The process by which the typical firm established marketing outlets and raw materials facilities in foreign countries was a logical
extension of the process by which it became vertically integrated
in structure and national in scope. As the market became international, the firms came into competition with firms from other
central countries that had also undergone the process of national
vertical integration. Metropolitan firms therefore began to compete with each other on each other's own home ground as well as
to compete for the markets and the raw materials of the peripheral
countries.

Hence, marketing subsidiaries and later refineries were set up
by American oil companies in Europe and by European companies
in America after the First World War. A French firm tried (and
failed) to penetrate Alcoa's preserve — the U.S. market — in the
second decade of the century. Subsequently, the American firm, in
turn, reached out to acquire hydroelectric power sites and aluminum-smelting facilities in France and Norway; it had already secured a large slice of Canada's hydroelectric power potential. On
the raw materials side, the American copper companies had secured control of all the important copper reserves of Chile and
Mexico by 1920. Congolese and Zambian copper was to be incorporated into the productive apparatus of English and European

companies. Alcoa's control of the important bauxite deposits of
Surinam and Guyana was also complete by 1920. American and
Anglo-Dutch firms fought spiritedly for Mexican oil at the turn of
the nineteenth century; in the 1920s, the battleground shifted to
Venezuela and the Middle East.

By the 1930s at the latest, the present-day pattern of transna-
tional-corporate ownership of these three mineral resource industries in the American periphery had been set. Chile's copper was
vertically integrated with the facilities of Anaconda and Kennecott,
Surinam's and Guyana's bauxite with the facilities of the Alcoa-
Aluminium, Limited, complex; most of Venezuela's oil formed part
of the transnational organizations of Jersey Standard (now Exxon),
Shell, Gulf, and Texaco. Subsequently, Jamaica's bauxite was
secured to the needs of Alcan Aluminium, Limited, Reynolds
Metals, and Kaiser Aluminum.

Growth, Development, and Resource Allocation of the Transnational Firm

It goes without saying that the process of the continued
growth and development of the transnational firm involves all
the dimensions of activity already outlined; that is, the continued drive for new markets and new raw materials reserves,
and the continued rounding out and extending of its integrated
structure. The institutionalization of research and development
for the reduction of costs and for product innovation is of course a
vital part of this process. Of particular importance to the present
analysis are two aspects of the firm's growth process: (a) how it
allocates its necessary raw materials production between different
raw-materials-producing subsidiaries; (b) how it allocates its production, financial, and research resources between different end
products. Both processes, as will subsequently be shown, have an
important influence on the determination of the level of output in
the mineral-export industry of the peripheral countries in the short,
medium, and long term.

Raw materials. Intuitively, it can be assumed that the first factor taken into account in determining the distribution of production
between raw materials subsidiaries is the structure of relative
costs (including taxes) in the different subsidiaries. Other things
being equal, we would expect the company to allocate its raw materials production so that the sum total of "tax paid" costs of all
subsidiaries represents the least costly way of obtaining the sum

total of the raw materials it needs to support its end-product output. Other things, of course, are usually unequal — so much so that one has to take explicit account of other factors in an abstract analysis if one is to hope to understand the actual raw materials policies of the firms.

The most important qualification to the least-cost rule arises out of certain factors that place a positive value on the firm's maintenance of a fairly wide geopolitical spread of raw materials supplies. Usually these factors involve the actions of national governments. Some supply sources are given preferential access to some markets because of neomercantilist policies (e.g., American oil on the American market). In most countries, the firms must develop and maintain some acceptable level of production of the resource as a condition of securing and keeping resource concessions. And there are differences — frequently wide differences — between the degree of political risks in different countries.

Such factors limit, but do not destroy, the operation of the least-cost principle. In the standard pattern, the firms maintain a certain geopolitical spread of raw materials production and, over time, allocate the bulk of incremental production to one or a small number of particular low-cost sources as their raw materials needs grow. At the same time, the firms are constantly seeking new sources of raw materials in order to widen their options, reduce their competitors' options, and displace depleted sources. The logic of this is that the firms' planning must include the planned displacement of any existing source of supply, including (and, for some reasons, especially) each one located in every peripheral country.

The planned displacement of each source operates both on the level of the firm's actual intentions and on the level of its contingency planning. Any given source may be abruptly lost to the firm because of a change in government policy, expropriation, war, or other such acts of men, which the firm might well put in the same category as "acts of God." Thus, there must be a contingency plan for such unforeseen developments. For some particular sources, the rate of extraction is relatively high because incremental production is being located there, and the firm must actively plan for that more or less foreseeable point in the future when it will locate incremental production at some other source or set of sources. The most important pressures giving rise to such a shift are the depletion of high-grade or easily extracted reserves of the natural resource and the associated growth in extraction costs, and the

17

growth of the tax rate and perhaps of state intervention, as the peripheral government struggles to obtain a growing share of the large surpluses realized by the industry.

The history of the oil companies provides the most sharply defined cases of planned displacement of supply sources. American oil companies shifted incremental production from the United States to Mexico in the early twentieth century, from Mexico to Venezuela between the 1920s and 1940s, and from Venezuela to the Middle East in the 1950s and 1960s. But the copper and aluminum firms behave in analogous ways. Anaconda and Kennecott located incremental output in Chile from the 1920s to the 1940s, and then shifted back to United States sources when they got into trouble with the Chilean government. Alcoa and Alcan shifted from the United States to Guyana and Surinam for their bauxite supplies from the 1920s to the 1940s and to Jamaica and the Dominican Republic after the Second World War, and have shifted increasingly to Australia and Africa in the 1970s.

There is a striking historical analogy here between the behavior of the corporations and the behavior of the plantation economies of the New World over time. Best has noted that plantation capitalism tended to "shift terrain" — that is, incremental production — from one peripheral country to another.[2] The pressures for such shifts were (1) the exhaustion of the soil and the attraction of virgin lands in other peripheral countries; (2) the restlessness of the slave or low-wage labor force; and (3) changing patterns of metropolitan preferential trade policy. The first two are clearly analogous to the depletion of high-grade reserves and the growing interventions of the peripheral government in transnational mineral economy.

End products. The fact that any given commodity tends to experience a low-high-low growth cycle over the long run has certain important implications for the relative specialization and diversification of the firm's product mix. It is widely accepted that the goals of the corporations are long-term profitability and growth. The pursuit of these objectives appears to lead the firms to specialize in a particular commodity that is undergoing its high-growth phase and then, as its growth rate levels off or falls, to shift incremental resources out of that commodity into another which is experiencing its period of rapid growth. By such means, the firms have benefited from the high-growth phase of a particular commodity, while their growth has transcended the fate of any one commodity and embraced those of many in their high-growth phases.

18

In the oil industry, the shifts have been to jointly produced commodities. First, the companies shifted incrementally from kerosene to gasoline in the early part of the century as electric lighting displaced the kerosene lamp and as the automobile revolution created a rapidly growing market for gasoline; since 1950, they have shifted incrementally into petrochemicals as the rate of growth of demand for gasoline leveled off in the United States and the demand for petrochemicals grew rapidly. In the copper industry, the shift has been to a competing commodity: Anaconda, Revere Copper, and Kennecott all acquired stakes in the aluminum industry in the post-World War II period, as this commodity ate hungrily into the incremental market for metals. It is not difficult to recognize the reasons for these incremental choices: shifting into jointly produced commodities makes use of the firms' existing production facilities; shifting into competing commodities makes use of their existing marketing facilities.

There is more to it, however. Basic to the process of growth and displacement of commodities are the twin engines of changing technology and changing demand. The firms are themselves deeply involved in influencing these changes: their large research and development establishments are constantly developing new products based on their resources and new ways in which customers can use their products; their heavy propaganda activities are geared to expanding demand for existing and new product lines. In other words, their technological and propaganda efforts necessarily include activities designed to promote products that are jointly produced or competitive with their main product lines. By such means they help protect themselves against losses and help assure themselves of the benefits of long-term shifts in technology and/or demand that affect the entire industry.

The logic of all this is that part of any firm's planning must include the planned incremental displacement of its main product line with another one, and that there have been, in the past, periods when the firms both planned and carried out such displacements. On the basis of this, it is not surprising to learn that the oil companies have diversified broadly into alternative sources of energy, such as coal, natural gas, and uranium. One would also expect — although no evidence of this seems to have appeared so far — that some part of the planning of the aluminum firms should include a strategy for that time when the demand for plastics becomes so great as to pose a real threat to the rapid growth of the firms specializing in the white metal.

All these factors — the process of allocating output between different raw materials subsidiaries and the phenomena of planned displacement of supply source and of produced commodity — are important in the analysis of long-run output determination of the mineral-export industry in the peripheral country, as we shall subsequently see. Also, they throw interesting light on changing patterns in the use made by metropolitan capital of the resources of the peripheral world through time. Finally, they point to a recasting of the mold of theories of international trade and international investment into institutional categories that are more relevant, at least insofar as these theories relate to trade and investment in raw materials and resource products.

Power Relations and Economic Relationships
Within the Transnational Corporation

As the corporation evolves from a plant to a factory to a national corporation to a multidivisional corporation to a transnational, multidivisional corporation,[3] it must adapt the structure of its internal power relations to meet the requirements of an organizational structure that is continually changing and growing ever more complex. Every single production unit must operate at optimum efficiency. In addition, raw materials production must be smoothly coordinated with fabrication and both of these with marketing. Finance and technical services must be available to all producing functions. Finally, long-term strategies must be generated and implemented for the firm as a whole. The basic problem is how simultaneously to ensure efficiency of operations, of coordination, and of strategic decision making. The fundamental principle developed to solve it can be called that of centralization-decentralization. That is, responsibility for operations is decentralized to the level of the individual producing unit; the coordination functions are centralized for all units within a particular product line or geographic area, while they are separated from the strategic function, which is in turn centralized absolutely for the firm as a whole.[4] Four main levels of administrative positions in the model corporation are distinguished by Chandler, on the basis of his research into the strategies and structures of American enterprise: (1) the field units, responsible for specific operations; (2) the departmental headquarters, each responsible for a particular function; (3) the divisional offices, each responsible for a particular product line or geographic area; and (4) the general office, responsible for overall strategy and planning. (See Fig. 1.)

20

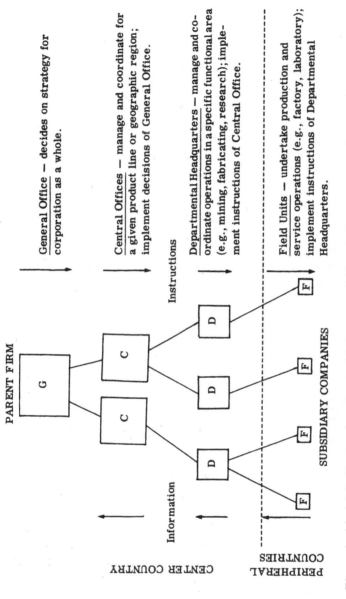

General Office — decides on strategy for corporation as a whole.

Central Offices — manage and coordinate for a given product line or geographic region; implement decisions of General Office.

Instructions

Departmental Headquarters — manage and co-ordinate operations in a specific functional area (e.g., mining, fabricating, research); imple-ment instructions of Central Office.

Field Units — undertake production and service operations (e.g., factory, laboratory); implement instructions of Departmental Headquarters.

PARENT FIRM

SUBSIDIARY COMPANIES

Information

CENTER COUNTRY

PERIPHERAL COUNTRIES

Figure 1. Administrative levels and associated power relations in the transnational corporation. (Adapted from Chandler [1962], especially pp. 11–13)

Only in the first, the field unit, are the managers primarily involved in carrying on or personally supervising day-to-day activities. Even here, if the volume of activity is large, they spend much of their time on administrative duties. But such duties are largely operational, carried out within the framework of policies and procedures set by departmental headquarters and the higher offices. The departmental and divisional offices may make some long-term decisions, but because their executives work within a comparable framework determined by the general office, their primary administrative activities also tend to be tactical or operational. The general office makes the broad strategic or entrepreneurial decisions as to policy and procedures and can do so largely because it has the final say in the allocation of the firm's resources — men, money and materials — necessary to carry out these administrative decisions and actions and others made with its approval at any level.[5] [Emphasis added.]

Transnational operations on the part of the firm do not change the fundamental nature of the management problem, nor do they alter in substance the principle developed to cope with it. The problem remains how to maintain the efficiency of local operations in many countries while ensuring product or geographic coordination and retaining overall global control. The solution adopted is to extend the principle of centralization-decentralization to the world level. To be sure, the precise nature of the solution varies widely from firm to firm — some allow a greater degree of local authority, others less; some adopt the product line principle of administration, others the geographic region principle, and many use a blend of both. But recent empirical research on the management of transnational enterprise agrees on an undisputed finding: the reality of centralized control of strategic decision making at the world level.[6] How far to expand production, of what products, in which countries, and by what principal methods — all these fall within the power of the top executives of the TNCs, the "earth managers" as they are sometimes called.

Not surprisingly, the petroleum, copper, and aluminum companies have been no exception to the general rule of centralization of power at the global level. Indeed, the vital role of raw materials production in the firms' total operations made it imperative that the raw materials subsidiaries be under absolute central authority. In Chandler's classic study of the strategy and structure of American industrial enterprises, it was found that Standard Oil of New Jersey (now Exxon) was among the first corporations to adopt the divisional structure embodying the principle of centralization-decentralization.[7] At Anaconda, "since World War 1, the over-all policy making was carried out in weekly meetings of the heads of functional subsidiaries"[8]; at Kennecott, "the story has been one of increasingly centralized administrative control."[9] At Alcoa, "overall appraisal and planning are carried out by the three Executive Vice-Presidents, the President, the Chairman of the Board, and the Chairman of the Executive and Finance Committee."[10] A recently published study revealed that at Alcan, the annual plan for the company is determined by an executive committee consisting of the president and four executive vice-presidents, with the president having the final word.[11] The other aluminum companies also employ the executive committee form for overall decision making.

Accompanying the typical structure of authority in the firm is a typical pattern of economic relationships between each subsidiary and the corporation as a whole. Many subsidiaries, especially those engaged in extractive and processing operations, may "buy" and "sell" far more with other subsidiaries of the same firm than with other firms. Raw materials subsidiaries sell to sister processing and manufacturing companies, who in turn sell to marketing affiliates; all operations buy from subsidiaries producing ancillary inputs, from those providing technical services, and from specially established purchasing subsidiary companies. Cash generation takes place at the level of the company as a whole, which acts as a bank to all the subsidiaries, receiving their sales proceeds, remitting them finances in accordance with the agreed plan, administering dividend and investment strategies, and managing the firm's liquid assets. The main relationships involved are shown in Figure 2.

The subsidiary, then, is not an autonomous entity to any significant extent. Especially for the raw materials subsidiaries, virtually every significant aspect of decision making over operations is outside the discretion of its "management." The parent company tells it how much to produce, of what product, by what methods, and where to send it. It tells it where to obtain its capital equipment and its inputs. It fixes the price of the product and of many of the inputs as intrafirm transactions; in so doing, it determines the value of "sales" and "costs" and therefore the amount of "profits." It also decides how much of these "imputed profits" will be reinvested locally and how much remitted for the use of the firm as a whole. The subsidiary's integration with the parent is comprehensive: its economic dependence is therefore total, and its subjugation to external authority absolute.

It is the imperialism of the parent over the subsidiary, as embodied in the power relationships and economic transactions char-

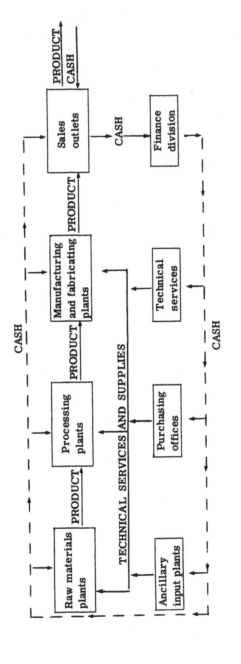

Figure 2. Model economic transactions among subsidiaries of the integrated transnational corporation.

acteristic of the transnational firm, which, when reproduced on a world scale and transposed onto the center-periphery pattern of the international capitalist economy, gives rise to the phenomenon that we have called corporate imperialism.

II. CORPORATE IMPERIALISM AND DEPENDENT UNDERDEVELOPMENT

The Anatomy of Dependence

Imagine, if you will, an economy that consists entirely of the operations of a single subsidiary firm. The firm produces a raw material for the transnational corporation to which it belongs, and all of its external relationships are with affiliates in other countries. Such a country represents a case of what we might call a pure subsidiary economy. All the important economic variables — the level, value, and rate of growth of output; the volume, value, and direction of imports and exports; the level of employment — are fixed by the parent transnational corporation. National income is nothing but the local value added of the subsidiary firm; it consists chiefly of the wages the firm pays to local labor and the taxes it pays to the national government. These, too, are virtually fixed by the parent corporation. Economic dependency and foreign domination are total in such an economy — they are the corollaries of the structural integration of the subsidiary with the parent transnational corporation.

An extreme case, perhaps, but an abstraction that is useful because it throws light on the anatomy of dependence in mineral-export economies. Such economies are, by definition, structured around the production and export of mineral products; the mineral industry is the hinge upon which everything else turns. And the mineral industry consists of a small number of subsidiary firms that are vertically integrated with large, oligopolistic transnational corporations. Dependent underdevelopment in these economies can therefore be analyzed with reference to (a) relationships between the subsidiary firms and their parent transnational corporations, and (b) relationships between the subsidiary firms and the host economy.

Let us begin by posing the question of why it is that ownership of the mineral industry in these countries is foreign in the first place. The conventional answers usually have to do with alleged capital shortage and technological backwardness in the "underdeveloped countries." Evidently such explanations are far too simplistic. Seen in historical perspective, foreign ownership in these industries is the effect of profound changes that took place in the industrial organization characteristic of the capitalist system. It is associated with the transition from a capitalism based on companies that are relatively small, unintegrated, competitive, and local or, at most, national in scope, to a capitalism based on companies that are large, integrated, monopolistic, and transnational in scope while being based in the center countries. In short, foreign ownership of the mineral industry in the periphery is the logical result of the emergence and spread of transnational monopoly capitalism based in the center.

We can see this very clearly when we examine actual historical cases that show how embryonic local capitalism in the periphery was overwhelmed by monopoly capitalism from the center in the latter part of the nineteenth century. As far as the colonial countries in Africa and the Caribbean are concerned, they never had a chance: it was precisely one of the objectives of colonial rule to guarantee by violence the free operation of imperial companies in the colonies. But even in the absence of formal colonization, as in Latin America, the essence of the process took place. In Venezuela and in Chile, for example, as in the United States, copper mining and oil extraction were in the hands of small producers in the middle of the nineteenth century. What then occurred was a revolution in economic organization that cut, virtually unresisted, across national boundaries, extending itself into the American periphery. Independent miners in the center and periphery alike were transformed into wage laborers of the large corporations, and small capitalists into their minority stockholders. For the miners of Montana, the enemy became the "capitalists from New York"; for the Venezuelans and Chileans, it was to become the "foreign capitalists" or the "Yankee imperialists." Both were attacking the same historical development. In Chile, the national lament over the denationalization of the copper industry that took place from the second decade of the twentieth century was clearly historically analogous to the attacks on big business that had begun to be heard in the United States a generation before. And those in Chile who sought to restore local capitalism in the copper industry were to suffer the same dismal failure as those in the United States, who, through trust busting, aimed at rehabilitating the competitive firm. The era of competitive capitalism had forever passed; the age of imperialism, as Lenin pointed out, had arrived.[12]

Dependency and Output Determination

To say that the mineral-export industries are dependent on external demand is to miss the point in an important sense. Output is rather dependent on the needs of the particular firms whose subsidiaries operate in the industry and the alternatives open to them. Let us assume the simplest possible case: a single metropolitan firm producing and selling the end product on a single metropolitan market, drawing its raw material from a single peripheral source. The cost conditions for the extraction of the raw material form part of the total cost conditions of the firm; these total cost conditions, in conjunction with demand conditions for the end product, determine the equilibrium quantity traded on the market. This equilibrium (given the ratio of raw material to end product) determines the level of output/exports of the mineral resource industry in the periphery.

In this, the simplest case, there is a clear and unambiguous relationship between the demand for the end product and the output (derived demand) for the raw material. Changes in the level of output will depend on changes in the structure of relative prices and in the level of income on the metropolitan market, in conjunction with the relevant elasticities of demand for the end product. They will also depend on changes in the firm's cost conditions and in the raw material/end product ratio.

In the real world, however, there are many markets, many firms, and many supply sources. Typically, there are a number of firms in each market, drawing their raw materials from a number of geopolitical sources, and in many cases more than one firm draws its raw material from the same peripheral country. To isolate the effects of these factors on the output determination picture, let us retain the assumption of a single metropolitan market that absorbs the entire end product output. Let us also take as given and fixed such factors as the level and rate of growth of metropolitan income, the income elasticity of demand for the end product, the structure of relative prices and the price elasticities of demand, and the raw material/end product ratio. The other assumptions of the simple case will be relaxed gradually to indicate the additional factors determining output. The original firm will be called firm X and the original peripheral country, country A.

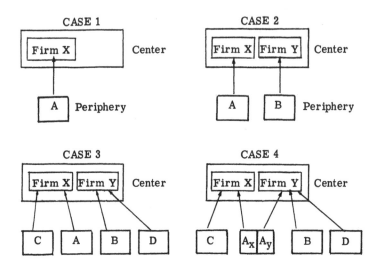

Figure 3. The framework of output determination.

The framework of output determination is represented diagrammatically in Figure 3 as case 1.

First, assume that there is another firm on the market — firm Y — drawing its raw materials from another peripheral country, called B. This is represented as case 2 in Figure 3. The additional factor determining A's output is the share of market supplies controlled by X. The larger X's share, the larger will be A's output, all other things being equal, and vice versa. It is true that A's extraction costs will affect X's market share through their effects on X's production costs. But a number of other factors will affect X's market share, such as its marketing ability, its rate of technological innovation, and possibly even market-sharing agreements. The interesting implication of this is that A's output relative to B's does not necessarily reflect its production costs relative to B's: it can be a relatively high-cost producer and yet enjoy a higher share of raw materials output, for example, because the non-raw-materials production costs of its parent are much lower than those of B's parent. Naturally, the opposite can also hold.

Another vital implication is that the rate of growth of A's output relative to B's depends exclusively on the rate of growth of firm X relative to firm Y. Thus, a peripheral country tied to a nondynamic firm will share the fate of that firm, and vice versa.

Now let us give each firm one additional peripheral country to choose from in satisfying its raw materials needs. Countries A and C are now attached to X and countries B and D to Y (case 3 in Fig. 3). In allocating its raw materials requirements between A and C, X will presumably use the least-cost principle. In effect, X's minimum cost curve for different levels of its end product output includes the optimum combinations of A's and C's output for the total raw materials requirements implied by the different levels of end product output. What is now happening is that country A is competing with country C within the structure of the firm; its output is determined, inter alia, by its production costs relative to C's. It also competes with other raw materials producers — B and D — but in a very indirect way.

One implication is that if X's alternative supply source were a different country with different cost conditions from C's, A would be competing with a different set of cost conditions and would almost certainly have a different level of output. In other words, since the level of raw materials output for any given country depends on the alternative suppliers with which it competes through the structure of the firm, a different combination of firms with countries implies a different distribution of raw materials output between countries.

Finally, let us assume that both X and Y draw supplies from A, with the other conditions unchanged. This is represented as case 4 in Figure 3. This brings us closest to the conditions in the real world, where many mineral-export countries have more than one firm drawing supplies from within their borders. A's output is now the sum total of the requirements of X and Y that are drawn from that country. That part of its reserves controlled by X competes with C, that part controlled by Y competes with B and D. Obviously, it is quite feasible for the least-cost considerations to yield a level of output in A which is higher for firm X and lower for firm Y, or a high rate of growth of output in A for firm Y and a low one for firm X, and so on.

These cases in the real world in which a country has experienced a period of high and sustained growth in its mineral exports — as have Chile, Venezuela, and Jamaica, for example — well illustrate the operation of these factors. For in all these cases, there were three conditions favorable to growth: (1) demand on the end product market was growing rapidly; (2) the companies controlling the bulk of reserves in the country controlled an important, and sometimes growing, share of the end product market; and (3) the al-

ternative raw materials supply sources available to these firms
were scarce or relatively high in cost. Similarly, when the boom
phases in the Venezuelan and Chilean mineral-export industries
ended in the 1950s, this reflected not so much changing demand
conditions for petroleum and copper, as the changing end product
and raw materials strategies of the firms. Venezuela, it can be
said, was feeling the effects of the oil companies' planned displace
ment of supply source; Chile was, to some degree, feeling the effects of the copper companies' planned displacement both of supply
source and of end product.

Since it is inherent in the nature of these booms that they taper
off as a result of deliberate corporate decisions, the question of
the extent to which the operations of the mineral-export industries
contribute to the attainment of self-sustaining growth in the periph
eral economies when they come to dominate the process of nationa.
income creation becomes all the more important. In other words,
we have seen that it is inherent in the dynamics of the system with
which we are dealing that the survival and growth of the transnational corporation as a whole transcends the survival and growth
of any one subsidiary, and sometimes of any one product line as
well, while the raw materials subsidiaries in a given peripheral
country that do enjoy a period of rapid growth enter eventually into
a phase of relative stagnation. This raises questions of critical
importance: What do the internal mechanics of the system imply
with regard to the ability of the national economy, in its growth
and development, to transcend the performance of the raw materials subsidiaries located within it, which provide it with much of
its dynamic? Does mineral industry initiate a process of self-
sustaining growth in the wider economy that can outlast the boom
period in mineral exports?

Dependent Underdevelopment in Mineral-Export Economies

The questions posed above are patently rhetorical. In fact, mineral industries in the peripheral countries have conspicuously failed
to act as a catalyst for the generation of self-sustaining growth.
They have remained economic enclaves within the host countries,
better integrated with the outside world than with the domestic economies of the periphery. They give rise to "growth without development," and typically, when the boom conditions in the mineral industry come to an end, the economy faces the prospect of endemic stagnation, while the transnational corporations, fattened but still

growing, move on to newer and greener pastures. What is more, this failure has occurred in spite of decades of active government intervention in these economies, using mineral-industry revenues to promote diversified development aimed at relieving economic dependence on mineral exports. Today, that goal is as far away as ever for most if not all of the mineral-export economies.

Venezuela is a classic case in this regard. Since 1947, when the government secured a fifty-fifty split of petroleum profits with the companies, the Venezuelan state has disposed of a large and growing revenue stream from the oil industry, which allegedly has been ploughed back into the country's development under the slogan "Sow the petroleum." In the early 1960s, however, the country faced a major recession due to the reduction of new capital investment by the oil companies. Today, the dependence of the Venezuelan economy on the oil industry is so absolute that it has been called an "open petroleum economy."[13] Huge oil revenues have conspicuously failed to solve any of the country's outstanding socioeconomic problems, while creating some new ones. Over 40 percent of the population of Caracas lives in slums; the proportion is greater in the interior. Roughly 55 percent of school-age children suffer from malnutrition, and some 1.2 million children out of a total population of 11.5 million suffer from mental retardation. Over one-half of the population, it is estimated, lives at the margin of economic life.[14]

Why the paradox? Partly, the answers are to be found in the nature of the specific socioeconomic formations of peripheral capitalism. In other words, the particular configuration of class structure, political power, and economic structure and organization in the host economy is to a large extent responsible. But part of the reason is also to be found in the relationships and processes that are typical of a mineral industry consisting of subsidiary firms of transnational corporations. In this section, we shall consider the "pure" role of the mineral industry in the peripheral economy — that is, the industry's role before state intervention aimed at skimming off mineral surpluses for investment in economic development. This corresponds to the first historical period of the implantation of the mineral industry into peripheral economies: roughly until about 1950 for many countries and until even 1960 and later for some.

We have said that the mineral industries remain economic enclaves within the host countries and do not catalyze balanced, self-sustaining growth. The specific manifestations of this have been the following: (1) few purchases of local agricultural and manufactured goods are made by the industry; (2) the capital/labor ratio in the industry is high relative to that in the rest of the national economy, and, as a result, labor productivity and wage rates are relatively high, but the total labor force and the total wage bill are low relative to the national labor force and the national wage bill, respectively; (3) profits and depreciation form a high proportion of the value of the industry's output (also as a result of the high capital/labor ratio), but this surplus is either repatriated to the foreign owners or reinvested within the mineral-export industry itself — it is not invested in other national industries, where it could contribute to diversified economic growth; finally, (4) as a result of (1) to (3) above, the value of the industry's output that is "returned" to the national economy (principally in the form of local purchases, wages, and taxes) is well below the total value of its "sales."

These features can be traced directly to characteristics of the subsidiary-parent relationship within the transnational corporation. Indeed, the subsidiary's lack of integration with the host economy is the correlate of its close integration with the parent firm. Take, first, the question of the locus of supply of inputs and capital equipment to the subsidiaries that comprise the industry. There is every reason to expect that such goods will be supplied to the subsidiary by the headquarters of the parent firm and will be obtained from metropolitan sources. First, some of the inputs may be produced by the parent firm itself, as a result of its horizontal integration. Some of the aluminum firms themselves, for example, produce the caustic soda for the alumina process and the cryolite for aluminum production. Second, the purchase of materials and capital equipment for all subsidiaries will in all probability be centralized by the firm's central office in order to effect economies and standardize the processes used and the goods produced at each stage of output. Under these circumstances, it is perfectly natural for the firm to use well-established metropolitan suppliers. Third, the transport of goods to the subsidiary overseas may involve little or no real cost to the firm, insofar as they can be shipped on the company's own empty ships on their return journey after offloading the raw materials from overseas. Both Anaconda and Alcan Aluminium, Limited, have used their shipping subsidiaries to carry fuel and other materials to their plants in Chile and Jamaica, respectively. Finally, it must be pointed out that, while the national economy of the peripheral country may experience a foreign exchange shortage, this may never be reflected in the transactions between the subsidiary and the parent firm. In terms of intrafirm accounting, the shipment of product from the subsidiary to the parent firm gives the subsidiary a credit in its accounts with the parent, against which are debited supplies and interest on the former's debt with the latter, as well as cash transfers to cover local purchases, wages, and local taxes. The residual forms the "surplus," which merely remains with the parent. On those occasions when the debits of the subsidiary with its parent exceed its credits — usually because of a large capital investment program — this deficit may be covered simply by an increase in the parent's stockholding or interest-bearing investment in the subsidiary; that is, by lending to the subsidiary. This type of economic organization ensures that foreign exchange automatically will be available to finance the imports of the mineral-export industry. The producing units in the industry feel no incentive to seek out local supplies or promote the development of supplying industries, even if they are independent enough from their head offices to be able to do so.

Closely associated with the question of the degree of linkage between the industry and local manufacturing is that of the degree to which the raw material is processed or refined into intermediate goods — not to speak of end products — within the national economy. Since some of the processes use considerable amounts of intermediate materials, they establish permissive conditions for the stimulation of supplying industries, as well as creating additional national value added in the form of wages and taxes. However, the history of the mineral-export industries of the periphery provides virtually a classic story of their relegation to those activities just necessary to get the materials out of the country. In Chile, the subsidiaries of Anaconda and Kennecott actually increased their production of low-valued blister (unrefined) copper and reduced their production of higher-valued fire-refined and electrolytic copper in the period after the Second World War. Guyana and Surinam were exporting bauxite for about forty years before production of alumina began. In Venezuela, the proportion of crude oil refined nationally had reached only one-quarter in the middle of the 1950 decade; ten years later, it was still only slightly higher than one-third.

In every case, the pattern can be traced to the vertical integration of raw materials output in the periphery with the refining capacity of the companies in the center. Both Anaconda and Kennecott built electrolytic copper refineries in the United States to process blister copper from their Chilean subsidiaries in the postwar period. Alcoa and Alcan Aluminium, Limited, built and expanded alumina and aluminum plants in the United States and Canada to process bauxite from the Guianas. Jersey Standard and Shell built huge refineries in Aruba and Curaçao to process their Venezuelan crude. It is therefore the pattern of locational allocation determined by the needs of the corporate economies which is responsible for the considerable underutilization of the potential of these industries to serve as growing points within the national economies.

It is true that the tariff policies of metropolitan governments in imposing higher duties on finished goods than on raw materials are partly responsible for the firms' location of processing capacity in their home countries. But these policies are by no means a full explanation. Powerful factors have operated at the level of the internal economics of the firm. In some cases, it was cheaper to expand processing plants originally built to handle metropolitan raw materials to process the materials coming from abroad, rather than to build new plants overseas. Operational economies of scale could also be realized from such a course of action. Another advantage was that it allowed the firms to adjust processing plants to accommodate to the desired distribution of raw materials production between different sources. Location at any one peripheral source might have committed the firm to drawing all the feed for the plant from that source, thereby precluding least-cost adjustments over time. Another factor arose out of the strategic significance of these materials during wartime. Shipments from Chile and the Caribbean were particularly susceptible to submarine attacks during the Second World War, and such fear was present during the Korean War as well. By shipping the unrefined rather than the refined product, the value of the material lost from any sinking was minimized: both the corporations and their home governments had identical interests in this regard. Finally, there was the well-known fact that the companies preferred (and still prefer) to risk as little capital as possible in countries where the political order cannot be relied upon to regard their existence as sacrosanct.

The next question concerns the adoption of techniques in these industries that are not only capital intensive relative to the national economy at the outset, but frequently become increasingly capital intensive over time. Outstanding examples are the Venezuelan and Dutch Antilles oil industries, which shed 33 and 70 percent of their labor force, respectively, between 1950 and 1966, although output

doubled in the former and remained the same in the latter over
the same period. The virtually total failure of the mineral-export
industry to adapt to the relatively labor-abundant, capital-scarce
nature of the peripheral economies becomes perfectly understandable if we consider the factor endowment situation of the corporate
economy of which each producing unit is an organic part. Capital
is relatively plentiful and cheap to the multinational corporation:
first, because of its large use of depreciation allowances and retained earnings for new investment; and, second, because it has
direct access to the highly developed capital markets of the centers. In contrast, the skilled labor needed to operate machinery
and equipment in the periphery is relatively scarce, and the firms
themselves often have to bear the costs of training this labor.
Moreover, the production technology embodied in the capital goods
the company must purchase for its new investment has become increasingly capital intensive in response to the increasingly capital-
rich nature of metropolitan economy. The absence of an indigenous capital goods sector in the periphery appropriate to the factor endowments there precludes the very availability of production
processes and capital goods that are relatively more labor intensive. In summary, the price of capital relative to that of labor to
the firms does not represent the social opportunity cost of using
capital relative to labor in the periphery (especially considering
the high costs of using direct foreign capital); and for the same
reasons that this is so, a labor-intensive technology is simply not
available.

It is to the structure of the corporation that we must also look
for an explanation of the failure to invest the surplus of the mineral-export industry in other sectors of the national economy. The
surplus is in reality tied to the needs and strategy of the corporation as a whole. Indeed, as we saw earlier, the surplus of the
raw material subsidiary is an accounting item that has neither
cash nor operational significance to the subsidiary itself; hence,
it is simply that part of the firm's total cash surplus which it
elects to "impute" to the subsidiary for purposes of tax minimization. How much it decides to reinvest there is a different question again: it depends on the determined expansion of end product
capacity and the determined location of new raw materials capacity. What is not reinvested in the given raw material subsidiary
is available not to the national economy but to the corporate economy. Hence, it is allocated in a manner consistent with the firm's
strategy: between different raw materials subsidiaries, different

refineries, fabricators, sales, and other departmental units, different end products, and dividends, debt reductions, and additions to working capital.

Finally, there is the question of the reliance on foreign capital in the industry, referred to earlier. Suffice it here to recall that, viewed in its historical perspective, the denationalization of the mineral industries of the periphery was merely the corollary of the transnationalization of the metropolitan corporations. Further, the practices of the corporations make it impossible for national capitalists to restore the industries to national ownership. The large fraction of the industry's sales value accruing abroad in the form of depreciation and net profits is only one of the more visible consequences of this.

In the pure case, therefore, the mineral industry remains a complete enclave. It sells and purchases very little from the host economy, it provides no stimulus to other industries, it uses very little labor and — if it can get away with it — it pays very little taxes. It is integrated internationally and isolated nationally. Under these circumstances, greater national integration can be secured only through the independent action of labor and the state — the two principal recipients of the industry's local income stream and the two principal social forces with which the transnational corporation has to deal in order to carry out production operations in the country.

III. A DIALECTIC OF DEPENDENCY: LABOR, THE STATE, AND THE TRANSNATIONAL CORPORATION

The transnational corporation embodies not only a pattern of economic relationships but also a pattern of domination, as expressed by the power relations within it. Raw materials operations have to be subjected to the absolute control of the parent firm, for they are the basis upon which rests the whole edifice of production and marketing, and hence of capital accumulation. Therefore, the social groups whose cooperation is indispensable for raw materials flows — principally labor and the state bureaucracy in the periphery — must be subjected, as far as possible, to the control of the firm. They must be relegated to a dominated and dependent status. They will not necessarily accept this. If an equilibrium is achieved, it will not necessarily be stable. The situation is dialectical and subject to sudden and frequent change.

A diagrammatic view of the principal relationships involved is given in Figure 4. The workers and the state bureaucracy in the periphery deal initially with the managers of the local subsidiaries. But these managers are themselves subject to the authority of the parent corporation. They can negotiate only within parameters set from above; especially in a situation of crisis and conflict, they frequently have to refer decisions back to the senior executives of the parent firm. Ultimately, then, labor and the government in the periphery have to deal with the management of the corporation as a whole. This implies a considerable weakening of their bargaining power. The transnational corporation not only has tremendous resources of finance and technology, it also has an enormous flexibility growing out of the fact that its operations are based in a large number of countries. Such flexibility and the integrated nature of its operations give it a wide range of options to shift accounting profits, and ultimately new investment and even existing production facilities, from one country to another. Furthermore, the transnational corporation normally enjoys a close relationship with the government of its home country — which means that the center country's government will bring pressure to bear on the peripheral government in the interests of the firm. This can mean, in turn, that the government in the peripheral country will pressure the labor force in the interests of the local subsidiary of the corporation.

With such formidable leverage deployed against government and the labor force in the periphery, it is no wonder that, at least in the early stages of the mineral-industry's operation in any given country, the transnational corporation more or less has its way. But as time passes and the corporation has a growing share of its capital assets and its raw materials production located in the country, the bargaining power shifts progressively to the latter. This sets the stage for the peripheral government and labor force to challenge the old arrangements in order to enlarge their "take" from the industry. At bottom, this represents an attempt to change the balance of power — both actual and perceived — between different groups involved in the industry in order to alter the way in which the income it generates is distributed among them. This is expressed in terms of the struggle to increase the national take from the industry and national control over it.

Depending on the circumstances, it may well be that it is labor which takes the initiative in challenging the power of the corporation and places itself in the vanguard of the struggle to increase

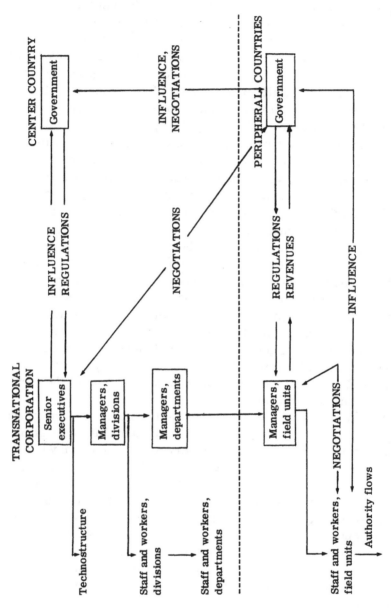

Figure 4. Center-periphery power relations as mediated by the transnational corporation.

the national take from the industry. However, there are limits to the extent to which the labor force can enlarge its share in the industry's value, as distinct from achieving higher wage <u>rates</u>. First, since the labor content per unit of physical output in the industry is low, large increases in wage rates can be conceded to militant mine workers with relatively small increases in labor's share — indeed, mechanization can and often does reduce the wage content of output even as wage rates increase. (In Venezuela, between 1950 and 1966, labor income per worker in the oil industry trebled, but total labor income as a share of the value of output fell from 15 to 11 percent because of the substitution of capital for labor.) The bargaining power of labor may also be weakened by the existence of a large reserve of unemployed labor.

Another important factor is that the struggles of labor may be met by deliberately repressive policies from the national government. The history of the mineral-export industries in the periphery shows that the fact that the wage bill is one of the chief components of the national take from the industry is no guarantee of government's support for efforts to increase it. Oil field workers in Venezuela were forcibly suppressed in the 1930s and 1940s, as were Chilean copper workers in the 1940s. For years, labor unions in the refineries of the Dutch islands faced official opposition, and in Trinidad and Tobago the passage of legislation to control strikes in 1965 was aimed mainly at the oil workers. The reasons for the militancy of the mine workers, on the one hand, and the frequent hostility of the national government toward them, on the other, arise directly out of the nature of the industry. The fact that the workers are well paid relative to the mass of the labor force and have relatively skilled tasks to perform gives them much greater confidence in their attitude toward management, compared to farm workers who are subject to traditional paternalistic relationships. At the same time, the fact that owners and managers in the industry are foreign, and frequently culturally and racially distinct from the national population, sharpens the inherent antagonism between labor and capital. Left-wing leadership is therefore frequently quite strong in the labor movement in the industry. Faced with the fact or the prospect of the emergence of an independent base of power in the political system, a national government unsure of its own popular support inevitably develops an insecurity complex. Moreover, when the government and the companies have reached an understanding on questions of taxation and the rate of expansion, militant labor demands threaten to upset the delicately balanced "partnership." Indeed, the very existence of a large-scale state apparatus in many cases is the direct outcome of the taxes paid by the industry; if militant labor demands threaten the rate of expansion of the industry determined by the companies, the rate of expansion of the state apparatus is threatened as well. Such factors may be reinforced by pressures the government of the center country brings to bear on the peripheral state in the interests of the corporation.

In any case, even where bargaining is relatively free, the capital intensity of the industry and the possibilities of continuing capital/labor substitution limit the possible growth of labor's share. Thus, the real locus of the struggle to increase the national take from the industry inevitably emerges as the distribution of the large surplus between the foreign company and the national government — that is, between depreciation cum net profits, on the one hand, and taxes, on the other.

In some important cases (Venezuela, Chile, Surinam, and Jamaica), it is possible to distinguish clearly an initial period of light and indifferent taxation followed by a period of growing tax rates and attentive regulation of the factors governing the tax take. In Venezuela and Chile, the first period lasted up to the depression years of the 1930s and was associated with the laissez-faire attitudes of contemporary governments and a low national awareness of the large surpluses accruing to the foreign owners of the industry. The depression years precipitated a radical change in the degree of state intervention in the economy and a rapid growth of national interest in increasing "returned value" by means of tax measures. In Surinam and Jamaica, the first period lasted up until the mid-1950s and was caused by ignorance of the real potential of extracting taxes from the industry, as well as the indifference and/or hostility of the Dutch and British colonial administrations to the question. Renegotiation of the tax arrangements was the work of the first generation of national politicians anxious to increase the spending power of the embryonic national state. In these countries, renegotiation was also facilitated by the additional leverage available to the state as a result of the considerable investment and production capacity established by the corporations during the time of low taxation.

The growth of the industry and of the government's tax take from it has profound implications for the national political economy. The tax payments become a major source of government revenue, usually the principal source. They become the basis for the expansion of the state apparatus — in effect, for the rapid growth of a state bureaucratic class under the formal leadership of the political managers. Furthermore, the economic system becomes progressively structured around the resource flows from the mineral industry. Imports of capital, intermediate, and consumption goods financed by the foreign-exchange stream sustain the maintenance and growth of real levels of investment, output, and consumption in the domestic economy. The current and capital expenditures of the government, financed largely by mineral revenues, assume a major role in the maintenance and growth of national income. Finally, the possibilities for structural transformation of the economy come to lie not so much with the direct economic effects of the industry as with the success of the government's economic development policies. These are themselves implemented by expenditures whose size and growth become critically dependent on mineral revenues. It is the attempt to implement a project for national economic development that will bring the buro-political class (bureaucrats under the leadership of the political managers) in the periphery into endemic conflict with the transnational corporation. In effect, the aspiration to establish a national economic system conflicts with the existence of the corporate economic system of the transnational firm.

We should pause at this point to note that the national economy is normally more dependent on the mineral subsidiary firms, both in degree and in kind, than are the transnational corporate economic systems themselves. The asymmetry of the dependency relationship arises in spite of — or perhaps because of — the fact that the subsidiary firm is an institutional part of the transnational corporation and not of the national economy. The reasons are as follows. First, most companies draw their raw materials from a number of different geopolitical supply sources and negotiate separately with the political authorities of each. The country, however, depends on one or at best a small number of subsidiaries; and, what is more important, the corporations commonly present a united front for purposes of negotiation with the government. Second, the profits imputed to the raw materials subsidiary by the parent firm form only a part of its total profits imputed at different stages of production, and the location of the different components of its total profits can be shifted from stage to stage and therefore from country to country with a large degree of corporate freedom. While it is true that there are other sources of tax revenue for the national economy, in all the mineral-export national economies, no other single industry has a taxable capacity of the size and growth potential of the mineral-export industry. But it is at the level of long-term growth and development that the asymmetrical nature of the dependence is most clearly shown. For while the strategic planning of the corporation ensures that its continued growth will not depend on the life of any one raw material subsidiary or even on any one product, the attempts of the governments to achieve the same thing for the national economy have invariably met with limited success. Let us therefore examine some of the factors involved in the persistent dependent underdevelopment of mineral-export economies where active state intervention has taken place.[15]

Government attempts to use the industry's tax revenues to diversify the bases of economic growth are fundamentally similar in strategy in all the economies, although the details of policies and programs vary from case to case. The basic strategy is to use government expenditures and policies to try to raise output and initiate new activities in the agricultural and manufacturing sectors. The targets are to substitute domestic output for imports in a considerable range of agricultural and manufactured goods and eventually to develop new export lines. The objective is that these two key sectors will develop a momentum of growth that can be internally sustained and that thereby the economy's dependence on the mineral-export industry will be reduced. The overall social goals are, of course, the elimination of structural unemployment and the raising of the level of material welfare of the mass of the population.

This strategy involves the government in heavy infrastructural expenditures designed to support and stimulate private capital investment in the required areas and to help provide buoyant markets for domestic output by stimulating internal demand. The main areas of spending are in such overhead facilities as roads and highways, ports, harbors, and railways, power and communications, and mass education. These are sometimes supplemented by a large public buildings program rationalized by the need for employment and income creation, but also used to provide the image of modernity judged necessary to attract foreign investment and to service the aspirations of the buro-political class to metropolitan life-styles.

This strategy has been followed in its essence since World War II by virtually all peripheral countries that have not opted for socialist central planning, and to discuss the reasons for their failure to solve any of the fundamental problems of peripheral economies is obviously beyond the scope of this work. Attention here is focused on some of the frustrations of applying this strategy under the particular conditions of mineral-export economies — frustrations that arise in spite of the fact that the mineral industries often give these governments large and growing revenues with which to finance such a policy.

One set of frustrations arises because of certain external diseconomies of the mineral industry in relation to agriculture and forestry. In the first place, the supply of land and labor to the agricultural sector may be adversely affected. Both the aluminum and the oil companies are in the habit of holding large areas of national territory with proven or probable reserves of the desired resources. The objectives are to maximize the long-term availability of raw materials to the parent firm and to minimize their availability to competitors. These objectives frequently lead to possession of holdings far in excess of what is used by the firm over a long period of time. Such holdings significantly reduce the actual or potential national acreage held or used principally for purposes of agriculture and forestry. The same is true of the use of associated natural resources such as water and local building materials.

The reduction of the supply of agricultural labor brought about by the mineral industry is one of its better-known external diseconomies. The relatively high wages paid by the companies and the quasi-urban areas established by them for extractive and administrative activities attract a heavy migration from the agricultural areas. In addition, when the government begins large-scale expenditure programs, the capital city usually absorbs a disproportionately large share of expenditures, and this acts as a magnet to rural labor as well. The result is that labor for the traditional low-productivity, low-income agricultural activities is in increasingly short supply at the going wage rate on the plantations and haciendas and at the going level of average real income on the minifundia. Farm workers and the younger members of farm families prefer to seek employment in the mining areas and in the capital city, or simply to remain unemployed, rather than work for what are considered to be unconscionably low returns. To bring about some degree of rationality in the structure of wages and incomes would require land reform and technical change in the agricultural sector, as well as the institutional integration of the mineral industry into the national economy. Both require fundamental institutional changes that are impossible without political changes as well.

The mineral industry also indirectly affects the pattern of commodity demand for agricultural products. The small group of well-paid mine workers and the growing group of relatively well-paid public sector employees give rise to patterns of food consumption in which the simple starchy staples traditionally produced by peasant farmers become progressively less important and experience low, falling, or even negative income elasticities.[16] Agricultural products with a higher and more balanced nutritional content, such as high protein foods, meat, and dairy products, and products associated with metropolitan urban and suburban life-styles, such as processed and precooked foods, are among those with high income elasticities. The initiation of activities to satisfy these demands is beyond the capacity of the traditional agricultural sector, especially peasant agriculture, acting by itself. They involve not only quantitative and qualitative changes in the supply of inputs to the sector, but also complementary investments in transport, storage, and distribution facilities and complementary marketing policies.

A second set of frustrations arises out of the external diseconomies of the mineral industry with regard to the manufacturing sector. In the first place, the most immediate and obvious possibilities for the establishment of a dynamic manufacturing industry in most cases lie precisely with the mineral industry itself; that is, with the creation of a whole network of backward and forward linkages centered on the processes and products of the industry, which would eventually acquire a dynamic of its own. This means initiating the production of capital and intermediate goods supplying the needs of and using the products of the industry, and carrying its vertical integration within the national economy forward to the production of final goods where possible.

It is precisely these possibilities that are to a large extent precluded by the vertically integrated structure of the corporation. The standardization of processes and products and the minimization of costs required by the corporate economic system mean that the purchase of all important supplies is centralized at the purchasing department or its equivalent in the center country and almost certainly obtained from suppliers there. Because the raw materials capacity in the periphery is geared to processing capacity in the center, the periphery's output is not free to be processed locally. In other words, the possibilities of utilizing the resource as a basis of backward and forward linkages within the national economy are restricted by its already existing use as a basis of backward and forward linkages within the corporate economy. The claims of the two systems are in fundamental opposition.

There are also diseconomies that, like those involving the agricultural sector, grow out of the effect of the industry on the structure of wage rates and consumer demand throughout the economy. The relatively high wage rates in the mineral industry tend to set the pattern of wage rates throughout the economy, especially in manufacturing, where an occupation-by-occupation comparison with the mine workers is often possible. Wage rates in the mineral industry display a persistent tendency to rise, as the mine workers compare their wage scales with those of metropolitan workers in the same industry and with their own rising average productivity due to capital/labor substitution. This exerts a continual upward pressure on wage rates in manufacturing, where the capital/labor ratio, and therefore average labor productivity, is lower and the weight of wages in total production costs is higher.

Two adverse results can immediately be seen to follow from this. One is that the consequently high structure of production costs in the sector severely weakens its ability to compete successfully with imports and achieve the overall objective of substantial import substitution that is self-sustaining. The second is that the structure of high labor costs, in particular, encourages the tendency toward capital/labor substitution already inherent in the dependence of peripheral economies on metropolitan technology and corporations from the center. This severely dampens the employment-creating capacity of the sector. Capital intensity also makes it more difficult for manufacturing plants to achieve low operational costs on the basis of the domestic market alone.

The effects of the industry in creating enclaves of high-income mining and government employees biases the structure of demand for manufactures in the direction of relatively expensive consumer durables such as automobiles and household equipment. These are precisely the kinds of goods that it is most difficult for indigenous enterprise using indigenous technology and indigenous inputs to undertake in the early stages of development. This is all the more true given the tying of consumption to particular brand names that the transnational manufacturing companies have popularized internationally. Indeed, this applies even to the simpler manufactures such as soft drinks (e.g., Coca-Cola) and cigarettes (e.g., Chesterfield). What therefore emerges under the rubric of a manufacturing industry is a set of tariff-hopping assembly plants established by transnational companies from the center and based on their capital, intermediate goods, and technology.[17]

These deficiencies in the structure and performance of the agricultural and manufacturing sectors, moreover, can be allowed to persist for some time without becoming a serious problem to the political economy, precisely because of the abundance of foreign exchange provided by the mineral industry itself. Imports of food are readily available to fill the gap between food demand and local food supplies; imports of capital equipment and intermediate goods are available to service the dependent manufacturing sector; and imports of finished consumer goods are available to meet the domestic demands that internal manufacturing fails to fill. In addition, the boom in imports and public spending does give rise to certain investment opportunities in which national capital can find secure, quick, and high returns. These include import trading, and its ancillary activity, internal transport; the promotion and construction of office buildings and residential accommodation; public work contract business; and personal and commercial services. The most important of these activities are those centered on physical construction, as can readily be confirmed by an inspection of the national accounts of Venezuela, Chile, Trinidad and Tobago, or Jamaica, or a visit to Caracas, Santiago, Port-of-Spain, or Kingston.

The overall result is that the most important structural changes taking place in association with the growth of the level of foreign exchange and tax revenue provided by the industry are those that assume the continued existence of these flows. In terms of the country's external accounts, this is reflected in the continued high weight of mineral exports in total exports and the rapid growth of imports both of final consumer goods and of intermediate goods for local assembly. In terms of the national accounts, it can be seen in the weight of the mining, government, and service sectors in the gross domestic product by industrial origin. In terms of the demand components, it is reflected in the importance of exports, foreign investment in the mineral industry, and government expenditure on current and capital account. Long-term growth is governed by the rate of expansion of the mineral-export industry. Structural dependence, rather than being reduced, has in an important sense been intensified by the partial incorporation of the industry into the national economy by means of the public sector.

As long as output in the mineral-export industry grows steadily and the prices on which taxes are based remain firm, this system is capable of continued expansion along the lines of what we might call "dependent growth without development." There will be high investment rates and a relatively high rate of growth of total and average per capita national income, although structural poverty and unemployment will remain widespread. But as we have seen, the mineral-export industry does not expand indefinitely; the very factors that make it important to the national economy — the high rate of growth of output and the growth of the tax take — are those that make it necessary for the company or companies ultimately to shift the location of new capacity elsewhere. The consequent reduction in the rate of growth of output is directly reflected in the decline in the growth of tax revenue and foreign exchange receipts. This puts pressure on the most important propulsive mechanism of the system — the growth of public spending — and the most important permissive mechanism — the growth of imports. Hence, the political economy will have either to contain these mechanisms or to find ways and means of allowing them continued operation.

Containing these mechanisms will not be easy, precisely because they become intrinsic parts of the political economy itself. The momentum of public spending is difficult to control because of both real and monetary factors. The real level of recurrent spending has to rise steadily because of the recurrent costs of servicing the continually growing stock of public assets, such as schools, hospitals, roads, and public buildings. Powerful political pressures exist for the maintenance and growth of capital spending as well, for neglected socioeconomic and geographic groups, whose expectations have been aroused, make their demands for their share of government services. The growth of population adds yet another factor for which public spending has to account. Finally, the steady growth of wage rates that occurs as a result of the internal example of the high wages of mine workers adds an important inflationary factor to public spending. Obviously, a political establishment that exists because of its ability to accommodate to such demands will find it very difficult to contain them.[18]

Neither will it be easy to contain the growth of imports without severe effects on the economy and therefore severe costs to the polity. It is precisely the growth of imports which permits the propulsive mechanism to operate without bringing about excessive costs in terms of domestic price inflation. Imports also sustain the level and growth of output in the fledgling manufacturing sector, by providing intermediate goods, as well as the level and growth

47

of activity in the internal trade and transport sectors. Hence, there is a limit to how much imports can be restricted without jeopardizing output, employment, and incomes in domestic manufacturing and import-based services, as well as internal price stability.

Thus, while some degree of internal containment may be attempted, the government is likely to seek ways and means of obtaining additional fiscal receipts in the form of foreign exchange to permit the continued growth of both public spending and imports. The two principal forms potentially available are foreign public borrowing and additional taxes on the mineral-export industry. Ironically, the very existence of the mineral-export industry makes it easier for the government to accumulate heavy foreign indebtedness, since its external credit worthiness is good. This is probably one reason why governments such as those of Venezuela, Chile, and Jamaica, which are relatively well off in peripheral America, have experienced a rapid growth in external public debt in the last two decades. This method is at best a temporary solution, however; foreign loans are not available indefinitely at a steadily high rate of growth in absolute level, and in any case they create obligations that grow proportionately to their use. Ultimately, the government finds itself with the need to try to extract even greater surpluses from the mineral-export industry.

Essentially, this was the position in which Chile found itself in the early 1950s, Venezuela in the early 1960s, and Jamaica in the early 1970s. Subsequent experience in these countries suggests that the attempt to increase revenues leads inevitably to the more basic questions of control over production, accounting, pricing, and marketing, since the variables determining the very size of the net profits to which the tax rate is being applied are to a large extent under the control of the corporation itself. In the first place, the company starts out with considerable leeway over the size of the depreciation, depletion, and amortization allowances it deducts from its income in declaring taxable profit — for example, whether exploration and development expenditures are capitalized or treated as operational costs, what rate of depreciation or depletion will be used, and whether and what kind of investment and depletion allowances will apply. Second, the company begins with almost total control over the price used to value the product, which is essentially an intrafirm accounting item used for tax-minimization purposes. The government eventually discovers that apparently minor changes in accounting procedures and prices can make as big a difference in its tax take as relatively large changes in the percentage rate of tax on profits.

The inevitable logic of this is that the government must assert its right to participate in those decisions which determine its tax take — accounting, pricing, and marketing. It is not difficult to see that, in addition to reducing profits, such moves go against the grain of the corporate system itself: its routines, its reflexes, its administrative structure, its decision-making procedures — the rules of the game, as it were. The companies respond by inten-sifying the strategy of utilizing alternative supply sources as a means of pressuring the governments and obtaining new supplies on relatively free terms. The logical counterresponse of the gov-ernments is to reduce the companies' area of maneuverability by international collective bargaining, that is, associations of produc-ing countries. This was to a large extent responsible for the lead-ing role played by Venezuela in the formation of the Organization of Petroleum Exporting Countries (OPEC), Chile in the formation of the Intergovernmental Council of Copper Exporting Countries (CIPEC is its French acronym), and Jamaica in the formation of the International Bauxite Association (IBA).

Such strategies by countries have evidently met with consider-able success, especially in the cases of oil and bauxite. To that extent, the success in raising additional mineral revenues enables the continuation of the pattern of "dependent growth without devel-opment." But the evidence also points to the fact that the national bureaucracies, having tasted the power of collective bargaining with the companies, are encouraged to place the issue of national ownership and control squarely on the agenda. A momentum is generated whose logical goal is the full nationalization of pricing, marketing, ownership, and decision making. By the early 1970s, this trend was well under way among virtually all the mineral-exporting states of the periphery.

There is an ironic twist in this development, however. National-ization, which is undertaken in the name of eliminating foreign im-perialist control and securing economic independence, is actually motivated by the wish to pursue the model of dependent growth. For the aim of nationalization in this context is to break the con-straints on the continued growth of state revenues and foreign-exchange flows represented by the structure and policies of the transnational corporation.

The transformation of the dependent model into a self-centered system together with the elimination of structural unemployment and material poverty for the mass of the population requires complementary institutional changes and policies in agriculture, manufacturing, the financial system, and the educational system. It involves, ultimately, a comprehensive disengagement from the international capitalist system. It may well be that the buro-political classes holding power in most mineral-exporting countries are incapable of carrying out the revolutionary changes required. And in the absence of such changes, it is quite easy to envisage a model of dependent growth based on a nationalized mineral-export industry.

But what will have changed is that investment, production, processing, and prices will no longer be institutionally tied to the needs and strategies of global enterprises. Nationalization may not be a sufficient condition for transcending the model of dependent growth, but it is certainly a necessary one.

Notes

1. The analysis in this section draws mainly on the following sources: petroleum — Williamson, Andrew, and Daum (1959); Williamson, Andrew, Daum, and Elose (1963); O'Connor (1937); Penrose (1968); Hartshorn (1967); copper — U.S., Department of the Interior, Materials Survey — Copper (Washington, D.C., 1952); Marcosson (1957); O'Connor (1937); Annual Reports of the Anaconda Mining Co. and the Kennecott Copper Corp.; aluminum — Donald Wallace, Market Control in the Aluminum Industry (Cambridge; Harvard, 1937); Peck (1961); U.S., Department of Commerce, Materials Survey — Aluminum (Washington, D.C., 1955); U.S., Bureau of Mines, Minerals Yearbook (annual), chapters on "Aluminum" and on "Bauxite," various dates; Annual Reports of the Aluminum Company of America, Alcan Aluminium, Ltd. (formerly Aluminium, Ltd.), Reynolds Metals Co., and Kaiser Aluminum and Chemical Corp., various dates.
2. Best (1968, pp. 290-92).
3. Hymer (1972).
4. Chandler (1966, especially the Introduction).
5. Ibid., pp. 11-13.
6. Brooke and Remmers (1970, especially chap. 1); Stopford and Wells (1972, especially chap. 1).
7. Chandler (1966, Introduction).
8. Ibid., p. 406.
9. Ibid., p. 407.
10. Ibid., p. 418.
11. Tugendhat (1973, pp. 126-134).
12. Lenin (1917).
13. Seers (1964). See also UN Economic Commission for Latin America, "Economic Developments in Latin America in the 1950s," Economic Bulletin for Latin America, Vol. 5, No. 1.
14. "Venezuela, ahora la nación mas rica de Latinoamérica, sumida en el subdesarrollo," Excelsior (Mexico), October 28, 1974, p. 2-A.

15. The following analysis draws on these sources: Chile: Pinto (1962; 1964); Machiavello (1923); Reynolds (1965); Vera (1962); see also essay 2 in this volume; Venezuela: Lieuwen (1954); Malave (1962); Cordova (1963); United Nations, Economic Commission for Latin America, "Economic Developments in Latin America in the 1950s"; Seers (1964); Venezuela, Ministry of Mines and Hydrocarbons (1966); Trinidad and Tobago: Frank Rampersad, Growth and Structural Change in the Economy of Trinidad and Tobago, 1951-1961 (Mona, Jamaica: Institute for Social and Economic Research); Trinidad and Tobago (1964; 1968); Harewood (1969); other Caribbean countries: Demas (1965); Girvan (1967; 1971b); Jefferson (1972). See also essay 3 in this volume.

16. The Jamaican case has been excellently documented by Adams (1968).

17. Some aspects of this are treated by Brewster and Thomas (1967); Girvan and Jefferson (1968); and Sunkel (1969).

18. The Chilean inflation appears to have been partly caused by a failure to contain precisely these mechanisms. See Osvaldo Sunkel, "Inflation in Chile: An Unorthodox View, International Economic Papers, No. 10.

CORPORATE IMPERIALISM
AND COPPER IN CHILE

2

Ahora, el cobre es Chileno
(Now, the copper industry is Chilean)

— Chilean revolutionary slogan

I don't see why we need to stand by and watch a country go communist due to the irresponsibility of its own people.

— Henry Kissinger,
referring to Chile

The case of copper in Chile involves every single aspect of the theme of corporate imperialism in the natural-resource industries of Third World countries. There is the expropriation of local capital by transnational corporations: Chilean copper passed from local to foreign ownership in the early years of the century. There is the massive export of surplus: between 1922 and 1968, the foreign copper companies generated some $2 billion in net profits and amortization allowances, of which the greater part — 63 percent — was exported abroad, all on initial capital investments that probably did not exceed $30 million. There is dependent underdevelopment: by the 1960s Chile, a major copper-exporting economy for nearly half a century, was in a state of profound and continuous social and economic crisis. There is endemic conflict: since the 1930s the Chilean state and the copper companies have been in a state of virtually permanent contentiousness with one another. There is state control of marketing and pricing without state participation in ownership, as took place in the early 1950s. There was the negotiated partial nationalization with compensation by the Frei government of 1964-70; and there was the unilateral complete expropriation without compensation by the Allende government of 1970-73.

Finally, there is imperialist intervention on behalf of the transnational corporations in Chile and American capitalism in general — an intervention that culminated in the violent and bloody overthrow of the Chilean government and the brutal destruction of one of the oldest constitutional democracies in the American hemisphere. This was followed by the "prompt and adequate" compensation for expropriated properties as demanded by the transnational copper companies. And the new Chilean regime has again thrown open the doors to foreign capital in the copper industry and in the economy in general.

The Chilean case is tragic; it is also instructive. One of the lessons to be learned is that conflict between the state and the transnational corporation grows in direct proportion to the development among the ruling groups of the aspiration to establish an authentically national economic system, an aspiration for which the state is an indispensable economic instrument. This can be seen through an analysis of the changing structure and role of the copper industry in the Chilean economy, and the changing attitude of the state toward it. Another lesson is that the integrated and diversified structure and transnational scope of the corporations' operations necessarily generate wide divergences between their own perspectives on investment and expansion strategies for the resource industry and those of the national state. For this reason, solutions based on partnerships between the state and the transnational corporation are of doubtful value. Finally, the transnational corporations are able to deploy formidable pressures against a Third World state, once that state decides to cease playing the game of negotiations and to behave like a sovereign entity by unilaterally fixing its own terms and imposing its own solutions upon the corporations.

I. COPPER, THE CHILEAN ECONOMY, AND THE CHILEAN STATE

Overview, 1810-1974

There is a sense in which the copper industry has historically acted as a barometer reflecting the state of the weather in the Chilean economy. When the export economy flourished under the control of national capitalists in the first postindependence period (1810-1870), so did the copper industry. When the export economy entered into crisis and was revived only under the control of foreign capital (1870-1930), the copper industry suffered the same fate. And when the collapse of the model of export-led growth brought about state interventionism, "developmentalism," and economic nationalism in the post-1930 period, the copper industry became one of the chief targets of state action, the principal locus of conflict between the state and foreign capital, and the main index of the government's general economic policy and the character of the groups in control of the state.[1]

Specific phases in the development of the industry and of the relationship between the state and the companies may be distinguished on the basis of: (1) the nature of ownership; (2) the rate of investment in new capacity; (3) the nature of state policy as expressed in the characteristics of the tax regime; and (4) the nature of state policy as expressed by the degree and forms of state intervention in the industry. In this light, six broad phases may be distinguished from 1900 to 1974, the major characteristics of each phase bearing a direct relationship to the characteristics of the previous one (see Table 1). In phase 1, which lasted from 1904 to 1933, the principal copper deposits were acquired by the U.S. transnational corporations, and the basis for the modern, large-scale Chilean copper industry was established. Government policy was strongly laissez-faire and taxes were low; as a result, Chile's share in the industry's value was very small. The world crisis of the 1930s resulted in the collapse of the model of export-led growth and radical political changes. The state now assumed an active role in the economy, and the development strategy now concentrated on production for the domestic market. In the new model, the state used a variety of techniques to extract more and more resources from the copper industry in order to support the expanded role of the public sector and the rapidly growing needs for foreign exchange. This was the chief characteristic of phase 2, which lasted from 1934 to 1954. The price of the additional resources was a low rate of investment in new capacity by the transnational copper companies, and by the early 1950s copper output was stagnating and Chile's share of world production was falling rapidly (see Table 2). To try to

Table 1

The Stages of Chilean Copper Policy, 1904-74

Phase	Years	Ownership	Tax regime	State intervention
1	1904-33	Denationalized (foreign ownership)	Light: a. 6 percent on profits, from 1904 b. additional 6 percent from 1925	None
2	1934-54	No change	Growing: a. additional 6 percent, 1934 b. additional 15 percent, 1939 c. additional 50 percent of all additional profits due to price rises, 1942 d. 1942 tax rate raised to 60 percent, 1952	Growing: a. special exchange rate for local costs, 1934-55 b. Central Bank pricing and marketing, 1952-55
3	1955-64	No change	Reduced, adoption of incentive mechanisms: a. 50 percent basic profits tax plus variable tax, depending on annual production, 1955 b. additional 8 percent and 6 percent, 1961	Reduced: a. removal of special exchange rate and Central Bank pricing and marketing, 1955 b. imposition of import controls, 1955 c. establishment of Copper Department, 1955
4	1965-70	51 percent state ownership	Reduced, incentive principle retained	Growing: a. reimposition of government pricing, 1965 b. nominal government ownership, control, and marketing acquired
5	1971-73	Full expropriation with little or no compensation		Full state control
6	1974	State ownership maintained but generous compensation paid; new copper deposits opened to foreign companies		General relaxation

Table 2

Chile's Share in World Copper Output, 1915-68

Period	Five-year copper output (thousand metric tons)			Percent world output	
	World	Chile	Gran Mineria in Chile	Chile	Gran Mineria in Chile
1915-19	6,298	412	264	6.5	4.2
1920-24	5,094	660	541	12.9	10.6
1925-29	8,094	1,246	1,124	15.4	13.9
1930-34	6,140	967	889	15.7	14.4
1935-39	9,575	1,629	1,498	17.0	15.6
1940-44	13,118	2,311	2,187	17.6	16.7
1945-49	11,464	2,037	1,993	17.8	17.3
1950-54	14,954	1,860	1,728	12.5	11.5
1955-59	17,419	2,414	2,187	13.8	12.6
1960-64	21,962	2,918	2,508	13.2	11.4
1965-68[a]	20,273	2,540	2,072	12.5	10.2

Source: From data in Chile, Senado, Cobre: Antecedentes económicos y estadísticos relacionados con la Gran Minería del Cobre, Oficina de Informaciones, Boletín de información económica, No. 157 (Santiago, 1969).
a. Four-year period.

turn the trend, the state reversed its policies in the 1955-64 period (phase 3); the burden of taxation was steeply cut and the forms of state intervention the companies found most objectionable were removed. But the companies still failed to engage in substantial new investment. Thus, under the Frei government of 1964-70, which forms phase 4 for the industry, there was a return to nationalistic policies. Fifty-one percent state participation was negotiated with the companies, together with a large expansion program. The nationalistic policy was intensified under the Allende government of 1970-73 (phase 5), which completely expropriated the companies with little or no compensation. Finally, the military regime which overthrew the Allende government in 1973 has handsomely compensated the companies and invited foreign investment to come in to exploit new deposits.

An analysis of each phase will show how the changing character of the Chilean political economy implied changing functions assigned to the copper industry, or demanded of it, by the state. These functions were, at critical periods, to come into violent

conflict with the functions assigned to the industry by the transnational corporations, and these conflicts were, in turn, to have
profound repercussions on the evolution of the Chilean political
economy itself.

Phase 1: Denationalization and Laissez Faire, 1904-33

In the mid-nineteenth century, Chilean copper played a leading
role in the country's economic growth. By the 1860s the industry,
which was entirely in the hands of national capitalists, accounted
for 40 percent of world production. Yet by the 1880s the industry
had collapsed. When it was rehabilitated to its former glory in
the 1920s, it was no longer under national ownership but rather in
the hands of two giant U.S. copper companies. What accounts for
the failure of national capital to maintain a place for Chilean-
owned copper in the world industry? How is it that powerful
American concerns were able to expropriate the Chilean deposits
and establish a traditional, enclave export industry in spite of the
existence of a tradition of local entrepreneurship?

These were questions which also preoccupied contemporary observers. In a celebrated work called Nuestra inferioridad económica [Our Economic Inferiority], Encina lamented the foreign
takeovers of the most important sectors of the Chilean economy,
blaming them on the disappearance of the enterprising spirit shown
by Chilean capitalists of previous generations.[2] In 1918 the leading
national newspaper published a series of articles on the causes of
the denationalization of the copper industry.[3] The author also
blamed Chilean capitalists, who he claimed did not have the necessary patience and persistence to make a success of large-scale
copper enterprise that would yield a profit only after some years.
Perhaps the most important contemporary comment was made in
a study on the economic and social implications of the copper industry by Santiago Machiavello, a university professor, published
in 1923.[4] His thesis was as follows: (1) copper had an enormous
potential for the Chilean economy, not only in the direct generation
of income, but also as a basis for stimulating other industries
linked to it on the supply and demand side, such as petroleum,
coal, iron and steel, sulfuric acid, agriculture, and manufacturing;
(2) it was not playing this role, basically because it had been de-
nationalized; (3) denationalization was due not to lack of Chilean

capital (there was a lot of Chilean capital invested in Bolivia and Argentina, for example), but rather to a lack of interest in forming large firms and in waiting for long-term profits, as well as a lack of state policy for technological development; and (4) means should be devised to "nationalize" the industry, not by state takeovers of the foreign companies, but rather by policies to foster the growth of local capital.

In retrospect, it can be said that the comments of contemporary observers were true, but not the whole truth. It was indeed the case that the changed conditions of the copper industry required large-scale enterprise with long-term profit horizons and a secure technological base, and that these were precisely the advantages possessed by the foreign copper companies. But to ascribe denationalization to "national" deficiencies on the part of Chilean capitalists is to miss an important point. Capitalism underwent profound changes in the latter part of the nineteenth century: the system of small, competitive firms was superseded by that of large monopolistic corporations based in the center countries — that is, monopoly capitalism emerged. For copper, the chief catalyst of the change was the emergence of electricity as a growth industry in the 1880s in the United States. The resulting derived demand for copper transmission wire transformed the metal into an important industrial material with a high growth potential. Since the bulk of potential new supplies was contained in vast, low-grade ore deposits, a technological revolution was induced in the large-scale production and processing of such low-grade ores. The division of the functions of mining, concentration, smelting, refining, and marketing became sharply demarcated; such division was geographic as well, since ores were not always found at the same place as the sources of abundant electric power needed to refine them, nor was abundant power always near the markets for refined copper. Successful production now required a much larger quantity of capital and a higher scale of production than before. Under these conditions, the individual miner and the small, independent, single-process firm were not destined to survive. Aggressive capitalists consolidated copper deposits to control raw materials supplies, vertically integrated their enterprises from mining through refining and marketing, and sought to control the market through either outright monopoly or cartel agreements with a small number of peers. By 1910 this process had been completed in the United States: four groups dominated that country's copper industry. The individual miners and the small companies had all been absorbed or driven out.[5]

By the end of the following decade, this process had been extended from the United States to Chile. Two of the four dominant American groups — Anaconda and Kennecott — acquired the deposits that became the basis of the modern, large-scale Chilean copper industry. The <u>national</u> Chilean copper industry had disappeared after the 1870s because Chile had failed to participate in the technological and organizational revolution that took place in the United States. It failed, that is, to develop a monopoly capitalism of its own; and this was principally because, as a peripheral country, it did not have the social and economic base to do so. Even when an American engineer, William Braden, tried to develop the famous El Teniente deposits in Chile independently of the dominant American enterprises, he failed and sold out to the Guggenheims (Kennecott group) after four years.

The same fate befell Braden with the smaller but nonetheless valuable Potrerillos deposits, which he sold to Anaconda in 1912, as well as to another American who consolidated the huge Chuquicamata deposits, the largest of the three, only to sell them in 1911 to the Guggenheims.[6] Both these men, especially Braden, had access to foreign technology, capital, and markets, but they could not break the tight control of the established copper oligopolies. We can also see the essential futility of government policies to foster local capital in the industry, as advocated by Machiavello in 1923. With the U.S. corporations in control of the bulk of the good Chilean deposits, local capital would simply not have had a sufficient resource base to challenge their hegemony. And since the American companies, as a matter of deliberate policy, fully owned their Chilean subsidiaries and never issued their stock on the Chilean capital market, any possibility of equity participation by local private capital was automatically ruled out. Henceforth, the only path to renationalization lay through state action.

But the Chilean state played a passive role in the economy during the entire period from the nineteenth century to the 1930s. The philosophy was laissez faire and nonintervention, the strategy was to rely on the international market and foreign capital. The groups that benefited from this policy and therefore favored it — the landed oligarchy and the commercial bourgeoisie — were in firm control of the state. Balmaceda, the only president favoring protectionism for Chilean industry and a more active role for the state, was driven from office by a civil war in 1891. Thus, the copper industry was not only allowed to pass into foreign hands, but it was also permitted to function as a classic enclave within the economy. The rate of tax on its profits was only 6 percent up to 1925 (the general rate within Chile) and only 12 percent between 1925 and 1934. The industry generated little income for local business, as it imported most of its current and capital inputs. The transnational firms, after all, had no need or incentive to substitute Chilean products for products imported from the center, or to develop such production where it did not yet exist. Similarly, the income generated for Chilean labor accounted for a relatively small share of the total value of production, since the companies tended to employ the capital-intensive techniques in use in their own operations in the center rather than adapt to the factor endowments of the Chilean economy. Hence, as the overall result of low taxes, local purchases, and labor incomes, the Chilean economy had a low share in the total value of the industry's production. In the 1925-34 decade, for example, the returned value[7] acounted for only 38 percent of copper exports (see Table 3), and even this is partly illusory because of the low copper prices prevailing in 1929 and after.

A low returned value was not a problem to the political economy, as long as the model of export-propelled growth flourished and its basis was provided not by copper but rather by the nitrate industry. But in time of foreign exchange crisis, it was inevitable that the huge drainage of foreign exchange through the copper industry, represented by the outflow of profits and amortization allowances and payments for imported inputs, would attract attention. This was exactly what took place in 1925: an external crisis was the occasion for the state to impose a special additional 6 percent tax on copper profits. This was the first time the industry was singled out for special treatment and to provide foreign exchange, and it anticipated the plethora of special measures to be imposed on copper as a result of the changes provoked by the great crisis of 1929.

Phase 2: Growing Taxes, State Interventionism, and the Emergence of Open Conflict, 1934-54

The world crisis that began in 1929 was calamitous for Chile. The export economy collapsed. For nitrate, the dominant export until then, the collapse was permanent, for synthetics replaced the natural material in the 1930s. Prices, output, incomes, and employment in the export industries fell, and the contraction was transmitted to the whole economy through multiplier effects. The model of export-led growth was no more. The political economy associated with it was discredited, and the groups involved with it

Table 3

Foreign-Owned Gran Minería: Total Value of Production and Value Returned to Chile, 1922-68, by Ten-Year Period

Period	Total value	Returned				Not returned			Foreign charges
		Total	Taxes	Local costs	Miscellaneous	Total	Profits	Amortization	
					Million current U.S. dollars				
1922-24[a]	81.0	19.2	3.4	15.8	—	61.7	29.4	7.6	n.a.
1925-34	493.6	186.9	34.2	152.7	—	306.7	160.2	43.6	n.a.
1935-44	876.0	376.9	129.1	245.4	2.4	499.0	266.2	54.3	31.0
1945-54	1,654.3	1,173.0	328.3	627.7	217.1	481.3	284.3	46.7	60.3
1955-64	3,095.7	1,893.5	915.5	861.3	116.7	1,202.2	464.7	172.9	295.5
1965-68[b]	2,102.1	1,283.4	589.5	634.3	59.6	818.7	398.1	105.8	136.6
Total	8,302.6	4,932.9	2,000.0	2,537.2	395.8	3,369.7	1,603.0	431.0	n.a.
					Percent distribution				
1922-24[a]	100.0	23.7	4.2	19.5	—	76.3	36.2	10.7	n.a.
1925-34	100.0	37.9	6.9	30.9	—	62.1	32.5	8.8	n.a.
1935-44	100.0	43.0	14.7	28.0	0.6	57.0	30.4	6.2	3.5
1945-54	100.0	70.9	19.9	38.1	13.2	29.1	17.3	2.8	3.7
1955-64	100.0	61.2	29.6	27.8	3.8	38.8	15.0	5.6	9.5
1965-68[b]	100.0	61.0	28.0	30.2	2.8	39.0	18.9	5.0	6.5
Total	100.0	59.4	24.1	30.6	4.8	40.6	19.3	5.2	n.a.

Source: As for Table 1, and Clark Reynolds, "Development Problems of an Export Economy: The Case of Chile and Copper," in Essays on the Chilean Economy, by M. Mamalakis and C. Reynolds (New Haven, 1965).

a. Excludes Braden Copper Co. — refers to Chile Exploration Co. only.

b. Includes Kennecott's share only of taxes and profits of new mixed company formed on April 14, 1967.

lost their hegemonic power. Political changes in the 1930s brought new groups into partial control of the state — urban professional or petty bourgeois groups who sought the political involvement and support of the popular masses. These groups were compelled, by the sheer severity of the internal economic depression, to abandon laissez faire and adopt a more interventionist role for the state to try and cushion the effects of the crisis. Further impetus was provided by a disastrous earthquake in 1939; after the quake, the government established the Corporación de Fomento (CORFO), a relief agency whose functions were progressively expanded to include the promotion of economic development. From then on, the public sector was to play the leading role in generating incremental national income and new employment and in defining the development strategy; in the private sector, the emphasis was on manufacturing industry to substitute for imports. The model of "externally oriented development" had been transformed into one of "internally oriented development" and substitutive industrialization.

The enclave nature of the copper industry could hardly have survived such profound changes. Indeed, since nitrate never recovered its former leading role in the Chilean export economy, copper was soon to become the major export industry. Hence, a large part of the burden of providing additional resources needed to support the new growth model was to fall on copper. Taxing the copper industry meant the simultaneous solution of two conceptually separate and distinct resource problems: (1) the need to secure additional government revenues to support the much enlarged role of the public sector; and (2) the need for additional foreign exchange to replace nitrate earnings and to finance the imports needed for development. For Chile, the returned value of the copper industry now became the hinge around which the whole economy turned; and over the next two decades a variety of techniques was utilized to maximize this critical resource flow. Largely as a result, the 1934-54 period was marked by the emergence of open conflict between the state and the copper companies.

This period also witnessed the introduction of the United States government as a protagonist in the conflict. From the 1920s through the 1950s, the bulk of Chilean copper went to the United States, and these exports accounted for a significant fraction of U.S. copper supplies. Through its copper industry and by means of the instrumentality of the U.S. transnational companies, Chile became a periphery not just of central capitalism but of the United States in particular. As a matter of course, the U.S. government works to protect and enlarge the interests of U.S. corporations overseas. But in the case of copper, there was an additional strategic interest on behalf of the American economy in general and the American military machine in particular. In wartime, the U.S. copper companies functioned virtually as agencies of their government in providing and pricing Chilean copper to the United States. At all times, the companies and the U.S. government worked closely together in their relations with the Chilean government. For Chile, imperialism had a concrete and tangible meaning: it was manifested in the presence and power of U.S. companies and government in the industry that had become the basis of the national economy, and the continuing pressure to constrain Chilean copper policies in the interests of the profitability of U.S. companies and the military security of the American state.

The conflict issues were generated by the methods Chile used to extract additional resources from the industry. These issues had to do mainly with (1) direct taxation; (2) the exchange rate; and (3) pricing and marketing.

The issue of direct taxation. The first special copper tax was levied in 1925, as a result of the foreign-exchange crisis in that year. In 1934 an additional general tax of 6 percent was imposed on all industry, as an anticrisis measure. Following the 1939 earthquake, another special copper tax of 15 percent of net profits was levied to finance CORFO. This brought the industry's tax rate up to 33 percent of net profits. In 1942 the government devised a new kind of copper tax, designed to cream off some of the windfall gains accruing to the companies from copper price increases. The tax was fixed at 50 percent of any profit increases resulting from rises above a base price; the rate was raised to 60 percent in 1953 to help finance a government deficit. The result of these measures was to raise the direct tax take to over 65 percent of net profits, and quite substantial additional revenues were raised. The new direct taxes, however, did not generate as much new returned value, nor as much conflict, as another fiscal device — the use of a special exchange rate applied to the companies.

The exchange rate issue. As a result of a chronic shortage of foreign exchange, the Chilean peso continually depreciated against the dollar. The government was concerned to prevent this from resulting in windfall gains to the companies in the form of lower local dollar expenditures for their peso production costs. Thus, from 1934 on it obliged the companies to buy pesos from the central bank at a special "copper exchange rate" to cover part of their local production costs. As the free market exchange rate for the peso declined, the implicit subsidy resulting from the special exchange rate grew substantially. Thus, by the end of 1954 the dollar bought 110 pesos on the free market but only 60 pesos for the companies.[8] As the internal value of the peso declined with rampant inflation, the companies had to spend more and more dollars to meet their local production costs. This resulted in a much increased inflow of dollars into the economy: the companies' local expenditures grew from $245 million in the 1935-44 decade to $628 million in the 1945-54 decade, for virtually the same level of production. The increase was far more than that of direct taxes, which grew from $129 million to $328 million from the first decade to the next (see Table 3). The result of the two sets of measures — but especially the special exchange rate — was to make production in Chile far less attractive than before, relative to other sources, and also to erode the competitiveness of Chilean copper relative to African copper on the European market. In the years after the Second World War, particularly the early 1950s, Chile's share of world copper production declined steeply; it fell from just under 20 percent in 1945 to 11 percent by 1954 (see Table 2). The country's share of the copper cake had increased substantially, but it seemed that the cake was shrinking relatively. The companies exerted strong pressure on Chile to remove the special exchange rate and to reduce direct taxes, as the price of increasing production and investing in new capacity. But the issue that brought matters to a head in the early 1950s was that of pricing and marketing.

The pricing and marketing issue. Being firmly tied to the U.S. copper market was at best a mixed blessing for Chile, if indeed it can be called a blessing at all. The United States, unlike Europe, has a domestic copper industry to protect; and when the crisis of the 1930s produced severe market gluts, the U.S. government imposed a tariff that virtually excluded copper imports from Chile. This delayed the recovery of the Chilean industry. On the other hand, when the Second World War generated enormous requirements for copper in the United States, Chile was assigned the role of providing much of the new supplies — but the American government and the companies agreed to freeze the price of Chilean copper at the low level of 12 cents per pound for the duration of the war. According to one estimate, Chile lost as much as $500 million of returned value during this period[9]; this was the price of being subjected to the strategic needs of the United States. When the same thing happened at the outbreak of the Korean War, Chile had had enough. In June 1950, the U.S. government froze the copper price at 24.5 cents, and the companies promptly applied that price to Chilean copper. Chile protested, and in May 1951 the U.S. government allowed a price increase of 3 cents to be credited entirely to the Chilean treasury. But in 1952 Chile repudiated this arrangement and proceeded to set the price unilaterally. In effect, the Central Bank now "bought" the copper from the companies at the agreed domestic U.S. price of 24.5 cents and "sold" it to the companies' customers at a price of 35.5 cents[10] (the copper actually continued to be transported and marketed by the companies). This measure brought in considerable amounts of additional returned value during the Korean War. Moreover, Chile had successfully asserted its authority over an area normally reserved to transnational firms and their home governments. This challenge to the traditional distribution of authority within the system of corporate imperialism was probably perceived to be just as dangerous to the system as the issue of returned value itself.

But Chile's leverage over the American companies and the U.S. government declined considerably with the end of the Korean War in 1953. The American government ceased stockpile purchases, and the companies reduced shipments drastically. Massive stocks of unsold copper accumulated in the country. The companies and the U.S. government demanded the removal of state pricing and the special exchange rate as well as the reduction of the steep taxes. Faced with these pressures, Chile capitulated within a year. The Chilean Senate threatened that if the United States would not buy Chilean copper for its strategic stockpile, it would no longer consider the country bound by its agreement not to sell to the Soviet bloc; at the same time, it indicated its readiness to approve drastic changes in the copper regime in favor of the companies. The stage for a reconciliation was set. In early 1954 the U.S. government agreed to purchase the unsold copper; the Central Bank of Chile, in turn, abandoned its plans to take over copper marketing, and by 1955 the Nuevo Trato (New Deal) on copper had been approved, embodying large concessions to the companies. Phase 3 in the evolution of company-state relations had begun.

Phase 3: Reduced Taxes and State Intervention, and the Persistence of Conflict, 1955-64

The Nuevo Trato was a classic piece of conventional applied

economics. It was based on the theory that the rate of foreign investment is a direct function of the expected rate of return after taxes and of the "favorability" of the "investment climate." A single profits tax of 50 percent was imposed, which would increase up to a maximum of 75 percent depending on how far production fell below a certain base level. Accelerated depreciation allowances on new capital expenditures were granted. The special exchange rate was removed, thereby lowering dollar production costs. State controls over pricing and the proportion of copper to be refined locally before exportation were removed.[11] Thus, dollar returns to the companies were increased and a "good investment climate" was created. Chile's returned value as a proportion of the industry's total value declined, but the theory was that this would be more than made up for by the expected production increases and new investment that would result.

The Nuevo Trato failed miserably. Its failure exposed the bankruptcy of conventional development economics, contributed to the deepening of the Chilean politicoeconomic crisis of the 1960s, and laid the basis for a return to policies of economic nationalism in copper which culminated in the expropriations undertaken by the Allende government.

After 1955 the companies did increase production, but they did not invest substantially in new capacity. Production increases were apparently made principally to take advantage of the variable tax provisions. As Vera showed, the base production level was set so low that the companies could secure substantial benefit from the variable tax without expanding capacity.[12] Indeed, the production levels achieved in the late 1950s were just sufficient to restore output to the levels of the Second World War. Anaconda did engage in substantial capital expenditures, but these were principally to replace the depleted Potrerillos mine with a new one, and to construct employee housing. Anaconda thus benefited from accelerated depreciation allowances without any significant capacity increase! Kennecott's capital spending after the Nuevo Trato was even less than Anaconda's, and was in the nature of maintenance and replacement expenditures only. Chilean copper output failed to grow significantly, and the country's share of world production was not recovered.

Moreover, the companies took advantage of their new freedom to increase exports of low-value blister (unrefined) copper and to engage in financial manipulations that deprived Chile of returned value.[13] Up to the Second World War, some 90 percent of the Gran

Minería's copper was exported in refined form (fire refined or electrolytically refined). With the removal of presidential authority to limit the export of unrefined copper under the Nuevo Trato, the share of refined copper in total copper exports declined to 53 percent by 1960, while that of blister copper increased to 47 percent. This increased the charges imposed by the parent companies on their Chilean subsidiaries for the refining of copper, which in turn reduced taxable profits. In addition, there were mysterious increases in the "costs" of shipping and insuring a pound of copper, which were to a large extent charges imposed by the parent companies. The companies also appeared to manipulate copper prices in order to minimize taxes. Thus, the subsidiaries incurring the highest tax rates "received" the lowest prices from their parent companies, and vice versa.

The result of Chile's fiscal concessions and the companies' financial manipulations was a steep drop in returned value per ton of copper exports, as well as in returned value as a share of export value. Production increases only barely compensated for these falls, and the absolute level of returned value in the latter part of the 1950s remained about the same as it had been before the Nuevo Trato (see Table 4). But since the foreign-exchange constraint was the major factor in Chilean economic life, and since the copper industry was the major source of foreign exchange, the stagnation of copper's returned value implied an intensification of economic and therefore political crisis. The rate of real per capita income growth declined, external indebtedness increased, and inflation became endemic. Economic policy became an unhappy alternation between periods of public sector expansion financed by external borrowing and money creation and accompanied by runaway inflation, and periods of severe contraction accompanied by growing unemployment, with hardly any containment of the inflationary process. The model of "internally oriented development" had been exhausted; it could not function successfully without a dynamic export sector, and this was exactly what the copper industry was not.

In a sense, the death knell for the transnational copper companies in Chile came when they were deserted by their traditional domestic allies, the landed oligarchy. Moran[14] has shown that until 1960 the Chilean latifundists and the conservative political groups supported the copper companies and were, in turn, supported by them. Pressure from these groups supplied a critical input into the decision to adopt the Nuevo Trato, for the state's treatment of the copper companies was regarded as an index of its

Table 4

Production and Returned Value Before and After the Nuevo Trato

Five-year period	(1) Production per year (thousand metric tons)	(2) Average value per ton (dollars)	(3) Average returned value per ton (dollars)	(4) (3) as percent of (2)	(5) Average returned value per year (million dollars)
1946-50	377	428.7	258.3	60.2	97.4
1951-55	355	582.2	485.4	83.7	172.1
1956-60	455	649.6	382.6	58.9	174.1

Source: Same as for Table 3.

attitude toward private capital and private property. When in 1960 the Kennedy administration adopted the Alliance for Progress, with its emphasis on land reform, the conservative groups interpreted this as a hostile shift in American policy and support. They suddenly became some of the most ardent critics of the copper companies — partly, argues Moran, to hold them hostage to the course of land reform in Chile, and partly, presumably, to divert attention from the land reform issue to the copper question. At any rate, by 1962, when Kennecott indicated its willingness to engage in large-scale expansion in Chile on condition that the provisions of the Nuevo Trato be frozen for twenty years, no political groups remained that would support its demands or defend the copper companies in any way. In the 1964 presidential election, the only differences between the major candidates was in the degree of nationalization advocated, with Allende calling for expropriation and Frei for state participation. The stage was set for the renationalization of Chilean copper, for decades the dream of Chilean nationalists.

Phases 4 and 5: Chileanization, Expansion, and Expropriation, 1964-73

When Eduardo Frei narrowly defeated Salvador Allende to gain the presidency in 1964, there was no question about the existence of a national consensus that the copper industry should be subjected to some form of state ownership and control. This was required, first, to stop the huge drainage of surplus from Chile in the form of profits and other charges, and second, to ensure that decisions

in the industry would be taken in the interests of the Chilean economy. The specific expression of decision making adverse to Chile
was the failure of the foreign companies to engage in any substantial expansion for the better part of two decades; this, in turn, constrained the growth of the economy as a whole because of the foreign-exchange bottleneck. The Frei solution for copper was simultaneously to secure both expansion and a measure of control. The
package involved the active cooperation of the copper companies
and the U.S. government, so much so that it is more properly regarded as a tripartite plan than a purely Chilean creation.

"Chileanization"[15] involved the acquisition by the state of a 51
percent share in the Gran Minería, the assertion of state control
over the pricing of copper, and state participation in marketing.[16]
Kennecott willingly agreed to Chileanization — indeed, the company
claimed to have taken the initiative in suggesting it to the government — and it secured a favorable price considerably in excess of
the book value for the equity sold to the government.[17] Further,
payment for the equity was made within two years after 1967, the
year the agreement received final approval from the Chilean Congress. Anaconda, on the other hand, resisted Chileanization at the
outset, preferring to commit its subsidiary to the expansion program as a fully foreign-owned company. It was not until 1969,
when copper price rises sent Anaconda's Chilean profits soaring,
that the public demand for the nationalization of Anaconda became
so great as to be irresistible. Then Anaconda did a complete volte-
face: it asked to be fully nationalized. The government agreed to
purchase 51 percent of the equity at book value for deferred payments, with provision for the purchase of the remaining 49 percent
at some time between 1973 and 1982.[18]

Chileanization therefore brought about majority state ownership;
but it cannot be said to have secured state control. Kennecott retained administrative control over its former subsidiary by means
of a management contract, which was one of the conditions of a
U.S. Export-Import Bank loan for the expansion program. In the
agreement with Anaconda, the company retained veto rights over
the naming of top management staff and over certain critical areas
of decision making. Anaconda also secured an advisory contract
to advise on plant operation, management, and marketing. Thus
Chilean control was at best shared and decidedly diluted; at worst,
it can have been considered as purely nominal. Indeed, it appears
certain that the Frei government decided to trade off complete
control in return for the cooperation of the companies and the

U.S. government, particularly in the expansion program.

It was the expansion program that stood out as the most concrete achievement of the package. It provided for massive investments totaling $527 million to raise the Gran Mineria's output by 75 percent between 1964 and 1970, most of it in the form of refined copper. The bulk of the investment was to be financed by the U.S. Export-Import Bank and the companies, which put up $169 million and $237 million, respectively.[19] Chile contributed some $31 million to the program, but its main input was to agree to slash tax rates on the companies' remaining 49 percent interest in the Gran Mineria and to freeze the provisions of the agreement for twenty years. In fact, the massive commitment by the transnational copper companies and the U.S. government could only have been the result of a deliberate political decision by the American interests to invest heavily in the Frei government. The Frei project of "Revolution in Liberty" — that is, for reforms more substantial than the conservative groups were capable of undertaking but less threatening to U.S. interests than the changes proposed by the socialists and communists — was regarded by the United States as the "hope" for Chile and a model for the rest of Latin America. It was of critical importance to the United States that Mr. Frei should succeed.

Mr. Frei did not succeed. However, the reasons for this lie far more in the profound contradictions that rend Chilean society than to any failure of his copper policy as such. In fact, within its own terms and especially as regards the objective of increasing copper's returned value, the Frei package must be credited with succeeding where the Nuevo Trato of 1955 had failed. According to one estimate, the 1964 agreement (expansion of the whole industry with Chileanization of Kennecott only) would yield an additional $81 million per year in state revenue,[20] representing an extra 40 percent on the average total returned value over the previous ten years. The 1969 agreement with Anaconda was estimated to be worth yet an additional $53 million to $112 million per year to the government.[21] At long last, it seemed that the interests of the transnational copper companies had been reconciled with those of Chile, and a solution had been devised which pleased everybody.

The harmony turned out to be short-lived. Even the Frei government itself could not stick to the provisions of the 1964 agreement. In 1969, when copper prices skyrocketed, it imposed a surtax to cream off the windfall gains for the state; and later that year it Chileanized Anaconda, which the original 1964 agreement did not envisage. But in any case, Frei's solution failed to command unanimity, even within his own Christian Democrat Party. It was clear that the Chilean state had not acquired real control over the copper industry. And the majority of Chileans found it offensive that compensation should be paid to companies that had drained so many millions of dollars out of the country for such a long time. One of the basic features of Allende's platform in the 1970 presidential elections was the complete expropriation of the Gran Minería without compensation; and when he assumed the presidency in October of that year, one of his first political acts was to proceed to carry out his promise.

Allende presented to Congress a constitutional amendment that allowed the nationalization of the companies on terms authorizing the comptroller-general of the Republic to determine the value of the assets on which compensation should be based. At the same time, the amendment gave the president the power to fix the amount of past excess profits earned by the companies, which would be regarded as the property of the Chilean state. The amendment was passed unanimously in July 1971; not only the Christian Democrats but also the conservative parties joined the Popular Unity coalition in approving it. The comptroller-general fixed the value of the three biggest mines in the Gran Minería at $386 million — the net book value minus deductions for plant and equipment in bad repair. President Allende determined the companies' excess profits by comparing the rate of profit in their non-Chilean operations with their profit rates in Chile, which were considerably higher. The "fair" profit rate was fixed at 12 percent; all earnings in excess of that in the 1955-70 period were regarded as excess profits. These totaled $774 million. Thus, the companies ended up owing Chile some $388 million on account of the three largest and oldest mines; only on account of two smaller and newer mines — Andina and Exotica — did Chile acknowledge a net debt to the companies, amounting to $28 million.[22] The companies, on the other hand, claimed that Chile's liability to them for the nationalized properties amounted to nearly $500 million. There can be few more dramatic examples of the gulf in values and perspectives that can separate the state in the Third World from the transnational corporation.

II. CHILEAN COPPER AND THE TRANSNATIONAL CORPORATIONS

Why, over such a large part of the history of the copper industry, did it prove so difficult to reconcile the interests of the transnational copper companies with the demands of the Chilean state? We have seen that since the 1930s Chile sought to extract as much returned value as possible from copper, because of the strategic importance of foreign exchange as an input in the postcrisis development model. But Chilean copper was also a strategic input for the transnational corporations: it was basic to their systems of production and marketing and ultimately to their systems of capital accumulation. Therein lay the kernel of the problem; the copper industry, which represented the nexus between the Chilean economy and the systems of the transnational corporations, inevitably became a point of conflict.

Insofar as the demands by Chile for greater copper revenues conflicted with the objectives of the companies to extract surpluses from their Chilean operations, this was one of the most important factors in the conflict. But there are other questions that need to be answered. Why did the companies fail to engage in substantial new investments from the 1940s to the mid-1960s? If it was due to burdensome taxation, why did they fail to take advantage of the enormous concessions granted in the 1955 Nuevo Trato? Why did Kennecott agree so readily to Chileanization, and why did Anaconda resist until it was almost too late?

The answers to these questions require a profile history of the companies — their origins, the growth strategies they pursued, the structures that resulted, and the role played by Chilean copper. Chilean copper was certainly important to the companies as a source of direct cash profits. But its importance went beyond that: it played an important role in the overall profit strategy and the corporate structure of each company as a whole. Throughout their history, the exercise of oligopolistic market power has been fundamental to the profit strategies of the companies. Market power involved two principal strategies: (1) control over raw materials supplies; and (2) direct access to and control over the market through vertical integration. After the Second World War, a third strategy was added in response to the need to ensure long-term survival and growth in the face of growing competition encountered from substitutes for copper, especially aluminum: this was the strategy of diversification. The strategies of oligopolistic control over copper, vertical integration, and diversification were important factors conditioning the companies' policies for Chilean copper. They made it even more certain that the companies and the Chilean state could not arrive at common perspectives on the

72

industry. For, inasmuch as the strategies and structure of the Chilean political economy diverged widely from those of the companies, conflict over copper policy was bound to ensue. Furthermore, this implied that the "partnership" between the state and the companies established through the Chileanization agreements was based on fragile foundations.

Anaconda and Chilean Copper

It is useful to start our examination with Anaconda, which owned two of the three mines in the Gran Minería (including the largest, Chuquicamata) and regularly produced about two-thirds of its output from the 1920s. Anaconda's production and investment policies were therefore the greatest single influence on what happened in the Gran Minería (see Table 5).

Anaconda's birth was a direct result of the revolution in the demand for copper arising out of the growth of the electric power industry in the United States in the 1870s.[23] The company was founded by Marcus Daly, an Irish immigrant who acquired some experience as an independent miner in the United States and who had secured financial backing for the development of a silver mine, called Anaconda, in Butte, Montana. In 1882, copper was discovered in the mine, and Daly was quick to recognize its potential in the context of the rapidly growing demand for copper conducting wire. He set about building a powerful copper enterprise with single-minded determination. All ancillary investments were made in the facilities needed to service a rapid growth of copper output: a smelter and refinery, a railroad to carry the ore from the mine to the smelter, timberlands to supply materials for mine supports and sawmills to process the timber, coal mines to provide fuel, a water company to supply the growing city of Butte. All this was carried out by 1895, and Daly boasted that his company was "without peer among the copper producers in the world."[24]

Next followed a phase of combination. Copper had been discovered at other mines in Butte, and this gave rise to a welter of claims and counterclaims among owners of adjacent deposits. To eliminate these, the various properties were brought together within the Amalgamated Trust. Anaconda was one of the partners, but the company subsequently bought out the trust in its entirety in 1911. Anaconda's energies were then devoted to securing the market for its primary copper by vertical integration "from mine to consumer." Under this strategy, a smelting and refining firm was

Table 5

Gran Minería: Gross Capital Expenditure by Company, Total, and Percentage
of Net Profits Plus Depreciation (in millions of U.S. dollars)

	Total		Anaconda		Kennecott	
1922–24	40.1a		40.1		21.6b	
1925–29	69.5		65.6		3.9	
1930–34	7.1		4.0		3.1	
1922–34	116.7	(48.4)	109.7	(69.1)	28.6	(20.6)c
1935–39	5.8		2.5		3.3	
1940–44	12.0		10.1		1.8	
1935–44	17.8	(5.6)	12.6	(6.1)	5.2	(4.6)
1945–49	33.9		29.4		4.5	
1950–54	115.0		106.4		8.6	
1945–54	148.9	(45.0)	135.8	(62.6)	13.0	(11.4)
1955–59	168.6		155.8		12.8	
1960–64	82.4		55.1		27.4	
1955–64	251.1	(39.4)	210.9	(46.3)	40.2	(22.0)
1965–68	181.6	(43.3)	173.1	(46.4)	8.5d	(18.4)
Total	737.6e	(36.7)	642.1	(45.5)	95.5	(16.1)f

Note: All figures in parentheses are percentage of net profits and depreciation.
Discrepancies in totals are due to rounding.
 Source: Same as for Table 2 and Braden Copper Co., Annual Report, 1915 to 1924.
 a. Anaconda only.
 b. 1915–24.
 c. 1915–34, excluding 1926.
 d. 1965–67 (April 13).
 e. Includes Kennecott, 1915–67, excluding 1926.
 f. 1915–67.

acquired in 1914, a marketing firm in 1915, and the largest and
best established copper fabricating firm in the United States in 1922.
As a result of this last purchase, Anaconda claimed to be both the
largest producer and the largest fabricator of copper in the world.

The company acquired its two Chilean properties during the
phase of vertical integration. The first — the Potrerillos mine —
was a relatively small operation acquired in 1916 but not fully operational until 1927. Its acquisition seems to have been the result
of a generalized search by the company for copper outside of the
United States, following the absorption of the Amalgamated Trust
properties. Of much greater importance was the second mine —

Chuquicamata — which is by far the largest of the three mines in
the Chilean Gran Minería and was for decades considered to be the
largest single copper deposit in the world. It was this mine that
was destined to tie the fate of Anaconda and the Chilean copper industry firmly to each other. The property was acquired by the
company from the Guggenheims in 1923[25] as a direct result of the
additional needs for primary copper generated by the acquisition
of the fabricating firm in the preceding year. Thus, Chuquicamata
(and, to a lesser extent, Potrerillos) was required to support an
overall strategy characterized not only by control over large deposits of domestic and foreign copper, but also by strong vertical
integration into fabrication.

One of the paradoxes of Anaconda's investment strategies in
Chile was that during the 1920s and 1930s, when Chilean tax rates
were generally low, reinvestment was small, but during the late
1940s when Chilean tax rates were rising, the company carried
out the largest capital projects since the early 1920s. This can
be easily explained if we look at the position of the company as a
whole. From its foundation in the 1880s until 1923, Anaconda's
growth had been rapid: for example, its assets grew from $40 million
in 1905 to $460 million in 1924. This growth was financed by high
reinvestment rates and, toward the end of this period, by considerable borrowing. Thus, its bonded debt stood at $249 million in
1926, a figure representing over 40 percent of its total liabilities.
Hence, from this time until the war years it concentrated on con-
solidating its position operationally and, on the financial side, reducing the burden of its bonded debt. In any case, the demand for
copper shrank considerably in the depression years of the 1930s,
and the stimulus provided by the war seemed merely to take up the
slack created by the massive expansion of the 1920s and the following depression.[26] Thus, from the early 1920s right up until
World War II, Anaconda's overall reinvestment was very low; its
reinvestment performance in Chile was representative of its overall reinvestment performance. In the latter half of the 1940s, on
the other hand, it embarked on a relatively large capital project in
Chile, designed to replace the depletion of oxide ores at Chuquicamata by opening up new deposits. That this significant project
took place in spite of growing tax rates in Chile can be explained
largely in terms of the company's need to maintain production levels
at Chuquicamata. This was necessary in order to keep plant and equipment in productive use and to guarantee the flow of copper necessary
for U.S. fabricators and for the company's overall marketing position.

Another paradox lies in Anaconda's failure to take advantage of the 1955 Nuevo Trato by undertaking substantial investment to increase capacity in Chile. The reason appears to have been the company's prior commitment to heavy alternative investments arising out of its decision to diversify its interests by entering the aluminum industry. The diversification strategy was impelled by the steady incremental substitution of aluminum for copper in a variety of copper's traditional markets. The use and consumption of aluminum had been enormously stimulated by the world war and demand showed every sign of continuing to grow at a high rate. Diversification into aluminum offered the company prospects for a higher rate of growth than did continuing exclusive dependence on copper. Further, a substantial part of Anaconda's existing resources could be utilized in the effort: primary aluminum could be fed into the company's fabricating plants and could be marketed together with its copper products. Finally, the timing was very propitious. Under the Korean War expansion program for strategic materials, the U.S. government undertook to subsidize a doubling of the country's capacity in primary aluminum, and Anaconda secured rights to participate in this expansion.

It can, of course, be speculated that diversification was chosen by Anaconda as an alternative to large-scale expansion in Chile in the early 1950s, as the tax burden in that country had grown steeply by that time. It is indeed a reasonable conclusion that the growing burden of direct and indirect taxation, and Chilean government intervention in pricing and marketing, made large-scale expansion in that country highly unattractive for Anaconda. On the other hand, it is difficult to see how the company could have avoided the powerful pressures for diversification then existing. The diversification strategy was characteristic of large integrated corporations in the United States at the time, arising out of well-known diversification economies, and Anaconda (and, as we shall see, Kennecott) was in a sense merely following a general trend.[27] And in the copper industry there were special, compelling reasons growing out of the competition from aluminum. In this connection, the remarks of one of the company's directors at the opening of the new aluminum plant are worthy of quotation:

... I wish to distinguish between the terms growth of a company, and development of a company.

Many times a company will grow merely because of production from physical resources it already owns, just as it may deteriorate from lack of proper use of these resources. On the other hand the development of a company, such as I have in mind, and as has occurred with Anaconda, means imaginative and aggressive management with an enquiring mind and with a determination to go into fields of endeavour that are compatible with its organization and the purposes for which it was endowed.[28] [Emphasis added.]

Once it had made the decision to diversify into aluminum, Anaconda was not in a position to undertake large-scale expansion in Chile in the years immediately following the Nuevo Trato of 1955. The diversification effort, in the form of the construction and operation of aluminum production and (subsequently) fabricating facilities, occupied a significant part of the company's attention and resources in the 1950 decade. Some copper expansion projects were undertaken at this time in the United States, but these were relatively small. Also, in the latter part of the 1950s, the company replaced the depleted Potrerillos mine in Chile by opening up the new El Salvador mine. But, as in the case of the project undertaken ten years earlier at Chuquicamata, this was designed for the maintenance of existing production levels, rather than for expansion proper. And even with the El Salvador and Chuquicamata expenditures, Anaconda allocated only 19 percent of its new investment to Chile in the forty-four years between 1925 and 1968, although its Chilean operations produced over 50 percent of the company's cash flow and were, on a cash flow/sales basis, much more profitable than its other operations (see Table 6).

It was not until its 1965 agreement with the Chilean government that Anaconda undertook its first major postwar expansion of copper-producing capacity, designed to increase production levels in Chile by 53 percent and the company's total production by 34 percent over the 1964 levels. That this was agreed upon at this time can be seen as due to the coincidence of the needs of the Chilean economy and those of Anaconda at that particular juncture. Having successfully established a base for itself in the aluminum industry, Anaconda was then in a position to continue to preserve its place as a dominant firm in the world copper industry by renewed capacity expansion, especially in the context of the excess demand situation prevailing in the industry in the mid-1960s. Further, Chile had agreed to reduce tax rates and to freeze them for twenty years. The agreement seemed to be a way of weakening the demand for expropriation coming from President Frei's chief opposition contenders on the left.

Why did Anaconda resist Chileanization in 1964 and then ask to be fully nationalized in 1969? It must be remembered that the

Table 6

Profits and Chilean Investments of the Anaconda Company and Its Chilean Subsidiaries

| | Surplus[a] as % of revenues | | Surplus in Chile as % of total surplus | New investment in Chile | |
	For company as a whole	For company in Chile		As % of net profit and depreciation of Chilean subsid.	As % of co.'s total new investment
1922–24	n.a.	47	n.a.	} 69	n.a.
1925–34	10	40	64		11
1935–44	14	36	51	6	3
1945–54	12	21	44	63	22
1955–64	15	22	47	46	25
1965–68	14	26	59	46	24
Total		25	52	46	19

Source: Calculated from data in the Anaconda Co. (formerly Anaconda Copper Mining Co.), Annual Reports and sources for Table 2.

a. Surplus is net profit plus depreciation.

company was highly dependent on Chile, drawing more than half of its copper supplies from that source. In 1964 it preferred to retain undisputed control over its Chilean mines, perhaps making the political judgment that its expansion program would neutralize the demand for nationalization. By 1969 it had become clear that this judgment was erroneous. At the same time, other growth possibilities had appeared as a result of the discovery of nickel-copper deposits in Montana and high-grade nickel sulfides in western Australia. The company evidently decided that the best course was to provide for full disinvestment from Chile and to strike the best possible bargain with the Frei government rather than face the risks associated with a possible Allende victory in 1970.

But it was as if Anaconda had done too little to salvage its Chilean operation, and too late. The Allende expropriation found the company unprepared and virtually defenseless, unlike Kennecott (as we shall soon see). Moran describes the company's position in early 1972, after its Chilean properties had been taken over, as follows:

Despite Anaconda's huge losses, the Hickenlooper amendment was not applied. That unhappy company, with writs of attachment only against the assets of Corfo and Codelco, with a disputed claim to any United States government insurance, and with long-term contracts and debts made in its own name, had few options for mobilizing either national or international support. Payments for the nationalized properties were cut off under Allende, and the company received no promise of compensation. The only reasonable course for Anaconda's board of directors — which it took — was to fire the entire top management and hire a new set of executive officers who would do their best to forget about Chile.[29]

As it turned out, Moran's judgment was premature in one important respect. For whereas Anaconda as an individual company had failed to make the provisions and erect the defenses against expropriation that Kennecott had, the politicoeconomic system of which Anaconda was merely a part had already decided that Allende must go. And in the aftermath of his overthrow, Anaconda did indeed receive generous compensation for its assets. It was only then that it can be said that the book on Anaconda in Chile was closed.

Kennecott and Chilean Copper

Kennecott's Chilean subsidiary, the Braden Copper Company, operated the El Teniente mine, which regularly produced about one-third of the Gran Minería's output and about the same proportion of Kennecott's total copper supplies. This company's reinvestment policies in Chile were historically even more conservative than Anaconda's: whereas Anaconda reinvested 45 percent of its Chilean-generated surplus within Chile (1922-68), Kennecott reinvested only 16 percent; while Anaconda did engage in significant capital expenditures between 1945 and 1960, Kennecott engaged in virtually none. On the other hand, Kennecott agreed much more readily to Chileanization, and, when expropriation came, the company was much more prepared for it — Kennecott actually received a promise of substantial compensation from Allende.

To explain these differences, as well as the similarities, we have to go into the Kennecott company history.[30] Kennecott grew out of the activities of the Guggenheims, a family of Swiss Jews who migrated to the United States in the middle of the nineteenth century. The family had accumulated some capital from import trading by the 1880s, which was then used in part to finance speculative gold, silver, and copper mining ventures. With the demand for copper wire growing rapidly, it was not long before the family began to concentrate its efforts in this area. Large-scale copper mining and smelting was started in Mexico in the 1890s, under an agreement with the Porfirio Díaz regime, with refining for the output carried out in New Jersey. In the first fifteen years of the present century, the Guggenheims (like Anaconda) concentrated on securing a strong controlling position in ore supplies, as well as smelting and refining. The family's U.S. smelters and refineries were merged with those of the American Smelting and Refining Company (ASARCO), the largest smelting and refining trust in the United States, in exchange for a sizable holding of stock in this company. Important copper properties were acquired in Utah, Alaska, and elsewhere in the United States, making the family the largest single copper group in the country. At the same time, the Guggenheims were supporting speculative explorations for and exploitation of copper deposits in other parts of the world, notably in Chile and the Belgian Congo. In Chile the family provided financial support for an American engineer, William Braden, in his attempts to successfully exploit the El Teniente mine after 1904. Financial difficulties forced Braden to sell out to the Guggenheims in 1908. The great deposits at Chuquicamata were consolidated into a single block by another American by the name of John Burrage, who sold them to the family in 1911. In 1915 the Guggenheims consolidated these Chilean properties and their U.S. copper mines into a single company, the

Kennecott Copper Corporation. The immediate economy to be gained from consolidation appears to have been the spreading of the losses of an Alaskan railroad operation over all the copper operations, thereby "sharing" them with the general public through public stock issues of the new company on the capital market.

Unlike Anaconda, Kennecott did not exert a notable effort toward forward vertical integration in its early life. Part of the reason was undoubtedly the Guggenheims' important stake in ASARCO, which smelted and refined most of Kennecott's copper under long-term contract. Another reason may be found in the fact that the skills, experience, and inclinations of the men who controlled the company lay in the field of mining proper, rather than in copper as such. The Guggenheims were the mining financiers par excellence of the United States. Stephen Birch, President of Kennecott from 1915 to 1933 and an important influence until his death in 1940, was a mining engineer; and Jackling and Smith, the men who pioneered the techniques of mass mining of low-grade ores and developed the methods of processing Chuquicamata's oxide ores, were close associates of the Guggenheims. This helps to explain why, in the 1920s, when other copper producers were integrating aggressively, the Guggenheims chose instead to sink enormous sums of money into the redevelopment of the Chilean nitrate industry along the lines of large-scale production and new processing methods, which had proved so successful in the copper industry. It was partly to finance this venture that the valuable Chuquicamata property was sold to Anaconda in 1923. But the Guggenheim magic did not work for this project. It demanded more and more capital during the 1920s but yielded no returns as the price of nitrate fell steadily; finally, the depression of the 1930s put an end to the hopes of great profits that had been held out for it.

Nonetheless, in certain other important respects Kennecott's experience from the 1920s to the end of the 1950s was basically similar to Anaconda's. Kennecott engaged in no substantial new investments for the expansion of copper-producing capacity from the 1920s until the end of the 1940s, largely as a result of the prior establishment of a massive production capacity and the contraction of demand associated with the depression. This helps to explain why, in a period of relatively high profitability in its Chilean operations, little new investment took place there.[31] Also like Anaconda, Kennecott's options for postwar expansion from a position of high liquidity did not include expansion of its basic copper-producing capacity. Rather, Kennecott opted for a series of dispersed diversification ventures, and a belated attempt at forward vertical integration.

The diversification effort took the form of both direct and portfolio investments. They included joint exploration for oil with the Continental Oil Company, two South African gold mining ventures, and a large effort to develop an iron-titanium project in Canada. A fairly large purchase was made of the stock of Kaiser Aluminum, a fast-growing aluminum company. But these ventures yielded disappointing results. The oil and gold mining activities were eventually abandoned, and the iron-titanium project took ten years to begin to show a profit. Perhaps because of the disappointing experience of spreading its diversification efforts over a wide range of uncertain ventures, the company's next significant diversification move took the form of concentrating its resources in an already well-established and fast-growing field. In 1968 it acquired one of the largest coal companies in the United States, Peabody Coal, whose assets and total sales amounted to about one-third of Kennecott's.

The integration effort had had a modest start immediately after the war with the construction of a refinery. In the middle 1950s, with the diversification ventures doing badly, the company decided to embark upon a comprehensive $100 million program of vertical integration. This included the establishment and/or acquisition of new mines, smelters, and mills, and the construction of another refinery. The latter step enabled the company to phase down drastically its commitments to have its copper refined by ASARCO. A move into fabrication was also made by the acquisition of a wire- and cable-fabricating firm in 1958.

Kennecott's preoccupation with diversification and vertical integration in the 1950s meant that it did not expand its basic copper-producing capacity in this period. It also meant that the company was hardly in a position to embark on large-scale expansion in Chile after the Nuevo Trato of 1955. And, unlike Anaconda, Kennecott did not have to engage in substantial capital expenditures in Chile after the Second World War to open up new ore deposits as replacements for depleted ones — a fact which explains Kennecott's much lower reinvestment ratio. The company was content merely to maintain its plant and equipment, while enjoying the substantial quasi rents accruing from its low-cost mines in the United States and its ownership of the rich El Teniente mine in Chile. Thus, although Kennecott's Chilean operation generated 20 percent

Table 7

Profits and Chilean Investments of the Kennecott Copper Corporation and Its Chilean Subsidiaries

	Surplus[a] as % of revenues			New investment in Chile	
	For company as a whole	For company in Chile	Surplus in Chile as % of total surplus	As % of net profit and depreciation of Chilean subsid.	As % of co.'s total new investment
1915–24	n.a.	47	n.a.	⎱ 21	
1925–34	34	43	39c	⎰	
1935–44	25	38	26	5	8
1945–54	22	19	14	11	11
1955–64	19	17	19	22	11
1965–69	20	14b	14d	18e	5d
Total	22	23	20	16	9f

Sources: Calculated from data in Kennecott Copper Corp., Annual Reports, and sources for Table 2.

a. Surplus is net profit plus depreciation.
b. 1965–67.
c. Excludes 1926.
d. 1965–66.
e. 1965–68
f. 1935–66.

of its cash flow (1925-66), only 10 percent of the company's new investment was allocated to Chile in the 1935-66 period (see Table 7).

The accession of the Frei government in 1964 presented Kennecott with a singular opportunity. The Chileanization-expansion package proposed by the company and accepted by the government allowed Kennecott (1) to secure a much-increased profit flow from Chile without any infusion of fresh capital; (2) to undertake the expansion program proposed in 1962 as managing agent and 49 percent owner but at no capital cost to the firm; (3) to provide for disinvestment of 51 percent of its Chilean holdings on favorable terms; and (4) to protect itself against expropriation of the remaining 49 percent by making a number of powerful alliances outside Chile.

Before Chileanization, Kennecott's share in the profits of the El Teniente mine was only 21 percent; taxes took the remainder. But taxes were cut so steeply in the 1964 agreement that Kennecott's share in profits, even as a 49 percent owner, increased to 27 percent. Moreover, the total amount of profits would increase because of expansion. And the expansion was financed almost entirely by the U.S. Export-Import Bank and the government of Chile. The latter made part of its contribution directly and provided the greater amount by compensating Kennecott handsomely for its 51 percent participation. This compensation was used to finance the bulk of Kennecott's share of the costs of the expansion. Finally, Kennecott made a string of alliances to protect itself in the event of a future expropriation. These were with the U.S. Agency for International Development, the U.S. Export-Import Bank, European and Asian customers for copper, and consortia of European and Japanese banks. The method adopted was (1) to insure Kennecott's $93 million contribution to the expansion program with the U.S. AID; (2) to secure unconditional guarantees from the Chilean state for the Kennecott contribution and the Export-Import Bank loan, submitted to the law of the State of New York; (3) to enter into long-term contracts for the sale of the additional output with European and Asian customers; and (4) to sell these contracts for a total of $45 million to two banking consortia, one in Europe and one in Japan. [32] The first two devices ensured that an expropriation would bring the Chilean government into confrontation with the U.S. government, which would be faced with substantial capital losses; the second two meant that the termination of Kennecott's management contract consequent on expropriation would generate anxieties among and pressures from customers and the banks. As a Kennecott executive explained, "The aim of these arrangements is to ensure that nobody expropriates Kennecott without upsetting relations to customers, creditors and governments in three continents."[33]

The Kennecott strategy was wildly successful. When Allende proposed to pay no compensation for the remaining 49 percent on the grounds that Kennecott's excess profits exceeded the value of its assets by $310 million,[34] a chorus of protests and an orchestration of pressure was generated, particularly in the United States and Europe. The U.S. government, with the full backing of Congress, adopted a strong position against Chile.[35] The U.S. assets of the Chilean national airline and the Copper Corporation, both state enterprises, were attached because of the guarantees of the Chilean state. The European and Asian creditors brought strong pressure on the "Paris Club" of creditors to use the renegotiation of Chile's external debt as a lever to secure compensation for Kennecott. Faced with these pressures, the Allende government yielded inch by inch. In October 1971, one month after his "no-compensation" decision, Allende agreed to accept the international obligations of El Teniente (formerly Kennecott's); that is, the loans from the European and Japanese banks and the Export-Import Bank, and the sales contracts. Finally, in February 1972, on the eve of meetings in Paris to renegotiate Chile's external debt, the Allende government announced it would compensate Kennecott for the amount guaranteed by the Chilean state — $84.6 million[36] — representing the proceeds from the sale of its 51 percent share committed to the expansion program, plus accumulated interest. These decisions were perfectly consistent with the Allende government's decision to honor its external debts in order to try to maintain its credit worthiness. But it meant that, since Kennecott had had the foresight to convert 51 percent of its interests in Chile into a Chilean state obligation, it received compensation in spite of the Chilean deduction of excess profits. By a strange and ironic twist, Kennecott, which had reinvested far less of its profits within the country than Anaconda, received more direct support from abroad for its claims and actually secured some compensation from the Allende government.

III. COPPER, REVOLUTION, AND COUNTERREVOLUTION, 1970-74

Chile entered the 1970s in a condition of profound economic and

social crisis.[37] For two decades, the rate of economic growth had
been stagnant: real per capita GDP growth had averaged 1.1 percent per year in the 1950s and 1.9 percent in the 1960s, well below
the average for Latin America, which was not itself impressive.
The agricultural sector had failed to generate the food production
required to support urbanization. It was riddled with inequalities
in land ownership that made for rural poverty and income inequi-
ties, eroded incentives, and hurt the balance of payments. The
growth of manufacturing industry was only sluggish; the phase of
easy import substitution had been passed since the early 1950s.
Manufacturing industry failed to generate substantial employment
growth, had a high-cost structure, was geared mainly to an elite
market, and failed to sustain its own growth inasmuch as there was
no indigenous capital-goods sector and manufacturing exports
failed to grow in such a way as to permit the sector to import its
capital-goods requirements. Income distribution was highly unequal: on the average, the top 1 percent of the Chilean population
received ninety-one times the average income of the bottom 10
percent, and 71 percent of the population received less than the
average national income. Fiscal disequilibria and balance of payments deficits had become a way of life. External dependence was
intensifying rather than decreasing and was particularly manifested
in the crushing burden of external indebtedness: in the 1960s,
Chile's foreign debt grew from $598 million to $2,025 million, an
annual rate of 14.5 percent; the drainage of profits and debt financing amounted to some $513 million in 1969, about 40 percent of
export receipts. Finally, runaway inflation had become endemic
to the economy. In the latter half of the 1960 decade, the average
rate of price increases amounted to some 26 percent per year.

The Chilean crisis emerged out of the conjunction of a stagnant
and inflationary economy and a society characterized by growing
expectation among the people for a better way of life as well as a
growing class and group consciousness and political organization
among the masses of the population, which traditionally had either
been excluded from the political process or had participated only
as pawns of politicians from the oiligarchy or the middle class.
The changes initiated in the 1930s matured in the 1960s, which
saw the arrival of Chilean workers, peasants, and "marginalized"
groups onto the political scene as strong and autonomous actors.
The political expression of this development was the presidential
elections of 1964 and 1970. The Socialist Allende narrowly lost to
the Christian Democrat Frei in 1964 and narrowly beat the con-

servative Alessandri in 1970, but on both occasions the vast majority of the populace voted either for the Popular Unity or the
Christian Democratic candidates, both of whom stood for revolutionary changes. The steady movement to the left in Chilean politics in the 1960s was thus the result of the growth of populist politics in the context of economic crisis, with an electoral and political system that faithfully recorded the trend in popular feeling.

In many respects, the policies of the Allende government represented an intensification and radicalization of the changes initiated
under Frei, rather than a total break with the past as such. The
Frei government had carried out a land reform; it had Chileanized
copper; it had extended the public sector; and it had undertaken
some redistribution of income. But, by comparison with the Allende
period, the measures were moderate and half-hearted, in the sense
that they were not fundamental enough to effect basic changes in
the structure of property and therefore of socioeconomic power,
and they were considerably watered down in the face of opposition
from the vested interests. Thus, after its first three years, the
Frei government faced the classic dilemma of reformism: its
changes went far enough to incur the hostility of the right, but,
while they aroused the expectations of the left and of the general
population, they did not go far enough to please them. The contradictions were expressed within the Christian Democrat Party itself, which split into bitterly warring factions of the left and right.
Some of these factions eventually left the party and joined what was
to become the Popular Unity coalition, which backed Allende for
the presidency in 1970. Popular frustration with the futile reformism of the Frei regime was reflected in the shift of support to the
Popular Unity coalition in 1970, and in the fact that the candidate
eventually selected to represent the Christian Democrats in the
election — Radomiro Tomic — was regarded as much further to
the left than Eduardo Frei and almost indistinguishable ideologically from Salvador Allende.

The immediate concern of the Allende administration was to
capitalize on its electoral victory to push through the greatest
number of fundamental changes as quickly as possible. Within the
first year, copper was expropriated without compensation and the
iron, nitrate, and coal industries were nationalized, as was a large
part of manufacturing industry and most of the banking system.
By the end of 1971, the public sector controlled the bulk of foreign
trade. The land reform was rapidly accelerated; by late 1972
virtually all farms over the maximum of eighty hectares had been

expropriated and the bulk of farmland was in the hands of either the peasantry or state or para-state organizations. Massive income redistribution was undertaken through both monetary and nonmonetary measures: wage increases were decreed while prices were rigidly controlled, and in one year the share of labor in the national income grew by an astonishing 8 percentage points, from 51 to 59 percent. There was also a huge expansion of educational and housing facilities for the masses. Most of these measures were adopted within the first eighteen months of the government's term.[38]

When Allende took office, the economy was operating with considerable slack, as private capital reduced production because of "political uncertainty." A margin of excess capacity was therefore available to support the expanded production required by the increased purchasing power of the low-income groups and the huge expansion in public expenditure. Thus the Allende regime was able to point to considerable economic success by conventional standards in its first full year in office (1971): real GNP grew by some 8.6 percent and by 6.6 percent in per capita terms. Employment grew by 6.8 percent; in the Santiago area, the unemployment rate dropped from 8.3 percent to 3.8 percent. Chile, it seemed, was demonstrating that it was possible to have a socialist revolution with bread and without blood. But by early 1972 the supply of goods and services appeared to have reached the limits of its expansion, while money demand from the mass of the population and from the public sector continued to grow. The resulting disequilibria were manifested in growing shortages of basic consumer goods and productive inputs and in the reemergence of an intense inflationary process.[39] As a result, political life became sharply polarized and the "rules of the game" of bourgeois democracy began to be breached on all sides. Opponents of the regime, on the one hand, were encouraged to go on the political offensive as the economic difficulties of the government multiplied; supporters of the government, on the other, began to take matters into their own hands: peasants seized farms, workers seized factories, and consumers expropriated supermarkets. The Allende government was sandwiched in the middle. It was increasingly forced to act against sections of its own support to uphold the constitutional order that had brought it into office in the first place; at the same time, it was under severe attack from its opponents. It was the same dilemma the Frei government had come to face, but it was much more intense and acute and had certain important differences.

What brought about the rapid deterioration in the economic situation and the economic disorganization in 1972-73, which paved the way for the overthrow of Allende? There were at least three levels of contradiction which contributed greatly to the crisis. First, contradictions at the economic structural level; second, contradictions within the revolutionary movement; and third, contradictions between the revolutionary movement and the counterrevolution.

The first level of contradictions was those resulting from the attempt to change rapidly an economy that is structurally integrated with the international capitalist system. The Chilean productive system cannot function without imports — imports of machinery, components, spare parts, fuel, and other producer and consumer goods. Food cannot be grown without imported tractors, seed, and fertilizer; it cannot be transported to the towns without imported fuel and spare parts for the trucks and trains; and manufacturing industry cannot function without imported equipment, spare parts, and components, nor can its products be distributed if the transport system is paralyzed. Imports require foreign exchange, and the supply of foreign exchange in Chile is dependent principally on the prices for and production of copper, the availability of credit, and the amounts that have to be used to pay for past borrowing. All these factors turned against the Allende government within a year; foreign exchange reserves were depleted, the price of copper fell while production failed to grow substantially, and foreign credit dried up.[40] Then the burden of servicing the foreign debt inherited from previous administrations assumed crushing proportions, and Chile's creditors came knocking at the door. Suddenly, the government that had pledged itself to bring economic independence to Chile found itself going to Paris in the spring of 1972, virtually cap in hand, to account for its actions to the biggest capitalist countries in order to negotiate the rescheduling of its external debt payments.[41]

The second level of contradictions was those that emerged between the government and its own supporters. Discipline and productivity on farms and in factories fell, as the workers and peasants became more preoccupied with changing the structure of property relations and power than with winning the so-called battle of production.[42] The primacy of politics over economics did not constitute a problem in itself; it only became so in a context where the revolutionary government operated within an electoral system in which it continually sought to demonstrate its superiority over its opponents in delivering material gains. Thus, apart from rhetorical appeals to the workers and peasants to increase productivity, the government's principal response to shortages and inflationary prices was to decree further wage increases to "compensate" the workers — a compensation that was entirely illusory and indeed exacerbated the problem by injecting fresh purchasing power into the system. Moreover, the shortages and the general deceleration in the pace of the revolutionary process stimulated sections of the population to take direct actions such as the seizure of rural and urban enterprises, the direct appropriation of production, and the direct capture and redistribution of food. The government had to demonstrate its commitment to law and order to its opponents in order to remove any pretext on their part for resort to violence; therefore, it acted against the most militant sections of its own support. Naturally, this increased the contradictions within the Popular Unity coalition and made it increasingly impossible for the government to mobilize active, physical mass support in its defense in the event of a threat to it. It is significant that when the army finally overthrew Allende in September 1973, there was no mass resistance — not even a general strike.

The third — and decisive — level of contradictions was those generated between the Popular Unity government and the counterrevolutionary forces, both inside and outside of Chile. In all the uproar over ITT's crude attempt to prevent the election of Allende or to secure his overthrow soon after his election, it seems to have been forgotten that there was no disagreement among ITT, the U.S. government, and the Chilean opponents of Allende over objectives: all were agreed that Allende should not be allowed to succeed and that sufficient chaos should be created to make it impossible for him to govern and to pave the way for a military coup.

In the Chilean case covert political action was an element of U.S. foreign policy — although there were substantial tactical differences between the C.I.A., the State Department, and the White House over the measures to be adopted and over the timing of events. Nixon's position and the measures, speeches and behavior of the lame-duck Frei Administration were intended to create economic collapse over a protracted period of time — while the C.I.A. and I.T.T. seemed to see that as their immediate goal. The prudent course chosen — limited to economic pressure — was based on a long-term strategy of political and economic attrition.... While the extreme "military" measures proposed by the C.I.A. and the I.T.T. to policy-makers were rejected, many of the economic proposals were put into practice by private businessmen and public policy-makers. Banks have not renewed credits and/or are delaying any new decisions. Companies are not making any new investments. Delays of deliveries and shipping of spare parts have occurred. Technical assistance has been withdrawn.[43]

In this scenario, the domestic opponents of Allende played the active role of harassing him politically and economically at every turn. The Christian Democrats and conservatives in the Congress impeached his ministers and frustrated his legislation. Private capital stopped investing, cut production, and engaged in hoarding, black marketing, illegal capital transfers, and widespread acts of economic sabotage. Shopkeepers and truck drivers went on strike, thereby paralyzing the distribution of essential commodities. Indeed, it was the six-week-long strike of truck drivers, joined by the shopkeepers, in September 1973 that signaled the political incapacity of the government to govern and the final, brutal military intervention. To be sure, it can be said that these sectors within Chile were merely defending their own political and economic interests. But it is highly unlikely that they would have succeeded in putting an end to the regime had that not been the will and intention of United States imperialism. What was critical in the economic and political defeat of the Popular Unity government was the widespread economic disorganization generated by the American-engineered drying up of credits for essential imports and delays in shipments, as well as the direct CIA financing provided to opposition newspapers and radio stations and — the coup de grace — to the six-week-long truckers' strike which brought the government down.[44] In the middle of this "strategy of political and economic attrition," in June 1973, President Nixon approved the sale of U.S.-made jet fighters to the Chilean air force,[45] a decision that surprised many and caused one letter writer to the New York Times to comment acidly:

The people of Chile must be jubilant today. The prospect of being able to buy F-5E supersonic jets will surely make them forget that shortly after Mr. Allende's election the Export-Import Bank turned down a loan for the purchase of Boeing passenger liners for LAN-Chile. It will also no doubt console them for the acute shortages of wheat, edible oil, sugar, petroleum products, spare parts, etc., etc., for which they are no longer able to obtain even short-term commercial credit from this country. And the military credit should go a long way toward compensating Chile for the U.S.-sponsored blocking of development loans by international lending institutions since 1971. Let 'em eat jets.[46] [Emphasis added.]

The decision might have appeared inconsistent to some, but actually it had a vicious rationality behind it. Evidently, in selling jets to the Chilean air force, the United States was maintaining its connections with its domestic Chilean allies: the jets, in other words, were meant to be used against Mr. Allende himself. U.S. government officials expressed lack of surprise when the coup finally took place three months later.[47] To many, this demonstration of the efficiency of U.S. intelligence services must have seemed the height of specious hypocrisy; it is easy to have foreknowledge of events if you yourself initiate them.

It is tempting to regard the wish to defend the financial interests of Anaconda and Kennecott in securing adequate compensation as the motivating force behind the U.S. intervention. But it is unlikely — indeed inconceivable — that fundamental policy strategies should be determined by the interests of two individual corporations. The Chilean copper expropriations became an issue not so much for their intrinsic as for their symbolic significance. The United States was concerned, to begin with, that if Chile got away with it, the rest of the Third World might be tempted to follow.

The New York Times reported:

Senior United States policy makers are reliably reported to fear that if the United States continues to appear "soft" toward underdeveloped countries that expropriate private American assets, this will precipitate a rash of similar actions.

In Africa United States private investments total $3 billion... in Latin America... $12 billion.... The African governments are closely watching how we react to expropriations by Latin-American states... [they]... are looking everywhere for development funds... and some of them believe that expropriations... may provide them with such funds.[48]

Apart from the expropriation issue itself, the United States was obviously concerned that the Allende government, as a political experiment, should not succeed. Why did Dr. Kissinger, the very architect and chief exponent of the policy of détente with the communist powers, take such a personal interest and involvement in the actions against the socialist government of Dr. Allende?[49] There is no paradox: if détente means anything, it means that each power respects the other's sphere of influence and accepts and seeks to maintain the prevailing balance of power between the socialist and capitalist worlds. Thus, détente means that there should be no more Cubas in the American Hemisphere — not only, it should be noted, that the United States will not tolerate another Cuba, but also that the Soviet Union will not support any future attempts in that direction. At the height of its foreign-exchange crisis in early 1972, Chile was reported to have received an offer of $50 million in credits from the Soviet Union — a piddling sum in relation to its needs.[50] President Allende is reported to have told workers in a speech that they could not expect that food and other consumer goods would be provided by the Soviet Union to eliminate the shortages.[51] In that sense, the copper expropriation issue became a convenient peg upon which the United States could hang the rationale of a policy that was also based on wider, more global strategic considerations.

In the Allende period, copper therefore became a kind of a proxy in Chile's internal and international politics, to an even greater degree than before. Expropriation without compensation was the government's proof to its followers of its integrity in carrying out its campaign promises and the seriousness of its revolutionary intent, as well as a symbol of Chile's economic independence. To the Americans, it set a dangerous and intolerable precedent and provided final proof that Allende, in spite of being elected to high office, was not capable of "responsible" behavior.

The final and convincing demonstration of copper's proxy role came after the military coup. Within literally a few hours after the news of Allende's death had reached New York, U.S. corporations whose Chilean subsidiaries had been expropriated indicated readiness to resume operations "if [the new] government were receptive to investment." Within a week the welcoming noises started coming from Chile: the military junta announced it would reopen the copper industry to private foreign investment, adding that the new government "would pursue liberal economic policies based on private enterprise." Within two weeks it announced that it was ready to make a new settlement for compensation of Anaconda and Kennecott. And within a month the new government began the process of returning to their former owners the vast majority of the companies that had been nationalized by the Allende government.[52]

This was apparently all that international capital was waiting for. By November 1973, the New York Times was able to report that American and Canadian banks were rushing to lend money to the new government. Short-term commercial credits, which had been cut from $300 million when Allende took office to virtually nothing afterward, were up to $150 million only two months after his overthrow. Noting the measures taken by the regime to restore "confidence," the newspaper commented that "perhaps most important, as far as the American Government and private companies are concerned, the junta has announced that it is prepared to resume negotiations on compensation to the United States copper companies."[53]

By March 1974, Chile's creditors — led by the United States — had agreed to allow the new government to defer payment of some $760 million of Chile's debts falling due in 1973-74, in return for a Chilean commitment to settle with the U.S. copper companies. The same month, the International Monetary Fund approved a $94 million loan to the new regime.[54] Two months later, the settlement with Anaconda was reached; Chile paid $65 million in cash and $188 million in promissory notes. Noting that the new government was compensating Anaconda even though the U.S. Overseas Private Investment Corporation had turned down the company's insurance claim after the Allende expropriation, the American magazine Newsweek commented,

Nonetheless, the new Chilean Government was apparently eager to settle with Anaconda because it wants to improve its international credit standing. A higher credit rating, the junta hopes, will make it easier for Chile to attract new foreign investment. For the same reason, Chilean officials predict that a similar agreement will be signed shortly with the Kennecott Copper Corp.[55]

The settlement with Kennecott was announced six months later.[56] Chile agreed to pay some $54 million in nineteen semiannual installments. In August 1974, after a year of widespread executions, mass imprisonment, torture, and the complete abrogation of political rights of all parties and of trade unions, the Chilean junta announced that it had proposals from U.S., Canadian, West German, and Japanese firms for investments totaling $1 billion in new copper-mining projects. Reported Newsweek, "Santiago now says that any firms investing in Chilean mining will be allowed to choose their share of investment participation, including up to 100 percent ownership in their ventures."[57]

The Chilean copper wheel had come full circle. But not quite, for Chile will never be the same again. Few more comprehensive cases of the imperialism associated with transnational corporations have ever occurred. Few have ended as tragically. The lessons should not be forgotten.

Notes

1. My interpretation of Chile's economic history has drawn heavily on Pinto (1962; 1964), and on Comisión Económica para América Latina (1953). On the more recent evolution of the economy and the crisis of the 1960s, I have used

mainly Muñoz (1973). On the history of copper, I have relied on the above and Machiavello (1923); Chile, Departamento del Cobre (1959); Vera (1962); Reynolds 1965). Readers may also wish to consult Mamalakis (1971); Mikesell, "Conflict and Accommodation in Chilean Copper," in Mikesell et al. (1971); Moran (1974).

2. Encina (1911), cited by Pinto (1962, p. 52).

3. Adrian Palomino, "Causas de la desnacionalización de la industria del cobre," El mercurio, December 1918; cited by Machiavello (1923, chap. 7).

4. Machiavello (1923).

5. See U.S., Department of the Interior (1952); also Marcosson (1957).

6. See Hiriart (1964, pp. 14-116); Marcosson (1957, chap. 9); Reynolds (1965, chap. 1). The Guggenheims sold Chuquicamata to Anaconda in 1923. The three mines came to be known as the Chilean Gran Minería [large mining industry]; Chuquicamata and Potrerillos belonged to Anaconda and El Teniente belonged to Kennecott.

7. That is, the value of copper exports "returned" to Chile. As used here, the term refers to the sum of local noncapital payments of the industry, comprising (1) taxes; (2) local labor income; (3) local purchases and payments on current account. The estimates for the period 1922 to 1969 used in this essay are taken from Girvan (1972); these were based on data from Chile, Senado (1969). Estimates are also provided in Reynolds (1965).

8. Vera (1962, p. 62). This is the weighted average of the companies' peso purchases both at the free market rate of 110 to the dollar and the special rate of 19.37 to the dollar.

9. Vera (1962, p. 55); Reynolds (1965, p. 240); both are referring to Chile, Departamento del Cobre (1959, p. 34), as the source. Moreover, it was estimated that an additional $120 million would have been paid to the companies in Chile had they received the same bonuses paid to the U.S. domestic producers by the U.S. government during the time of the price freeze.

10. The price applies to electrolytically refined copper; a small discount of $0.25 was allowed for fire-refined copper.

11. For more details on the features of the Nuevo Trato, see Vera (1962); Reynolds (1965); Girvan (1972).

12. At full capacity, the Gran Minería would pay only 13 percent of the 25 percent variable tax, for a total rate of 63 percent (Vera [1962, p. 75]).

13. Ibid., pp. 82-83, 112-13.

14. Moran (1973).

15. Information on Chileanization and the expansion program was drawn mainly from the following: Griffin (1969, chap. IV); Saez (1965); "El cobre: Entre 'la gran estafa' y 'el segundo 1810,'" Panorama económico (Santiago), July 1969; Corporación del Cobre (1969); and mimeographed material from the Corporación del Cobre.

16. The government's Corporación del Cobre [Copper Corporation] — CODELCO for short — was the institutional vehicle for state holdings in the copper enterprises and state participation in pricing and marketing.

17. Book value was $66 million, but Kennecott succeeded in getting a value based on the "going concern" — $160 million. Chile therefore paid $81.6 million.

18. Payment for the 51 percent was to be made over six years beginning in 1970, at a 6 percent interest rate on the unpaid balance. The remaining 49 percent could be acquired between 1973 and 1982, but at market value (using a price/ earnings ratio), which would be higher the earlier Chile's option was exercised.

19. However, most of the Kennecott contribution — $81.6 million out of $92.7 million — was financed by the Chilean government's payment for its 51 percent equity.

20. Saez (1965). It was not made clear whether the cost of purchasing the 51 percent interest in the Kennecott mine was deducted from this estimate.

21. Corporación del Cobre (1969). The cost of purchasing the 51 percent share in the Anaconda subsidiaries was deducted.

22. See Corporación del Cobre (1972); Lillich (1973).

23. The following account of Anaconda's history is based on Marcosson (1957); Anaconda Co. (formerly Anaconda Copper Mining Co.), Annual Reports, 1905 to 1969; and articles in Fortune, December 1936, January 1937, and May 1966.

24. "The policy of the company... has not been so much to realize immediate returns as it has been to try to lay the foundations for a long life of activity and usefulness" (Marcosson [1957, pp. 88-89]).

25. Actually, 51 percent was acquired in 1923, the remainder in 1929.

26. Thus, at the end of 1944, the book value of Anaconda's fixed assets was actually lower than in 1934.

27. See, for example, Chandler (1966, Introduction). It is interesting to note that the two major new entrants into the U.S. aluminum industry after the Second World War — Reynolds Metals and Kaiser Aluminum — were also doing so as a result of diversification and integration decisions. Also, it may be significant that in Marcosson's company history, Anaconda's decision to go into aluminum was not discussed in terms of the problems the company was encountering in Chile.

28. Marcosson (1957, p. 336).

29. Moran (1973, p. 283).

30. The following account of Kennecott's history is based on O'Connor (1937); Hiriart (1964); Kennecott Copper Corp., Annual Reports, 1915 to 1968; and articles in Fortune, April 1930 and November 1951, and Business Week, December 7, 1968.

31. For example, in the 1935-44 decade, Kennecott's Chilean operations had a surplus to sales ratio of 38 percent, compared to 25 percent for the company as a whole, but new capital expenditure in Chile amounted to only 5 percent of the surplus generated there (see Table 6).

32. Moran (1973).

33. Ibid., pp. 279-80, citing an interview in Santiago on May 27, 1970.

34. Lillich (1973, pp. 124-25).

35. See the next section.

36. Juan de Onís, "Chile Says She Will Pay $84.6 Million to Kennecott," New York Times, February 26, 1972.

37. The following brief analysis of developments in the 1960s is based mainly on data and analysis found in Muñoz (1972) and Molina (1972).

38. See Vuscovitch (1972).

39. See Universidad de Chile (1972).

40. See, for example, Vuscovitch (1972).

41. "According to financial sources, Chile has reluctantly agreed to allow the International Monetary Fund to periodically review Chile's monetary, credit and trade performance as part of a deal to obtain refinancing of her debt" (Onís, "Chile Says She Will Pay"). "The United States and eleven other creditor nations agreed early today to grant Chile a major degree of credit relief, while obtaining a promise of 'just compensation for all nationalizations, in conformity with international law' " (John L. Hess, "U.S. Joins in Credit Accord with Chile,"

New York Times, April 20, 1972). See also "Chile, Reserves Low, Will Seek Renegotiation of Payments on Her $3 Billion Foreign Debt," New York Times, November 10, 1971; "Chile Meets with International Creditors to Renegotiate Payments on $1.3 Billion," Wall Street Journal, January 10, 1972, p. 12; "Two More Meetings on Chilean Debt Slated by 'Paris Club'," Wall Street Journal, February 7, 1972; "Accord on Loans Reported," New York Times, January 27, 1972; "Allende Confers with Foreign Officials on Debts," New York Times, April 15, 1972.

42. See, for example, Leoncio (1974).

43. Petras and Laporte (1972, pp. 132-33). For an interesting contrast in U.S. policy in the case of Algeria, see Quandt (1972).

44. Petras and Laporte (1972); also "Kissinger Reportedly Led Anti-Chile Moves," International Herald Tribune, September 16, 1974, p. 4; "The CIA's New Bay of Bucks," Newsweek, September 23, 1974, pp. 12-13; "CIA Reportedly Subsidized Chilean Strikers," International Herald Tribune, September 22-23, 1974, p. 4.

45. "Nixon Authorizes Jet Fighter Sales to Five Latin Nations," New York Times, June 6, 1973, p. 1.

46. Eric B. Shearer, in a letter to the Editor, New York Times, June 12, 1973, p. 44.

47. "U.S. Not Surprised," New York Times, September 12, 1973, p. 1.

48. "Aides Say Chile's Move Will Spur U.S. To 'Get Tough'," New York Times, September 30, 1971. See also "Chile's Take-Over Plans Hit by Javits," New York Times, February 2, 1971; "Rogers Reproves Chile on Seizures," New York Times, October 14, 1971; "U.S. Tells Chile Seizures Could Endanger Aid to Needy Countries," New York Times, October 16, 1971; "Six Concerns Embroiled in Chile Seizures Are Called in by Rogers," Wall Street Journal, October 25, 1971; "Nixon Announces Tough U.S. Stand on Expropriation," New York Times, January 20, 1972, p. 1.

49. See note 44 above.

50. "Debt-Ridden Chile Is Reported to Get Soviet Offer of $50 million in Credits," New York Times, January 16, 1972, p. 20.

51. Onís, "Chile Says She Will Pay."

52. "U.S. Companies Looking to Chile," New York Times, September 12, 1973, p. 19; "Plan on Copper Reported," New York Times, September 20, 1973; "Chile Offers to Reopen Talks on Copper," New York Times, September 24, 1973; "Chile to Return Seized Companies to Their Owners," New York Times, October 20, 1973.

53. "Private U.S. Loans in Chile Up Sharply," New York Times, November 12, 1973, p. 53.

54. "Chile and Creditors Reach an Accord," New York Times, February 24, 1974; "Chile Wins Extension of Part of Debt Owed to Twelve Creditor Nations," Wall Street Journal, March 8, 1974, p. 8; "Chile Wins Delay on Debt," Newsweek, April 8, 1974, p. 36; "Chile Gets IMF Approval to Borrow $94.8 Million," Wall Street Journal, March 31, 1974.

55. "Chile Settles Copper Claim with Anaconda," Newsweek, August 5, 1974, p. 34.

56. "Kennecott Settles Its Copper Claims with Chile," Newsweek, November 4, 1974, p. 46.

57. "Chile to Open Up for New Copper Mining," Newsweek, September 23, 1974, p. 46.

CORPORATE IMPERIALISM IN
THE CARIBBEAN BAUXITE INDUSTRY 3

> When Columbus landed in the Caribbean he thanked God and en-
> quired after gold. Nowadays the industrialists arrive by jet clip-
> per. They thank the Minister of Pioneer Industry and enquire
> after bauxite.
>
> — Lloyd Best

> ... it can be demonstrated that almost 20,000 jobs at Reynolds in
> the United States — two-thirds of our total — work with bauxite,
> alumina or aluminum derived from Jamaica. Since the U.S. alu-
> minum industry as a whole employs ... some 300,000 people —
> and since half of the domestic industry's bauxite comes from
> Jamaica — we are talking about 150,000 jobs in this country that
> trace back to raw materials from Jamaica.
>
> — Richard Reynolds,
> President of Reynolds Metals

Bauxite is the red gold of the Caribbean. The innocuous-looking
dirt that covers the islands of Jamaica and Hispaniola and the
mainland countries of Surinam and Guyana contains hundreds of
millions of tons of aluminum — the "miracle metal" of the twentieth century. In the last eighty years, aluminum has been transformed from a rare, expensive, and relatively unknown commodity
into the first of all industrial metals after steel. Aluminum's light
weight and great strength has given it wide and abundant uses as a
building material, in the manufacture of transport and electrical
equipment, and in all kinds of consumer goods used in everyday
life.[1] Aluminum helped to win two world wars for the Allied powers. Without it, the aeronautics industry could not exist in its
present form, nor could the arms industry; housing of all kinds
and automobiles would be heavier and more costly. The aluminum

industry generates incomes running into the thousands of millions of dollars and provides hundreds of thousands of jobs. Forty-four percent of the aluminum produced in the capitalist world is extracted from the soil of Jamaica, Surinam, Guyana, the Dominican Republic, and Haiti.

What do the people of these countries have to show for the riches drawn from their earth? This: unemployment racks these societies; the rate of joblessness runs from a minimum of around 15 percent to as high as 30 percent, and underemployment affects at least another 20 percent of the labor force. Malnutrition is endemic; it kills off many of the babies born every year and stunts the cerebral growth of many of those who survive. The majority of the people have no adequate or decent housing; their families crowd into single-room shacks and hovels made not of aluminum but of mud, thatch, or cardboard. Incomes are pitifully low; the majority earn no more than $10 per week or its equivalent.

Caribbean bauxite does produce great wealth, but for others outside of the region. A man named Arthur Vining Davis died in 1962 and left a fortune of $400 million. His wealth had been generated almost entirely on the basis of Caribbean bauxite, from which was extracted most of the aluminum produced by the Aluminum Company of America and Alcan Aluminium, Limited — the companies responsible for Davis's great wealth. Davis willed most of the money to a foundation, on one condition: its funds could not be used for the benefit of citizens of the Caribbean bauxite-producing countries or any country other than the United States and its possessions.[2] The Mellon family is reputed to be the richest in the United States, perhaps in the world: their wealth was estimated in 1967 to be at least $3 billion.[3] Some 21 percent of the Mellon fortune is derived from their large holdings of stock in Alcoa, a company that, since the 1930s, has produced most of its aluminum from Caribbean bauxite. The annual dividend income of the Mellon family was set at $78 million in 1967, about one-third of the total annual incomes of the 430,000 people of Surinam, the country that provides Alcoa with most of its raw materials.

In fact, the Caribbean bauxite industry is a classic case of economic imperialism. It is entirely owned and operated by a small number of vertically integrated North American transnational aluminum companies (except in Guyana, and then only since 1971). These companies also control the bulk of world production and reserves of bauxite and they dominate the world aluminum market. Capital and technology for the Caribbean bauxite industry come from the transnational aluminum companies. There is no "market" for its output other than the plants of the companies. Prices are fixed by the companies according to their convenience. Levels of production and the rates of investment and expansion are matters of company policy, determined by the global economics of the transnational firm. Only a part of the value of the industry's "sales" actually accrue to the Caribbean economies; and only an infinitesimal fraction of the value of the end products flows back to Caribbean people. Raw materials are shipped abroad for processing; they form the basis for the creation of income and value added abroad and permit the generation of surplus value and the compounded accumulation of capital, privately appropriated in the form of the transnational corporation. Thus, the Caribbean bauxite industry is entirely subject to the needs, policies, and authority of corporate monopoly capital based in North America. Total integration of the industry with the wider, global structures of the companies has been the instrument by which this has been achieved.

Moreover, the corporations have been so powerful that they have largely succeeded in molding the political economy of the Caribbean states concerned to their own needs. Historically, the only resistance to the complete hegemony of the corporations in the Caribbean has come from the workers in the industry and from peasants whose lands the companies have sought to expropriate in order to secure bauxite deposits. But even this resistance has been generally weak, because workers and peasants could not count on the state to act consistently and vigorously in their defense. On the contrary, the state has, more often than not, been a direct agent of the corporations in the countries concerned. When we speak of corporate integration in the Caribbean bauxite industry, we mean more than the integration of raw materials facilities in the Caribbean with overseas processing facilities within the authority framework of the transnational firm: we also mean the integration of the state in the bauxite-producing country into the network of power relations within the corporation.

But since the integration is a subordinate one, it also gives rise to contradictions. Recently, these contradictions have become heightened as a result of economic and political pressures within the countries concerned and within the wider international capitalist system. Governments have imposed higher taxes on the companies; they have formed an association of bauxite-producing countries; they have even nationalized the subsidiaries of the corporations. What factors have motivated such actions? How suc-

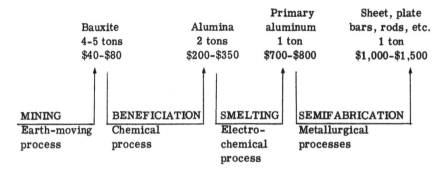

Figure 5. Processes, products, and values in the bauxite-aluminum industry.

cessful have they been, and do they promise to be? And how far do they imply an assault on the system of corporate imperialism within the world aluminum industry, rather than merely attempts to redefine the terms upon which the governments participate in it? These are some of the questions we will seek to answer.

I. CORPORATE INTEGRATION AND THE CARIBBEAN BAUXITE INDUSTRY

Corporate Integration and the Unequal International Division of Labor

With every stage in the transformation of bauxite deposits into aluminum products, the production process becomes more complex and the value added by the process higher (Fig. 5). Thus, mining bauxite is a relatively simple earth-moving process, but extracting aluminum oxide from the ore requires multiple-stage chemical treatment, and reducing the oxide to aluminum metal involves a costly electrolytic-chemical process. Consequently, the value of end products is very high in relation to that of the raw material. Bauxite valued at $50, say, yields aluminum products that can be sold for anything up to $2,000. Evidently, the crucial activities in the generation of value and of industrial external economies are the processes of reducing aluminum from alumina and transforming the primary metal into semifabricated products used by manufacturers. But the Caribbean countries, in spite of their possession of some of the world's largest bauxite deposits, have been confined to the simple low-value activities, and particularly to the extraction of the bauxite ore and to that alone. Thus, the region

101

Table 8

World Production of Bauxite, Alumina, and Aluminum, 1972[a]

	Bauxite		Alumina		Aluminum	
	Thousand tons	% world total	Thousand tons	% world total	Thousand tons	% world total
Jamaica	14,318	19.0	3,297	10.5	—	—
Surinam	8,573	11.4	1,323	4.2	58	0.5
Guyana	4,108	5.4	385	1.2	—	—
Dominican Republic	1,142	1.5	—	—	—	—
Haiti	863	1.1	—	—	—	—
Total Caribbean	29,004	38.4	5,005	15.9	58	0.5
Australia	15,910	21.1	3,894	12.4	227	1.8
Guinea	3,000	4.0	772	2.5	—	—
Yugoslavia	2,421	3.2	374	1.2	80	0.6
Sierra Leone	765	1.0	—	—	—	—
Ghana	349	0.5	—	—	146	1.2
Total IBA countries	51,449	68.2	10,045	32.0	511	4.1
France	3,591	4.8	1,340	4.3	434	3.5
Greece	2,978	3.9	529	1.7	143	1.1
United States	2,125	2.8	7,760	24.7	4,122	32.9
India	1,829	2.4	453	1.4	196	1.6
Indonesia	1,407	1.9	—	—	—	—
Malaya	1,187	1.6	—	—	—	—
Brazil	550	0.7	231	0.7	107	0.9
Other Western Europe	—	—	2,215	7.1	2,070	16.5
Canada	—	—	1,387	4.4	1,000	8.0
Japan	—	—	2,638	8.4	1,119	8.9
Others	123	—	84	0.3	225	2.0
Total capitalist world	65,239	86.5	26,682	85.1	9,957	79.4
USSR	6,300	8.3	3,300	10.5	1,980	15.8
Other Eastern Europe	3,399	4.5	1,036	3.3	434	3.5
China	500	0.7	330	1.1	170	1.3
Total socialist world	10,199	13.5	4,666	14.9	2,584	20.6
World total	75,438	100.0	31,348	100.0	12,541	100.0

Sources: American Bureau of Metal Statistics and U.S. Bureau of Mines.

a. Bauxite and aluminum: production in short tons (2,000 lb.); alumina: capacity in short tons.

102

accounts for 38 percent of total world bauxite production, but only 16 percent of alumina production and an insignificant 0.5 percent of world primary aluminum production (Table 8). Its production of semifabricated aluminum products is infinitesimal. The overwhelming bulk of Caribbean bauxite and alumina is transformed into end products in the United States and Canada, which themselves produce very little bauxite. In fact, the industry is a perfect example of the unequal international division of labor characteristic of the international capitalist system.

This inequality is not accidental, nor does it result from the impersonal, objective operation of the laws of locational economics. It has been deliberately imposed. The instruments of its imposition are the transnational aluminum companies. Company-owned mines extract the ore within the Caribbean countries and subject it to first-stage processing (drying). Some of it is processed into alumina at company-owned plants on the spot; most of it is exported, more often than not in company-owned ships, for processing at company-owned alumina plants in the United States and Canada. The alumina is reduced to aluminum at company-owned smelters in North America and all over the world; a large part of the primary aluminum is itself used by the companies in their own semifabricating plants (Table 9, Fig. 6). Thus, the international vertical integration of the companies has been the means of securing a perfect structural integration of Caribbean raw materials with manufacturing industry in the central capitalist countries.

Factors Conditioning the Pattern of Corporate Integration

Historically, the pattern emerged as big, monopolistic U.S. corporations engaged in the production of aluminum sought to secure control over foreign sources of bauxite in order to bolster their monopolistic position.[4] Alcoa and its sister company Alcan had a complete monopoly over the aluminum industry of the United States and Canada clear up until the Second World War. Alcoa had secured control over the patent rights for electrolytic production of aluminum when it began production in 1888. By 1909, when the patents expired, Alcoa had acquired a virtual monopoly over bauxite deposits in the United States and had also come to control several important hydroelectric power sources that were crucial for reliable, low-cost aluminum production. The company was vertically integrated from bauxite mining through aluminum semifabrication and even the fabrication of finished goods such as kitchen utensils.

Table 9

The Caribbean Bauxite Industry and the Transnational Aluminum
Companies, 1972

	Alcoa	Alcan	Rey-nolds	Kaiser	Ana-conda	Revere	Billi-ton[a]	State company	Total country
Jamaica[b]									
Bauxite	1,150	2,570	3,000	6,700	1,005	460	—	—	14,885
Alumina	551	1,226	478	344	478	220	—	—	3,297
Surinam									
Bauxite	4,200	—	—	—	—	—	2,600	—	6,800
Alumina	1,400	—	—	—	—	—	—	—	1,400
Aluminum	58	—	—	—	—	—	—		58
Guyana									
Bauxite	—	—	707[c]	—	—	—	—	3,000	3,688
Alumina	—	—	—	—	—	—	—	385	385
Dominican Republic									
Bauxite	1,208	—	—	—	—	—	—	—	1,208
Haiti									
Bauxite	—	—	677	—	—	—	—	—	677
United States, Canada									
Bauxite	400	—	600	—	—	—	—	—	2,125[f]
Alumina	2,750	1,387	2,225	1,825	—	—	—	—	9,147[f]
Aluminum	1,545	1,035	975	710	180	237	—	—	5,122[f].
Caribbean raw materials as percentage of company requirements	48	29[d]	71	88	100	100[e]	n.a.	—	—
Company as percentage of capitalist world primary aluminum capacity	16	19	11	12	1	1	n.a.	—	—

Note: The figures are estimated from various sources. Figures for bauxite
are in thousands of long dry tons; for alumina and aluminum, in thousands of
short tons.

a. A member of the Royal Dutch-Shell transnational oil conglomerate.

b. Capacity, not production.

c. To be nationalized at the end of 1974.

d. The proportion was about 58 percent at the time of Guyana's nationalization of Demba in 1971.

e. It is assumed that Revere also purchases alumina made from Caribbean bauxite.

f. Includes other companies.

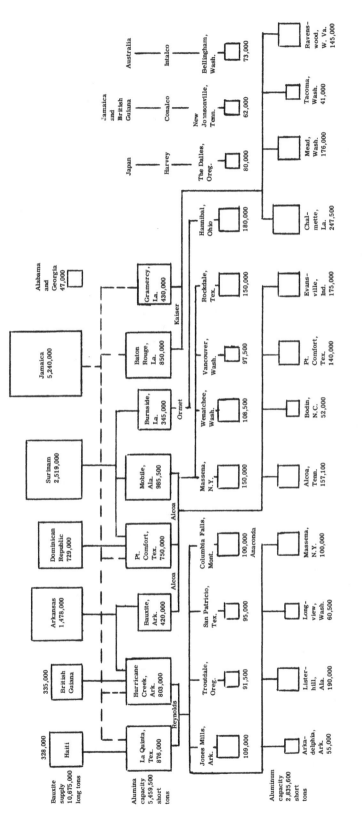

Figure 6. Vertical integration of Caribbean bauxite with United States processing plants, 1963. (From U.S. Bureau of Mines, Mineral Facts and Problems, 1965)

Alcoa continually sought to reinforce its position vis-à-vis potential competitors in North America as well as the European monopolies by acquiring foreign bauxite deposits and hydroelectric power sources. By the First World War, at the same time that Anaconda and Kennecott were busily buying up the Chilean copper deposits, Alcoa was aggressively acquiring the bauxite of Guyana (then British Guiana) and Surinam (Dutch Guiana). Between 1912 and 1925, Alcoa had secured virtual monopoly control over available bauxite deposits in these countries. Apart from outright purchase of bauxite lands, the methods used included litigation, negotiation, outright trickery and double-dealing, and alleged influence-mongering among the colonial administrations in British and Dutch Guiana and the imperial governments of Britain and the Netherlands. As Alcoa developed its bauxite production in the Guianas, it did not build plants to process the ore or aluminum smelters there; and it displayed no interest in developing the considerable hydroelectric power potential of the large rivers that drain from the Guianas into the southern Caribbean. The company found it cheaper, more convenient, and less risky to expand its alumina facilities and smelters in North America and gradually to develop the huge hydroelectric power sources it had acquired in the Canadian provinces of Quebec and Ontario and several states in the United States.

The Alcoa-Alcan monopoly in North America was finally broken after the Second World War. Reynolds Metals and Kaiser Aluminum entered the industry, using alumina plants and smelters virtually given to them by the United States government from its surplus war facilities. In their search for their own bauxite supplies independent of Alcoa, both countries made large discoveries in Jamaica. Reynolds also found bauxite in Haiti and acquired a small operation in Guyana. Reynolds and Kaiser simply fed their Caribbean bauxite production into the alumina plants they had acquired cheaply from the U.S. government. As their aluminum production grew rapidly in the 1950s, they each built a new alumina plant — but still in the United States, although the evidence is that it would have been more economical to build them next to their mines in the Caribbean, at least in Jamaica.[5] Why was the classic pattern of exporting the raw material without processing maintained, in spite of clear directions to the contrary by the conventional economics of location? A critical and probably decisive factor was the military security needs of the United States. Aluminum is a strategic war material, and the plants were built at the height of the cold war in the early 1950s. Shipments across the

Gulf of Mexico were particularly vulnerable to submarine action. From the American point of view, it was strategically more desirable to ship the low-valued bauxite than the higher-valued alumina, not to speak of aluminum. And the U.S. government had great leverage over the companies, through its taxation and financial policies and its stockpile purchases of bauxite and aluminum.

More recently, with the relaxation of cold war tensions and increasing pressure from Caribbean governments, the companies have shown willingness to build alumina plants in the Caribbean to process their incremental bauxite production. The initiative had been taken by Alcan, which built alumina plants in Jamaica and Guyana in the 1950s. Alcan's longer shipping routes, which include western Canada (British Columbia) and Norway, made it impossible to ignore the cost advantages of shipping one ton of alumina instead of two tons of bauxite. Alcoa followed by building plants in Surinam and Jamaica in the middle and late 1960s. In Jamaica, Reynolds and Kaiser were joined by a new entrant to the U.S. aluminum industry, Anaconda, in forming a consortium to build an alumina plant, which was completed in 1969. Anaconda had entered the aluminum industry in the 1950s as a result of a decision to diversify away from copper, in which it was highly dependent on its Chilean mines. Revere, another new entrant to the aluminum industry, also built an alumina plant in Jamaica at the turn of the 1960 decade. Apart from considerations of locational economics, the companies found that they could use the promise of alumina plants as a bargaining tool to extract considerable concessions from the governments. Nonetheless, the bulk of Caribbean bauxite production continues to be exported from the region without further processing. And, apart from a small smelter built in Surinam by Alcoa, the region has been completely deprived of the production of aluminum metal from its own natural resources. The Caribbean bauxite industry was developed in order to form the raw materials base for the aluminum industries of the United States — the world's largest aluminum-producing country — and Canada. It forms the natural-resource foundation upon which the entire global edifice of international production and marketing of the world's four largest aluminum companies has been built.

Corporate Integration and the State [6]

In extending their vertical integration from the North American center to the Caribbean periphery, the corporations have encountered one problem that is absent in the case of vertical integration within their national borders. That problem is the existence of the national state. The state has formal sovereignty over the natural resources found within its political borders. It levies taxes on income, on property, and on exports and imports. Its political system, laws, customs, and practices differ from those of the firms' home country. The state apparatus is a powerful influence on the degree of activity or passivity of other social groups — such as workers and peasants — whose labor and land are needed to carry out the extraction of the natural resource. But the imperatives of corporate vertical integration mean that raw materials facilities must be subjected to the absolute control of the firms' central authorities. This is required in order to permit smooth and efficient coordination of production, shipping, processing, and marketing, and to allow long-term strategic planning by and for the corporation as a whole. Thus, to the parent companies with bauxite-producing subsidiaries abroad, the foreign state represents an interposition across the control relationships and mechanisms of vertical integration. In effect, the state represents an irritating nuisance to the corporation. Its influence must be eliminated or neutralized or stabilized or — best of all — turned to the service of the corporations. In other words, the state must, if possible, become a part of the control system of the transnational corporation itself.

Diagrammatically, the situation is as depicted in Figure 7. The unbroken lines show the corporate boundary and the intrafirm relationships. They relate to the flow of instructions and cash from the parent to the subsidiary, and the flow of information and products from the subsidiary to the parent. These may be called the "control" relationships. The broken lines show the boundary of the foreign country in which the bauxite is being produced, and the relations between the bauxite subsidiary and the government of the country. The government establishes the regulations governing the operation of the subsidiary and receives a revenue stream composed of various taxes from it. These relationships may be called the "regulation and revenue" relationships; they cover such questions as the area of mining concessions and the taxation formula for bauxite. Finally, there is the direct relationship between the parent company and the national government, which might be called the ongoing "negotiation" relationship. It is this which defines the parameters and content of the regulations and revenue relationships between the government and the subsidiary.

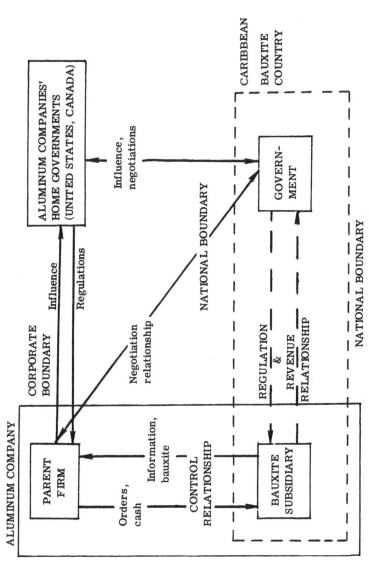

Figure 7. Company-government and government-government relationships in the Caribbean bauxite industry.

The balance of power in the negotiation relationship has lain overwhelmingly with the aluminum companies over most of the life of the Caribbean bauxite industry. In part, this has been due to the overall politicoeconomic framework within which the company-state relationship has unfolded — a framework characterized by Caribbean subordination to European and American imperialism. Guyana, Surinam, and Jamaica were all colonies of European powers at the time the U.S. companies first secured concessions to exploit their bauxite. Whatever secondary contradictions might have existed between Britain or Holland and the United States, these were submerged into the wider imperialist interests associated with the fight against communism and the conflict with fascism. Britain and Holland accepted a de facto U.S. economic dominance over their Caribbean colonies, especially as political decolonization took place after the Second World War. Moreover, the bauxite industries, geared as they are to the United States and Canada, were viewed as dollar earners to the dollar-starved British and Dutch in the 1940s and 1950s. The Dominican Republic and Haiti, although formally independent since the nineteenth century, are both quasi colonies of the United States. The significance of U.S. imperialism in the Caribbean bauxite industry is revealed by concrete episodes: the American-sponsored destabilization and eventual removal of Dr. Jagan's government in Guyana in the early 1960s; the military intervention in the Dominican Republic in 1965; and indirect political intervention in Jamaican politics at least since constitutional independence in 1962. All these actions were at least partly motivated by a wish to maintain security over bauxite supplies.

The aluminum companies also have the advantage of a certain intrinsic superiority in bargaining power over the governments. They possess superior financial resources: each of the four largest companies has a turnover greater than the national income of the largest producing country. To a large extent the companies themselves monopolize the very knowledge and information the government needs to negotiate with them — information about prices, costs, reserves, alternative expansion strategies, production conditions, and technology. The companies control the markets and the production technology, so that governments are often faced with a choice of having their bauxite exploited on the company's terms or not having it exploited at all. And the companies enjoy the flexibility that comes from having operations all over the world and diversified sources of raw materials supplies. The threat of shift-

ing operations and investment from one country to another has for
a long time been more than adequate to keep a government in line.

The companies have therefore succeeded historically in securing
access to Caribbean bauxite very much on their own terms. The
general principle is that these terms should maximize the "control"
relationship between the parent companies and the Caribbean subsidiaries and minimize and stabilize the "regulation and revenue"
relationship between the subsidiaries and the Caribbean states.
What techniques are employed by the companies to operationalize
this principle? The first point to note here is that the companies
always avoid operating under the general legislation and administrative law and practice in the Caribbean states. Instead, they
always negotiate special agreements with the governments, agreements which cover in a comprehensive way all the various aspects
of their operations in the country. This technique enables the companies to secure privileged and generally more favorable treatment than is available to other firms and individuals in the country. But its value goes beyond this. A special agreement establishes the company as a legal enclave within the state, which cannot be touched by government officers or actions except on terms
clearly set out in the agreement itself. It removes the bauxite subsidiary from the impact of changes in government policy and practice over time; in that sense, it freezes government treatment of
the industry and neutralizes the state as an autonomous actor in
the bauxite industry. Thus, it permits the parent company to control its Caribbean subsidiary; and by reducing the area of unpre-
dictability, it facilitates the parent company's long-term strategic
planning. The sovereignty of the state is constrained in order to
reinforce the sovereignty of the corporation. Finally, a special
agreement becomes part of the ongoing negotiation relationship
between the state and the transnational corporation. If the government wishes to change its policies in regard to bauxite, it must
seek to renegotiate the agreement. By agreeing to renegotiate at
all the company is making a concession, for which it will seek
some quid pro quo from the government.

An examination of special agreements between the aluminum
companies and the Caribbean bauxite-producing states indicates
that they consistently cover four main areas of the company-state
relationship. The first is the area of resource accessibility: this
concerns the specific rights of the company to the natural resources
of the country in a defined physical area. Such resources include
not only bauxite but other natural resources that might be needed

111

in operations, such as water, sand, and gravel. The company's objective here is to secure rights to as much bauxite and other natural resources as possible, and over the largest possible physical area, and to secure these rights on terms that exclude other users and especially other aluminum companies. Maximize and monopolize, then, is the strategy in the area of resource accessibility.

Second, the agreements cover the extent and limitations of the company's rights and responsibilities regarding operational conditions; that is, such matters as employment and the use of profits and of foreign exchange. More generally, operational conditions cover both those relating to physical production operations and those relating to financial transactions. In this area, the company's objectives are first to secure the maximum freedom from state regulation for its subsidiary, and second to ensure that such powers of regulation and intervention as the state is allowed are spelled out clearly and their limits clearly defined. Thus, the strategy for operational conditions is to minimize and stabilize state regulation and intervention.

The third area relates to the payment stream from the subsidiary to the government. It concerns taxes and all the different kinds of fiscal obligations the company agrees to accept in payment for its concession. Again, the company strategy here is to minimize and stabilize the payment stream as far as possible, both to minimize costs for the parent corporation and to make such costs predictable and therefore to facilitate long-term planning. It is important to note here that the payment stream concerns only one area of the total package covered by company-government agreements, and that the company normally uses it as a bargaining tool to secure a favorable result in other areas. Companies offer to pay more if the taxes are fixed for a long period of time, and if other components in the agreement are favorable and likewise fixed. Thus, the company bribes the government to accept a reduction in the sovereignty of the state; in this way it seeks to buy the stability it needs in its subsidiary's operations.

Finally, all agreements contain provisions that define their juridical status. The company seeks to have the duration of the agreement fixed for as long a period of time as possible; thus, in 1970 the average life of the agreements in force between the companies and Caribbean states was forty-one years, with a range from twenty-five to seventy-five years. Obviously, very few agreements actually last that long without any changes, but a company uses its consent or reluctance to renegotiate as a bargaining tool in its own right. Just as important, the company seeks to have the agreement defined as preeminent over all general statutory and administrative law in the state. Frequently, too, there are provisions for resolving disputes arising out of the agreement which remove jurisdiction entirely from the hands of the national authorities and place it under the authority of international bodies or the courts of the home country of the transnational corporation. Evidently, the company seeks to have the juridical status of the agreement established in such a way as to tie the hands of the state as tightly as possible and for as long a period of time as possible.

The companies have succeeded in meeting their objectives in agreements with the Caribbean bauxite-producing states with remarkable consistency, irrespective of the constitutional status of the country concerned — colony or independent state — and irrespective of the legal tradition — British, French, Dutch, or Spanish. These agreements put the seal of juridical and governmental approval on the divorce of the bauxite industries from the national economy and remove their industries virtually completely from the competence of the economic policy and the planning of the national governments. In effect, the state apparatus becomes an appendage of the transnational corporation: it is integrated into the control mechanisms through which the corporations operate in the country concerned. Thus, corporate integration is carried to the point where it subverts the institution of the state, insofar as we think of the state as a sovereign entity. So perfect has been the dominance of the companies that only in very recent years — since 1971, in fact — have some bauxite-producing states in the Caribbean felt strong enough to assert their sovereignty by unilaterally renouncing contracts with some of the aluminum companies and seeking to impose their own terms on bauxite without first asking the permission of the firms.

II. CORPORATE INTEGRATION AND DEPENDENT UNDERDEVELOPMENT AMONG CARIBBEAN BAUXITE PRODUCERS

Caribbean economy, society, and polity have evolved within the framework of European colonization and, more particularly, that of the plantation system.[7] Black people — first Africans and then Asians — were brought in by the colonial powers to work the

European-owned cane plantations that supplied sugar to the European market and generated profits for European planters, traders, and manufacturers. After the abolition of slavery and indentured labor, the blacks established an independent peasantry and artisan class, which diversified the economy somewhat. A small commercial bourgeoisie appeared, consisting mainly of the remnants of the white planter class, mulattoes, and immigrants from the Middle East. The embryo of a class of political managers was formed out of the elite of certificated blacks and mulattoes who received European-sponsored education. But the legacy of the plantation system persisted. The economies remained externally dependent and highly specialized, and the societies rigidly stratified. Overt colonial rule continued in the British, French, and Dutch territories; in those that were formally independent, U.S. imperialism assumed an active role. It was in this context that bauxite mining and processing activities were introduced — in Guyana and Surinam after the First World War, and in Jamaica, the Dominican Republic, and Haiti after the Second.

From the strictly technological point of view, bauxite ores hold a certain intrinsic potential as a basis for heavy industrialization and industrial diversification (Fig. 8). In transforming the ore into aluminum products, a market is created for all kinds of capital equipment, for steel and other products of the metallurgical industry, and for industrial chemicals, fuels, and electricity, to name but a few. Demands are generated for skilled labor, for engineering services, and for construction. The products of bauxite ore also form the basis of important industrial activities. Apart from the manufacture of alumina, some kinds of bauxite are used in the manufacture of a special type of cement and of refractory and abrasive products. Alumina is used not only for the production of aluminum but also in the manufacture of certain aluminous chemicals. And aluminum is of course a major input into the contemporary metallurgical industry, with a wide variety of applications. In other words, the remarkable industrial potential of bauxite materials is such that the resource could have represented the means for the Caribbean economies to escape from the underdevelopment trap imposed upon them by the plantation system.

But this was not to be. The bauxite industries have increased national incomes — in some countries rather more, in others less. But external dependence has in many respects increased. The ratio of exports, imports, and foreign investment to the national

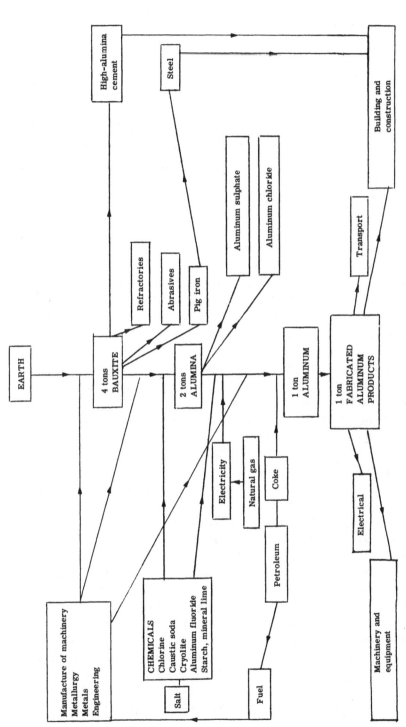

Figure 8. Industries based on and linked with bauxite. (From Norman Girvan, Foreign Capital and Economic Underdevelopment in Jamaica, Mona, University of the West Indies, Institute of Social and Economic Research, 1971, p. 77)

income has grown; the economy is more sensitive to external market conditions and foreign decision making than before; and the national authorities are probably even less capable of influencing the economic system. And underdevelopment has been intensified: the bauxite industries represent a new version of the historical Caribbean role of providing labor power and resources to meet the demands of capitalist accumulation in the central capitalist countries. Such dependent underdevelopment is in fact the corollary of the integration of the Caribbean bauxite industry into the structures of the transnational aluminum companies.

The first notable consequence of this integration is a characteristic pattern of production growth in individual producing countries. The countries can be classified into major suppliers (Jamaica, Surinam, Guyana), and reserve suppliers (the Dominican Republic and Haiti). The classification relates to the role assigned to the country by the principal aluminum companies engaged in mining its bauxite. Reserve suppliers, by definition, are not meant to develop large-scale production. Their production is deliberately kept low and stagnant by company fiat. Their role is to "top up" the company's bauxite supplies from other sources and to act as insurance and a bargaining counter in dealing with governments of the major suppliers. Thus, for these countries, the basic bauxite-producing potential is deliberately underdeveloped as a result of corporate integration.

Major suppliers are destined to enjoy a high rate of production growth and to develop large-scale production. But the pace of expansion is not maintained indefinitely. The high-growth phase corresponds to the period when the principal operating companies decide to draw a large part of their total or incremental supplies from that country. This may last for decades, but after a certain point the companies decide to stabilize their production or their rate of expansion in the country. The reason may be that the depletion of high-grade, easily worked reserves has increased production costs, or that the government of the country has acquired greater leverage as a result of large-scale production, or a combination of both. In any case, no company wishes to be overdependent on any one raw material source. For the country, the end of the high-growth phase signals the onset of maturity in its bauxite industry, perhaps even of stagnation. For Guyana and Surinam, the high-growth phase lasted roughly from 1920 to 1950, while for Jamaica it ran roughly from 1950 to 1970. At the end of the high-growth phase, the rate of production growth in each of these countries declined below that of the world as a whole; and the growth of the industry's value came less from the growth of bauxite production itself than from the growth of the processing of the ore; that is, the development of calcined bauxite, alumina, and (in Surinam) aluminum production.

But what happens to the economy during the high-growth phase? How far does the bauxite industry help to generate a process of self-sustaining growth in these countries that can outlast the onset of maturity in the industry? In fact, the onset of maturity in the industry has precipitated a crisis in the growth model in the countries concerned. And this crisis to a large extent underlies the outbreak of open conflict between the governments and the companies, as the governments strive to secure greater returns from the industry to allow the model of dependent growth to continue.

To begin with, although exports of bauxite and bauxite products account for the greater part of the total exports of the major suppliers, the economies of these countries receive far less than the value actually assigned to the exports in the trade accounts. In Jamaica, the returned value was normally between 36 and 43 percent of the value of bauxite and alumina exports between 1956 and 1967.[8] In Surinam, returned value was calculated at around 38 percent in 1969[9]; in Guyana, it was normally about 35 percent in the 1960s.[10] The fact is that, aside from wages and salaries and tax payments, the companies pay out very little to the national economies. Since the production technology is capital intensive, wage costs are a small proportion of the total value; while capital allowances, profits after tax, and other capital charges are high, since the capital is foreign owned, these accrue abroad rather than at home. Moreover, the companies purchase very little from local businesses. They often provide themselves with their own services, such as transport, construction, distribution, electric power, and water; and even where these are purchased, they do not amount to much in relation to total turnover. Virtually all capital goods and equipment are imported. Bauxite mining itself does not require substantial inputs of materials. Processing the ore into alumina does involve significant quantities of caustic soda and flour; yet these, too, are imported. Thus, the company-owned bauxite industries in the Caribbean started out, and remained, typical mineral-export enclaves almost completely isolated from the host economies.

Closely associated with this is the virtually complete lack of linkages between the bauxite industries and the national economies.

Guyana and Surinam, after fifty years of large-scale bauxite production, cannot point to a single industry of any importance that was established to supply the bauxite industry or to use its products. Nor can Jamaica, after twenty-five years. No mining or processing machinery or equipment is manufactured or even assembled; no chemicals for the processing of bauxite and alumina are produced and no by-products or joint products of the products and processes are utilized. Cement is made from Jamaican bauxite — but not in Jamaica; refractory and abrasive products are made from Guyanese bauxite — but not in Guyana; aluminous chemicals are made from Surinam bauxite — but not in Surinam. In fact, it is the central capitalist countries, especially North America, that have secured the benefits of the tremendous linkages and associated external economies based on Caribbean bauxite. It was estimated that in 1964 some $1.813 billion of valued added plus some $1.14 billion of input demand were generated abroad in the transformation of Caribbean bauxite into semifabricated aluminum products, compared to the $171 million total value of the region's bauxite and alumina exports in that year (see Table 10). The returned value is even less than the total export value; thus, only some 3 percent of the value of semifabricated aluminum contained in Caribbean exports actually filtered back to the people of the region.

The result is that the impressive potential of bauxite to serve as a basis for economic transformation in the Caribbean has been completely frustrated by the system of corporate integration. Rather than initiate a development process in the economies, the bauxite industries have reinforced the internal fragmentation and external dependence of their productive systems. The mining sector has been introduced with little or no economic transactions with agriculture or manufacturing or any other producing sector. It is completely dependent on foreign decision making, capital, technology, inputs, and demand. In such a context, the quantitative growth of productive activities and national income in no way reflects qualitative changes oriented toward improving the material welfare of the population at large or making the productive system more self-centered. Rather, quantitative growth implies greater integration with the international corporations, intensified dependent underdevelopment, and a growing divorce between the structure of resource use, on the one hand, and the material needs of the population, on the other.

Guyana provides an instructive case of the effects of the introduction of a bauxite industry into a modified plantation economy.

Table 10

Location of GDP Created and Input Demand Generated by
Processing of Caribbean Metal Grade Bauxite, 1964
(in million U.S. dollars)

	Mining		Benefi-ciation		Smelting		Semi-fabrication			
	GDP	Input demand	GDP	Input demand	GDP	Input demand	GDP	Input demand	Total	Percent of total
Caribbean	90	25	34	22	—	—	—	—	171	6
North America and rest of world	—	—	120	81	571	381	1,122	678	2,953	94
Total	90	25	154	103	571	381	1,122	678	3,124	100

Sources: Estimates calculated from input and value-added data from Caribbean producers, and from the United States as recorded in U.S. Bureau of the Census, Census of Manfactures, 1963. Estimate excludes calcined bauxite.

Mining began after the First World War, and over the decades the industry joined sugar as the basis of the national economy: in 1965, for example, it accounted for some 35 percent of merchandise exports, 19 percent of the GDP, and 10 percent of government revenues. But its effects on economic growth and development were extremely limited. Between 1917 and 1969 the transnational corporations extracted some 50 million tons of bauxite from the country, valued at some G$1.2 billion (G$1 = US$0.50 in 1969). The government's take from this amounted to only 1.6 percent in royalties; even when income taxes are included, the share was only 3.4 percent as late as the 1960s.[11] In all, the share of the country did not exceed some 39 percent, even when internal capital spending is included. No feeder industries were established to supply the mining activities. The main mining town grew up, willy-nilly, some sixty-five miles from the capital city up the Demerara River, isolated physically, economically, and socially from the rest of Guyana. It was one of the worst examples of a company town, ruled by the Demerara Bauxite Company (Demba), a subsidiary of Alcan Aluminium, Limited.

So limited was the economic impact of Demba that the Guyanese economy has suffered from endemic stagnation, at least since the 1940s. Between the 1940s and the 1960s, the average real income per person in the country declined; this was accompanied by a worsening in the distribution of income and a steady rise in unemployment, which was estimated to have reached 18 percent of the labor force by the mid-1960s.[12] In 1970 the average per capita income in Guyana was only $308. Yet between 1928 and 1950, Guyana's bauxite was the only source of raw material for Alcan, which grew during that period from virtually nothing to become the world's second largest aluminum company, with assets of over $400 million. After 1950 Jamaica was added to Guyana as the base for Alcan's aluminum production, and by the early 1970s the company's assets had grown to over $2 billion, while the Guyana economy stagnated and Guyanese became steadily poorer.

Jamaica provides a contrasting experience with that of Guyana. While Guyana's lot was stagnation with underdevelopment, Jamaica's was growth without development.[13] At the end of the Second World War, Jamaica was a typical colonial, modified plantation economy with high unemployment (27 percent). Between 1950 and 1972, the aluminum companies invested some $700 million in bauxite and alumina production in Jamaica. The country became the world's largest bauxite producer in the 1950s and 1960s; it also became, and remains, the principal source of bauxite and alumina for the U.S. aluminum industry. According to the statistics, profound changes took place in the Jamaican economy. The bauxite industry now accounts for 12 percent of the GDP and 66 percent of merchandise exports; during the late 1950s and 1960s, it produced between 11 and 18 percent of government revenue. Average real per capita income grew by roughly 4 percent per year in the 1950s and 1960s. Jamaica's per capita income of around $1,200 is one of the highest in the Third World today.

This has meant very little, however, in terms of the quality of life of the vast majority of the Jamaican people. Income distribution has worsened perceptibly, with the richest 5 percent earning some twenty-four times the average for the poorest 50 percent, estimated to be about $130 in 1968.[14] Unemployment, in spite of substantial economic growth and massive emigration, was 25 percent of the labor force in early 1972. And the Jamaican economy is far more dependent now than it was twenty-five years ago: the ratio of exports and imports to the national product has increased, and foreign trade is now highly concentrated with the United States, which also supplies most foreign investment. Basically, Jamaica's economic performance and the pattern of growth is determined by

decisions taken by the North American aluminum companies and
North American investors.

Both in Guyana, a case of stagnation and underdevelopment, and
in Jamaica, a case of growth without development, sharp social
and economic contradictions have emerged within the country. One
expression of these contradictions is the demand by disaffected
and excluded groups that the bauxite industries be integrated into
the economic and social life of the country and be made to serve
the interests of the population. Within the terms of the corporate
system, however, the principal method available for establishing
some links between the industry and the national economy is through
taxation. This means that it is the relationship between the transnational corporations and the state that establishes the parameters
of whatever integration is achieved between the industry and the
economy. In Guyana, Surinam, and Jamaica, the bauxite industries were first established in the colonial period, when the
state was in the direct service of imperialist interests. There
were therefore few, if any, contradictions between the corporations and the governments during this time. What in fact took
place is that the colonial state activity colluded in the rape of
natural resources by the companies. In Guyana, during the
1920s, the companies paid a royalty amounting to 2 percent of
the value of bauxite exported, and this value was itself under-
stated[15]; in Surinam the payments were also very small until
the late 1940s; and in Jamaica the initial agreement (1950) gave
the Treasury a total of $0.38 per long dry ton of bauxite valued
at between $7-$10 per ton.

It is when the embryonic national buro-political class begins to
inherit the state apparatus from the colonial administration that
the first opportunities for conflict with the corporations begin to
appear. Nonetheless, political developments by themselves do
not tilt the balance of power away from the corporations. The
companies still operate within the context of broad imperialist
relationships in the hemisphere, with control over information,
technology, capital, and markets, and with substantial international
flexibility. Moreover, the fledgling national state faces an additional problem when it seeks to place the taxation of the company-
owned bauxite industry on a more equitable basis. Income taxes,
the major potential source of revenue, are levied on profits. Profits are the difference between revenue and costs. Revenue is
the product of the number of units sold times the unit price of

sales. But suppose the product is not actually sold, and there is no real sales price. How, then, shall profits be computed? This problem results directly from the vertical integration of the aluminum companies, which means that, to all intents and purposes, the entire product of the Caribbean bauxite industry is merely transferred to the parent companies in North America for further processing in their own plants, rather than sold. It is not an unfamiliar problem to Caribbean plantation economies, for the historical relationship between West Indian planters and European merchants gave rise to the same phenomenon. It has come to be known as the problem of incalculability.[16]

The normal solution to the problem is to use a "tax-reference" price; that is, a notional value assigned to the product that is used for the purposes of taxation. But this prescription does little to help Caribbean governments. Tax-reference prices are usually based on actual market transactions, and in the world bauxite industry actual market transactions are few and far between, and the terms of those that do exist are held as closely guarded secrets by the companies. The full dimensions of the problem of incalculability are revealed when one examines actual prices and values used for bauxite in published sources. The range of prices reported is so wide and the methods used so numerous as to be quite inexplicable and bewildering (Table 11). The companies have used one set of prices for valuing the U.S.-produced bauxite used in their own plants, another set for imported bauxite, a different set for the sales of bauxite to the U.S. government stockpile, and a different set again for tax-reference purposes with Caribbean governments. In other words, they have simply used different prices depending on what is convenient to them at different times and on different occasions. However, if there is one consistency that emerges in the pricing pattern, it is that the prices more or less imposed by the companies on Caribbean governments for tax-reference purposes generally have been significantly less than those realized from actual sales of Caribbean ore. They have also been far less than the values for U.S. bauxite recorded by the companies, although U.S. bauxite is far inferior in quality to the Caribbean material.

The problem of incalculability together with the strong bargaining position of the companies helps to explain why, when Caribbean governments came to renegotiate bauxite taxes and terms of oper-

Table 11

Company Sales Prices for Metal Grade Bauxite Compared to Prices Used
to Value Exports for Tax Purposes in Bauxite Countries
(in U.S. dollars per long dry ton)

Company price		Country price	
1. For U.S. bauxite, purchased by U.S. government for stockpile during World War II	6.84[a]	Jamaica: By agreement with the companies (tax rate 40 percent)	
		1952-56	5.00
		1957-67	7.35
2. For Jamaican bauxite, purchased by U.S. government for stockpile, 1953-69; total quantity purchased, 8,858,881 tons		1968-70	12.00
		Dominican Republic: Price range, 1957-68 (tax rate 30 per-	
Average purchase price	15.05	cent)	9.87-15.26
Market value per ton	11.64		
		Haiti: Price range, 1959-68	
3. For Jamaican bauxite, purchased by Reynolds from its Jamaican subsidiary, 1952-72; with adjustments for changes in wage rates, taxes, and U.S. import duties			8.72-14.25
		Surinam: Prices during World	
		War II	$5.56- 4.00
	9.12[a]	Prices 1950-68	
			$6.43-10.28
4. For Jamaican bauxite, purchased by U.S. government for stockpile from Kaiser, mid-1950s, with adjustment for change in Jamaican royalty and U.S. import duty		Prices by agreement with Alcoa (metric ton):	
		1949-50	6.67
		1951-54	6.65[a]
	15.05[a]	1955-56	6.64[a]
		1960-2033[b] (tax	
5. For Surinam-type bauxite, purchased by U.S. government for stockpile, 1950-69; total quantity purchased, 7,889,881 tons		rate 35 percent) 11.13[a]	
		Guyana: Agreement with Alcan,	
Average purchase price	15.68	1965	10.40
Market value per ton	15.35	Agreement with Reynolds,	
		1965	10.44[a]
6. For Surinam bauxite, sold by Alcoa to Kaiser under 1949 contract (metric ton)		Guinea: Agreement with six companies, 1967	
1949-50	6.67[a]	(tax rate 65 per-	
1951-54	6.65[a]	cent)	4.35[a]
1955-56	6.64[a]		

Note: Standard grade is 56 percent Al_2O_3, 3 percent SiO_2, 6 percent Fe_2O_3, 1.5 percent free moisture. Jamaica-type bauxite is from Jamaica, the Dominican Republic, and Haiti; Surinam-type bauxite is from Surinam and Guyana.

a. At standard grade, with adjustments for content of ore.

b. As fixed in the seventy-five-year Brokopondo agreement made in 1958.

ation in the 1950s and 1960s, the results were usually less than satisfactory. Let us turn to a more detailed analysis of government actions and policies, and company reactions.

III. STATE RESPONSES AND COMPANY COUNTERSTRATEGIES: 1915-73

The cooptation of the Caribbean state into the control relationships of corporate vertical integration is not a stable process, free from contradictions. The basic contradiction is between the transnational corporations, as agencies of imperialist capital, and the mass of the Caribbean population — that is, the workers, whether employed or unemployed, and the peasants. In the colonial period the state is openly and formally an agent of imperialist capital; hence, in this context the contradictions between the Caribbean people and imperialist capital are expressed as conflicts between the people and the colonial state. But as decolonization took place in Jamaica, Surinam, and Guyana, the three major Caribbean bauxite producers, the state came — formally — to represent the people. Nonetheless, we have seen that in the period of decolonization and early postindependence (that is, in the 1950s and 1960s) the bargaining power of the companies was so strong that they were able to secure direct agreements with governments that juridically institutionalized their control. To the extent that the state authentically represents the interests of the population, however, conflict with the companies is structurally inevitable.

But there is another level at which contradictions emerge. The state apparatus is actually manned by what we have called a buropolitical class; that is, bureaucrats under the formal leadership and authority of the political managers. This class has vested economic interest in extracting more resources from the corporations in order to finance its expansion and secure higher incomes. This coincides with its political interest in demonstrating to the population that it is acting in their interest by securing higher returns from the nation's natural resources. To this should be added the economic interests of the private capitalist class engaged in businesses associated with the dependent economy, such as commerce, light assembly manufacturing, real estate, and construction. Such businesses cannot prosper without a steady growth of foreign exchange to finance imports and of public expenditure to finance business subsidies and overall monetary demand. Hence, there is a coincidence between the interests of the buro-political class and the private capitalist class in securing a steady growth of mineral revenues. When the mineral corporations are expanding the industry, there is a reasonably stable equilibrium, based on an alliance between the corporations and the buro-political and private capitalist class and on payouts by the state to selected segments among the mass of the population. But when expansion stops or fails to take place, this equilibrium is not feasible: the popular masses and the private capitalist class join to support the buro-political class in its use of the state machinery to pressure the mineral corporations for greater revenues. Under these circumstances, the conditions for company-country conflict are met; its actual intensity, however, varies widely from case to case depending on the particular characteristics of each.

To begin with, three broad sets of strategies by the governments may be distinguished. Strategy 1 is simply to seek to secure higher taxes from the companies, through either negotiation or unilateral action. A second strategy is to seek to induce the companies to establish processing facilities — alumina and aluminum plants — within the country, so that additional taxes, foreign exchange, and employment may be generated from the same level of bauxite production. Strategy 3 is to seek direct state participation in ownership and decision making in the subsidiary companies engaged in the industry. Strategy 1 (higher taxes) has been used by all of the governments at one time or another. The larger producers — Jamaica, Surinam, and Guyana — have also tried strategy 2 (greater processing). Strategy 3 — state participation — has been fully employed in Guyana and, more recently, partly employed in Jamaica, while Surinam has made a tentative step in that direction.

Naturally, the companies do not react passively to these strategies. In some cases they refuse the demands of the governments outright; in others they appear to accede but adopt new arrangements that turn the new agreement to their own advantage. Thus, the demands by the governments have sometimes had perverse results, contrary to those intended. The frustrations produced by such experiences have given rise to government attempts to alter the basic balance of bargaining power in the industry by forming an association of bauxite-producing countries. The formation of the International Bauxite Association (IBA) should be regarded as an additional measure — strategy 4 — designed to secure the objectives of the other three strategies by increasing the bargaining power of the governments.

We shall look at each of these strategies, analyzing the experiences of Haiti, Surinam, Guyana, and Jamaica, and examining the "1974 bauxite offensive," when the Caribbean countries, led by Jamaica, all moved to substantially increase their tax take from the industry.

Haiti: From Stage 1 to Stage 1[17]

Students of company-country agreements in the extractive industries perceive a tendency for the balance of bargaining power and benefits to shift progressively from company to country over the life of any given relationship. Thus, according to Wells,[18] the development of agreements progresses through three distinct stages, beginning with stage 1 when the company's bargaining power is strongest and it secures most of the economic rents and is allowed virtually free and unregulated operation in the country. Over time, the technical sophistication of the government grows and it acquires greater leverage over the company as a result of the fixed investments the latter has sunk in the country. The agreements evolve through a second and then a third stage, in which the government secures the bulk of the economic rents and exerts a growing degree of regulation and control over operations, such as purchasing and employment policies and marketing. In a recent analysis, Garrity suggests that the Haitian experience between 1944 and 1971 seems to disprove this general law.[19] In effect, during nearly thirty years of its relationship with the Reynolds Metals aluminum company, marked by four different agreements or amendments to agreements, the Haitian state remained in stage 1 of the company-country relationship.

The basic agreement, negotiated in 1944, was made at a time when American influence in Haiti was extremely strong. The country had been militarily occupied by the United States for twenty years between 1915 and 1934; American personnel still functioned in the Commercial Department, the Treasury, the National Bank of Haiti, and the Customs Administration. The Haitian lawyer who negotiated the agreement for Reynolds actually had close ties with the Lescot government, which was itself controlled by the mulatto elite, traditionally allied to European and North American interests. Small wonder, then, that the 1944 agreement amounted to little more than a juridical approval by the Haitian state of the demands of the company. Reynolds was given rights to prospect over practically the whole country with options to select some 600 square miles for mining, together with virtually unrestricted freedom of operations and total exemption from income taxes. Its sole fiscal liability was for the payment of a small royalty per metric ton of bauxite mined, equivalent to 1.25 times the price of one pound of aluminum ingot on the U.S. market. The company did not actually begin to produce bauxite until 1957, some thirteen years later, and until 1962 the Haitian state had received an average of only 30.5 cents per metric ton for bauxite exports from the country.

The subsequent amendments to the 1944 agreement made between 1944 and 1971 did little to improve the Haitian tax take substantially. The 1949 amendment stipulated that a minimum royalty based on a hypothetical output of 1 million tons per year should be paid, even if shipments were not made or were below that level. The 1963 amendment eliminated the linkage between the royalty and the aluminum price (the "escalator clause") and instead tied the royalty to the level of annual exports on a regressive scale; the result was that the average royalty payment dropped to a mere 20 cents per ton in the 1963-68 period. At the same time, the 1963 amendment imposed an income tax of 70 cents per long dry ton, which was 40 percent of a notional profit of $1.75. Finally, another amendment in 1971 raised the royalty to a flat rate of 50 cents per long dry ton and the income tax to 45 percent of the (unchanged) notional profit, with a minimum total payment by the company of $900,000 per year. After the 1971 amendment, the Haitian state was still receiving only $1.29 per long dry ton for bauxite exports, an amount well below the take negotiated by Jamaica in 1957 and Surinam in 1958. The total take of the Haitian economy — the returned value — amounted to only 28 percent of the value of bauxite exports. Thus, as Garrity points out, Haiti in 1971 could be regarded as still in stage 1 in the development of company-country agreements, with most of the advantages still on the side of the company.

Surinam: The Brokopondo Solution

Surinam has a much longer experience than Haiti with its bauxite industry, and one that is much more varied. The roughly fifty years of bauxite production in Surinam have been marked by a long first phase lasting over thirty years, during which Surinam came to be the principal source of bauxite for Alcoa and for the United States, and a large quantity of high-grade bauxite was mined out in return for relatively low tax payments. This was followed by a second, beginning in

1949, during which the terms of bauxite exploitation were renegotiated to yield greater taxes and increased domestic processing of bauxite — a renegotiation with decidedly limited results.

Phase 1: 1916-48. As early as 1916, a number of seventy-five-year mining leases were granted to Alcoa, and since that time Alcoa has been either the sole or the principal producing company in Surinam. A number of sources attest to the high grade of bauxite ore that the company was able to extract.[20] It appears that the company paid three main types of taxes: a royalty per ton of ore mined, a harbor and river maintenance tax per ton of bauxite shipped, and an income tax computed in the conventional way. These taxes could not have amounted to much; in 1939, for example, the first two levies were reported to be 12 cents and 10 cents per ton, respectively,[21] and since the price of bauxite exports was maintained at between $4 and $6 per ton, the income tax did not generate a substantial amount.

Phase 2: 1949-73. The terms of bauxite exploitation were renegotiated twice in this period, first in 1949 and then again in 1958, when the so-called Brokopondo agreement came into effect. The 1949 terms were as follows:[22]

1) the harbor and river maintenance tax was removed;

2) the royalty was increased from 13.25 cents to 53 cents per ton, but to only 26-1/2 cents per ton for bauxite mined at a depth of five meters or more;

3) a fee of 53 cents per hectare per year was payable for each mining concession;

4) the basic income tax on bauxite mining was altered so as to constitute an incentive for new bauxite producers; the schedule applied the highest rate of tax — 30 percent — only on profits earned in excess of $530,000 per annum, with lower tax rates applying to profits earned up to that amount;

5) an excess profits tax was imposed, computed progressively on profits as a percent of invested capital: the tax began at profits above 15 percent on invested capital; profit rates of 15-25 percent paid a 30 percent excess profits tax; the rate increased to 40 percent for profit rates between 25 and 40 percent and to 50 percent after that;

6) a formula for fixing the prices of metal-grade bauxite for income tax purposes was devised which varied the price according to alumina and silica content; the resulting price increases were made retroactive to 1946, and Alcoa paid some $2 million in back taxes.

Evidently, these terms can be regarded as moderate at best; the company would normally pay a basic 30 percent profits tax, and its rate of profit would have to exceed 40 percent of invested capital before it reached the highest tax bracket in the payment of excess profits tax, which was itself only 50 percent. As a result of the new terms, Surinam's tax receipts amounted to between $2.18 and $2.50 per ton in the early 1950s. Yet even these moderate terms were considerably better than those prevailing elsewhere in the Caribbean at the time: Guyana and Jamaica, for example, were earning about $1.60 and $0.38 per ton, respectively, from bauxite exports during this period.

Surinam's real ambition, however, was to marry its bauxite to the hydroelectric power potential represented by its large rivers for the creation of an aluminum-smelting industry. One ton of bauxite worth around $6 as ore increased in value to about $125 in the form of aluminum ingot at prices prevailing in the 1950s. Thus, aluminum smelting would simultaneously generate considerable value added, foreign exchange, and some employment and industrial skills, and would also permit the exploitation of hydroelectric power potential. It had been the dream of Surinam economic planners for decades. As early as 1925, reports were that Alcoa engineers had determined that a site on the Marowijne River could be developed for the generation of 200,000 horsepower to be utilized in a smelter at Albina.[23] But nothing ever came of this possibility; instead, Alcoa chose to develop the huge hydropower potentials it had acquired in the Saguenay region of Quebec and at other sites in both Canada and the United States.

After the Second World War attention was focused on the development of a site on the Surinam River — the Brokopondo development. The government tried to secure World Bank financing for the project, but failed when the Dutch government refused to guarantee the proposed loan. Surinam therefore had to agree to let Alcoa finance, construct, and operate the hydroelectric facility together with the aluminum smelter and the alumina plant. Dutch and American pressure had converted what should have been a public national development project into one that was private and foreign.

Moreover, Surinam had to pay dearly for the Alcoa investment.[24] Alcoa's ownership of the hydroelectric facility, smelter, and alumina plant are guaranteed for seventy-five years (after which, theoretically, they revert to the state!). The government bore all the costs of the preliminary work, including surveying, road construction, relocation of population, construction of housing, provision for hygienic needs, etc., and also provided land gratis to the company for ancillary facilities. Generous exploration concessions with options for exploitation were granted to Alcoa over a large area in the northeast of the country up to a total of seventy-five years, and Alcoa's existing concessions were renewed for a further forty-five years. During the seventy-five years of the agreement, Alcoa is exempted from all import and export duties for the facilities; the excess profits tax was repealed and in its place the government undertook to limit taxes on the facilities to 30 percent of taxable profit in the first twenty-five years of their operation and not more than 40 percent thereafter. Taxes on the company's bauxite operations were also limited to no more than 35 percent of taxable profit in the first thirty years and 40 percent thereafter. A new pricing formula for exported bauxite was adopted, and a minimum income tax of $1.85 to $2.38 per metric ton was fixed. Thus, in return for infrastructural expenditures and huge resource concessions, Surinam got facilities that offered relatively little employment (less than 2,000 people in the operations) and a tax-revenue flow that was itself limited by agreement to a low level.

Once the aluminum smelter and alumina plant came on-stream in the late 1960s, the full limitations of the Brokopondo agreement became evident. Through transfer pricing, Alcoa shifted profits from its bauxite operations, which pay a 35 percent tax rate, to its alumina and aluminum operations, which pay 30 percent. The agreement failed to provide a formula for fixing the prices of chemical grade, refractory grade, and abrasive grade bauxite, and of alumina and aluminum, but these had become Alcoa's most important exports from Surinam in value terms. The net result was that Surinam's total tax receipts from bauxite amounted to only about $2.50 per ton in 1973, although upwards of 40 percent of its production was converted into higher-valued calcined bauxite, alumina, and aluminum. The strategy of greater processing had been manipulated by the company to extract additional concessions without yielding greater tax revenue.

Jamaica: Tax Renegotiation and Greater Processing
Strategies, 1950-73

In many respects the Jamaican experience was similar to that of Surinam, condensed into a much shorter period. Until 1973 Jamaica had relied mainly on the renegotiation of bauxite taxes and on negotiations to secure alumina plants as strategies to increase revenues and raise the general economic benefits from the industry. Large quantities of bauxite had been discovered during and just after the Second World War. The first agreement — with Kaiser, Reynolds, and Alcan — was signed in 1950.[25] It provided for a total tax payment amounting to a minuscule 38 cents per ton of exported bauxite, comprised of 14 cents royalty and 24 cents income tax (40 percent of a fixed notional profit of 60 cents). The companies used to good advantage their monopoly over technical information as well as their leverage, represented by their ability to commit or withhold their investments and, through that, to determine whether Jamaica would have a bauxite industry at all.

By 1957 the Jamaican government had waked up to the fact that its tax receipts from bauxite were the lowest in the Caribbean, although Jamaican bauxite was evidently highly attractive to the companies, since they were taking it out on a large scale. Moreover, its leverage over the companies had increased, since the latter had now committed large investments to facilities in the country and Jamaica had now become the largest producer not only in the Caribbean but in the world. A new agreement negotiated in 1957[26] increased taxes on exported bauxite fivefold, to an average of around $1.85 per ton. This amount was composed of a royalty of between 40 and 20 cents, computed regressively on the level of annual production, and an income tax of $1.54 (40 percent of the new notional profit of $3.85). One-half of the royalty and income tax payment was to vary with the price of aluminum ingot on the U.S. market; the government expected this price to continue rising above its March 1957 level of 25 cents per pound, so that its total tax take would increase to around $2.80 per ton within a few years.

As it happened, the price of aluminum fell, rather than rose, after the 1957 agreement; indeed, it was not until the early 1970s that the price firmed up at a level above 25 cents per pound. On balance, Jamaica lost rather than gained from the price escalator clause. Moreover, during the 1960s serious deficiencies appeared in the agreement, which had seemed to be a triumph for the government at the outset and which had been designed to run for at least twenty-five years. There was no provision for increasing the taxable profit in accord with the quality of the ore mined, or with decreases in production costs or freight rates, or with general improvement in the profitability of the companies as integrated enterprises using Jamaican ore. In addition, the companies were valuing the Jamaican bauxite at up to $15 per ton in their reports to the U.S. customs authorities, although the notional profit was based on a price of $7.50 per ton. The Jamaican government came to realize that the 1957 agreement had tied its hands, but it was not until 1971 that it persuaded the companies to agree to increase tax payments.[27] Even then, the increase was relatively moderate, ranging from between $1.80 and $1.90 to about $2.40 per ton (the income tax was raised to $2.25, 40 percent of the new notional profit of $5.00). The companies also paid back taxes retroactive to 1966, amounting to $11 million.

In fact, during the 1960s the main emphasis of Jamaica's bauxite policy was on increased processing of the ore into alumina within the country. From the very outset, Alcan had built two plants to process its Jamaican bauxite into alumina before export; the U.S. companies, which had received subsidized alumina capacity from surplus government property, had opted to export the ore without further processing, following the traditional pattern in Guyana and Surinam. Research indicated that a ton of bauxite processed into alumina within Jamaica generated nearly three times more direct national income and foreign exchange and one and one-half times more government taxes than a ton of bauxite exported abroad.[28] The government therefore sought to induce the U.S. companies to build alumina plants within Jamaica. The opportunity came when the U.S. aluminum companies embarked on a large expansion program in the latter part of the 1960s and sought to increase bauxite extraction from Jamaica. The government was able to negotiate a total of three new alumina plants to be built by five companies (three of them in the form of a consortium). It was projected that the new plants would raise alumina exports to over 3 million tons per annum by 1975, increase the export value of the industry to around $250 million, and more than double tax revenues — from $19 million in 1967 to $43 million in 1975.[29]

The plants were built, Jamaica's alumina production increased to 2.3 million tons by 1972, and large additional export value was recorded. But the increased tax payments did not materialize. The Jamaican Prime Minister reported that, in 1972, 3.5 million tons of bauxite converted into alumina in the new plants yielded only $1 million in taxes[30]; astonishingly, this was only a fraction of the nearly $9 million in taxes the same bauxite would have generated if exported without processing! The reason for this incredibly perverse result was that the companies were recording virtually no taxable profit from the new plants. Since Alcan pays substantial taxes on its own alumina production in Jamaica, the presumption has been that the American companies have manipulated both prices and production costs in the new plants to achieve the desired results. [31] This remarkable phenomenon occasioned a frank if somewhat amusing exchange between members of the U.S. Senate subcommittee on transnational corporations and the President of Reynolds Metals, one of the companies involved:

Mr. Levinson: You have said that the Alpart plant has not yielded any profits to the partners. Has it yielded any revenues to the Jamaican Government?

Mr. Reynolds: As far as I know, that is one of the complaints that the Government has, since it hasn't made a profit, that they haven't got any revenue from it except from the mining.... The Prime Minister gets on me every time I see him; they are losing and we are losing more. It's a sad thing but we should be paying taxes and if we were paying taxes we would be very, very happy and I hope that day will soon be.... [later] ... I don't blame the Prime Minister. He says he should get something and I think he should. I am saying that the Lord only knows, I hope he gets a lot, because the more that will be the cheaper the better [sic]. [32]

As in the case of the Brokopondo agreement in Surinam, the companies had turned Jamaica's strategy of greater processing inside out: they had used it as a device for extracting a greater value of raw materials out of the country at reduced tax costs. Yet another compelling demonstration was provided of the maneuverability, flexibility, and strong bargaining position of the transnational integrated aluminum companies operating in the Caribbean bauxite industry.

Guyana: From Accommodation to Expropriation, 1915-73

If Jamaica and Surinam had problems with the aluminum companies, Guyana had profound and long-standing grievances. Guyana has the oldest bauxite industry in the Caribbean, and one that formed the raw materials base for the rapid growth of aluminum production in Canada and the emergence of Alcan Aluminium, Limited, as a major international aluminum company. Yet Guyana was unable to secure even the limited gains in tax-revenue increases and domestic processing recorded by the other two major Caribbean bauxite producers in the 1950s and 1960s. This helps to explain why, at the beginning of the 1970s, Guyana moved rapidly from accommodation to open confrontation in its relations with Alcan, culminating in the expropriation of the principal bauxite enterprise operating in the country.

The taxation issue was the basis of one of Guyana's historical grievances. Throughout the 1920s and 1930s, Alcan[33] paid a royalty amounting to 10 cents per ton for bauxite mined from Crown lands, plus a general export tax of 1.5 percent of the declared value of exports.[34] The total amounted to about 3.5 percent of export value; income taxes were kept low since the company maintained bauxite prices at between $5 and $6 per ton during the whole period from the early 1920s to the late 1940s. Undervaluation of Guyana bauxite continued in the 1950s and 1960s; the prices recorded for Guyanese metal grade bauxite exports during this period were significantly below those used in Surinam, where the grade of ore and shipping costs are roughly comparable, and the northern Caribbean, where shipping costs are lower but the grade of ore is inferior.[35] The undervaluation issue was especially strong in the case of Reynolds Guyana Mines: between 1952, when this company began operations, and the end of 1964, it paid no income taxes whatsoever to the Guyana government, on the grounds that it was sustaining operating losses. Indeed, it was not until 1965 that these two companies came to their first agreement with the Guyana government on a pricing formula for their bauxite exports, used for computing profit, to which the general company income tax of 45 percent was applied.[36]

Like Surinam and Jamaica, Guyana also attempted to secure greater domestic processing of bauxite as a means of increasing the economic benefits and government revenue generated by the industry. In the early 1950s Alcan, on its own initiative, had begun the production in Guyana of calcined bauxite, a product with a sales value per ton roughly double that of metal grade bauxite. Guyanese ore was especially suited to the production of calcined bauxite; furthermore, it gave Alcan the opportunity to generate an increased profit flow from its Guyana operation without substantial new investments. In the mid-1950s Alcan agreed to build a relatively small (220,000 tons per year) alumina plant in the country; under the terms of the agreement, which was made with a British-appointed administration, the plant was granted an outright five-year tax holiday to be followed by generous investment allowances. The plant was completed in 1961. Because of the generous terms accorded, it paid virtually no taxes at all until 1971. The similarities with the result of greater processing strategies in Surinam and Jamaica are too striking to need further emphasis.

Just as in Surinam, too, the Guyanese have had a historical dream of utilizing their bauxite in conjunction with their considerable hydroelectric power potential to develop an aluminum smelting industry. As early as 1917, only a few years after the discovery of bauxite in the country, government officers had spoken of these exciting possibilities. [37] But nothing ever came of the dream; Alcan preferred to develop its privately owned hydroelectric resources in the Saguenay region of Quebec to furnish power to its giant smelter at Arvida on the St. Lawrence River, which used Guyana bauxite as its chief raw material. After Guyana's independence in 1966, the government began to push the idea once more and secured a public commitment from Alcan to build a smelter in Guyana if sufficiently cheap and abundant power became available. But a World-Bank-sponsored investigation of the feasibility of hydroelectric power development turned in a negative report. The Guyanese were, to say the least, skeptical of the report; to declare that they felt intense frustration would be an understatement.

As the 1970 decade opened, Guyana, site of high-grade bauxite production on a large scale for over fifty years, had little to show for it. The country could not even point to the existence of a small aluminum smelter, as in Surinam, or to significant alumina production, as in Jamaica. Government revenues from the industry amounted to a pitiful $3 million per year, on a total production of nearly 5 million tons. No significant expansion was envisaged by the companies, and the economy had been stagnating for the better part of twenty years. The government was therefore impelled to undertake what at that time was the most radical strategy employed among Caribbean bauxite-producing countries: direct state involvement in ownership and decision making in the producing companies, in the belief that only such a change could meet the preconditions for the development of the industry in the national interest, rather than the interest of the transnational aluminum companies. In late 1970 Guyana began negotiations with Alcan for the acquisition of a majority interest in the latter's Guyana subsidiary (Demba), by far the largest of the two companies operating in the country, with assets of about $60 million and annual sales of $50 million. The basis of the government's proposals was that the assets should be acquired at their written-down book value and paid for out of the future profits of the enterprise, and that the government should acquire actual operating control. Alcan refused to accept these terms, and in February 1971 the government announced its intention to nationalize Demba outright. Alcan retained considerable leverage, however, for in the final settlement the government agreed to pay somewhat more than written-down book value and to remit the amount over twenty years in the form of deferred payments, which were not linked specifically to the future profits of the enterprise.[38]

Not surprisingly, the record of the new state enterprise — Guybau — has been a mixed one so far. In its first eighteen months of operation (to the end of 1972), it reported that the major problems of transition had been dealt with successfully and that profit levels had exceeded those of Demba.[39] But in 1973 it reported declining profits, due to escalating costs, price difficulties, and problems of employee discipline.[40] Guybau exists in the context of an international industry in which the "market" for metal grade bauxite and alumina is controlled almost entirely by the large, integrated transnational aluminum companies; moreover, it began operations at a time when the aluminum market was depressed. Thus it has experienced some difficulties in the marketing of its metal grade bauxite and alumina; indeed, in 1973 the alumina plant actually had to be closed for a few weeks to allow stocks to be cleared. Guybau's chief source of market leverage lies in calcined bauxite, in which it holds a near-complete world monopoly, and this is providing it with a useful breathing space. At the same time, the Guyana government has announced plans for a large combined hydroelectric and aluminum-smelting project to be completed in 1980, with Yugoslav assistance. Hopefully, the Guyanese dream of industrializing its natural resources will soon be realized.

IV. THE RISE OF GOVERNMENT MILITANCY IN 1974

The 1974 Caribbean Bauxite Offensive

As 1973 drew to a close, none of the Caribbean bauxite-producing countries had any reason to be satisfied with the situation in their bauxite industries. Guyana had taken the courageous step of alone nationalizing one of the big aluminum companies operating there; but the new state enterprise felt isolated and vulnerable, if not precarious, in a world in which the transnationals still held virtually undisputed sway in the industry. Surinam, a major producer, had seen no improvement in its per ton revenues from the industry since the 1950s, in spite of the construction of a large alumina plant and the prestige of having the only aluminum smelter among the Caribbean bauxite-producing countries. Jamaica, the leading producer, had been frustrated by the lack of significant revenues

from its large alumina output and could point to no prospects for
further significant expansion of its industry by the aluminum companies. It was in this context that the September 1973 nonaligned
summit in Algiers crystallized the ideological legitimacy of the
movement of Third World economic nationalism; it was followed
rapidly by the Ramadan war in October and the OPEC offensive
that doubled crude oil prices in October and then doubled them
again in December of that year.

The OPEC actions provided a dramatic demonstration of what
might be feasible in bauxite through the collective action of producing countries. But it also provided motivation and urgency for
the action, for the sudden and steep rise in oil prices posed severe
balance-of-payments and economic growth problems to the Caribbean countries. Jamaica, for example, faced the prospect of an
oil import bill of nearly $180 million in 1974 compared to $55 million in 1973. The Jamaican government, like the others, had three
options: (1) reduce oil imports severely, which would probably
imply zero or even negative economic growth; (2) reduce nonoil
imports, which would have a similar effect, since most capital and
intermediate goods are imported; or (3) raise the additional foreign exchange required by higher taxes on the bauxite industry.
Jamaica took the third option, a course of action followed with
varying degrees of success by the other four Caribbean bauxite
producers.

It is important to consider why it was Jamaica that acted as the
leader in seeking higher returns, not only among the Caribbean
bauxite-producing countries but in the world as a whole. (The
other important bauxite-exporting countries are Australia and
Guinea.) Alone among the bauxite-exporting nations, Jamaica had
both the motivation to seek higher returns and the leverage to secure them, even over the apparent opposition of the companies.
Jamaica's economic motivation has already been mentioned: the
disappointing returns from the strategy of greater processing
coupled with the shock effect of the rise in oil prices. The Jamaican government also had a political motivation, for the new government that took office in 1972 was anxious to demonstrate that it
was different from its predecessor, and especially that it was more
nationalistic and quicker to defend the nation's sovereignty. But
Jamaica had leverage as well as motivation, for it is the largest
source of bauxite and alumina for the U.S. and Canadian aluminum
industries, and all of the major North American companies draw a
significant share of their supplies from their Jamaican subsidi-

aries, which represent an investment of over $700 million. Other Caribbean bauxite-producing countries had as strong a motivation as Jamaica but lacked Jamaica's leverage, as did Guinea, whose large-scale bauxite production was only then coming on-stream. Australia's production is bigger than even Jamaica's; it is the major supplier to the Japanese aluminum industry and provides significant supplies to the United States. Australia therefore had similar leverage, but it lacked Jamaica's motivation because the bauxite industry plays a relatively insignificant role in the Australian economy as a whole, and also because, being self-sufficient in oil, Australia had no compelling urgency to increase foreign exchange earnings as a result of the OPEC action.

In early January 1974, the Jamaican government announced that it would seek to renegotiate the existing bauxite contracts, since the "doctrine of changed circumstances" had become applicable as a result of higher oil prices. The companies accepted the necessity for renegotiation, and meetings between the firms and the government began in March. Jamaica proposed a novel method of taxation — a production levy imposed on all bauxite produced, fixed as a percentage of the realized selling price of the equivalent quantity of primary aluminum shipments by the companies. The government's original proposal was to fix the levy at 8.75 percent for aluminum prices of up to 35 cents per pound and then to raise the percentage sharply for higher prices. The companies accepted the principle of the levy but countered with an offer of 3.5 percent. The government rejected this offer and in May 1974 proceeded to legislate its new terms, fixing the production levy at 7.5 percent for the financial year 1974-75, and raising it to 8.0 percent and 8.5 percent in the next two financial years. At the prevailing aluminum price of 31.5 cents per pound, the levy would yield approximately J$11 (J$1 = US$1.10) per ton of bauxite. The levy was applied to all bauxite production, whether exported or processed locally into alumina, and was also accompanied by a flat royalty of J$0.50 per ton on all production. The levy replaced the income tax on exported bauxite, but alumina production would also pay normal income taxes on taxable profit (if any). The new taxes were made retroactive to January 1974, and as a result the government's bauxite revenues for the January 1974-March 1975 period were expected to amount to J$210 million compared to the J$28 million that would have accrued under the previous arrangements. The total take would be around J$12 per ton compared to just over J$2 before.[41]

The companies — Alcan, Alcoa, Anaconda, Kaiser, Revere, and Reynolds — protested the Jamaican action and gave notice that they would seek arbitration by the International Center for the Settlement of Investment Disputes (ICSID) to which Jamaica was a signatory. But just before negotiations were broken off, Jamaica had withdrawn from that portion of the ICSID convention covering natural resources. In effect, the companies were left with no legal recourse, and within a few weeks it had become evident that they would pay the new taxes, albeit with verbal protests, without any significant confrontation with the Jamaican government. The companies had too much at stake in Jamaica; moreover, they were operating in a tight aluminum market where the additional taxes could easily be passed on to consumers in the form of higher prices. The additional taxes imposed by Jamaica represented only about 2 cents per pound of aluminum; the companies actually raised prices by that amount on June 1, 1974; prices were increased by that amount again in August, to 36 cents, and industry sources were predicting that the price could reach as high as 40 cents per pound by the end of the year.[42] As a matter of fact, the companies reported record third-quarter profits for 1974, after the Jamaican levy had become effective. If anything, the Jamaican action demonstrated how large a margin there was for the bauxite-exporting countries to increase returns without adversely affecting the companies' off-take.

The Jamaican production levy became a model for the other Caribbean bauxite-producing countries, each one of which sought to increase its revenues along the same lines during the remainder of 1974. The Jamaican government also provided technical help and advice to the other governments as they formulated their proposals. By the end of the year, Surinam had secured agreement from Alcoa for the payment of a Jamaican-type levy fixed at 6 percent, yielding a revenue of $11.02 per ton and raising Surinam's total take from Alcoa from $18 million to $45 million for 1974.[43] In December, Haiti announced that Reynolds had agreed to a Jamaican-type levy of 7.5 percent, which would raise per ton revenues to approximately $11 (compared to the previous $1.88) and total revenues to $11 million per year.[44] The Congress of the Dominican Republic proposed legislation that would almost double the bauxite royalty from $2.73 to $5 per ton, with a minimum tax-reference price of $12.08 per ton, but the President vetoed the legislation.[45] As before, Guyana proved to be an exceptional case in the Caribbean. When Guyana nationalized the Alcan subsidiary operating there in 1971, the much smaller Reynolds Guyana Mines had been left untouched. Early in 1974, the government began to negotiate with Reynolds for state participation in its Guyana subsidiary, but the negotiations dragged on without result during the time of Jamaica's own unsuccessful revenue negotiations with the companies, the imposition of the Jamaican production levy, and the formation of the International Bauxite Association. Between July and September, the Guyana government moved to impose a solution, announcing that (1) it would apply a Jamaican-type levy to Reynolds, yielding approximately the same amount per ton and applicable to the whole of 1974; and (2) it would nationalize Reynolds Guyana Mines by the end of 1974. The company promptly ceased negotiations on the ownership question, refused to pay the levy, and withdrew its five North American employees from the operation.[46] Reynolds Guyana Mines had been insured with the U.S. Overseas Private Investment Corporation (OPIC), and the Reynolds strategy was apparently to shift the negotiations on the compensation question from itself to OPIC, presumably because of the greater leverage of the latter due to its status as a U.S. government agency. The Guyana strategy was to use the production levy as leverage on the compensation issue. In the final agreement reached between OPIC and the Guyana government, the latter agreed to pay some $10 million over thirteen years at 8.5 percent interest. The written-down book value of the enterprise was $14.5 million (this was also the amount of the OPIC insurance) but some $4.5 million was deducted because of the amount due from Reynolds for payment of the production levy.[47]

The Jamaican action thus worked as a catalyst for Caribbean-wide changes on bauxite tax arrangements. But the Jamaican action was not limited to taxes; the government indicated that it proposed a total revision of the terms of the aluminum companies' operations in the country. Specifically, the government also proposed to (1) find ways of increasing the foreign-exchange contribution of the industry (apparently, other than the higher taxes themselves); (2) reacquire for Jamaica the large areas of land owned by the companies; and (3) secure government participation in the ownership of the enterprises.[48] Negotiations with the companies on these matters were started after the tax negotiations broke down. In November 1974, the government announced an agreement with Kaiser Aluminum for state participation in the latter's bauxite-mining facilities (the largest in Jamaica) and government acquisition of company-owned lands. A 51 percent share in the mines will be acquired at a cost of J$15 million (US$16.5 million), payable over ten years at 8.5 percent interest. The government is guaranteed a profit equivalent to 12 percent per annum on the purchase price of the assets. Kaiser dropped its opposition to the production levy, which was fixed at 7.5 percent for the first three years (rather than the 8.5 percent which became applicable to the other companies in April 1975), to be increased subsequently to a rate equivalent to the national levy minus 1 percent if the national levy is above 8.5 percent. Kaiser is to continue to manage the enterprise for an initial seven-year period, "subject to policy directives" from an executive committee in which it has equal representation with the government. Company-owned lands amounting to 40,000 acres were acquired by the government under the agreement for a price of J$7.5 million, payable in ten equal annual installments with an interest rate of 7 percent per annum. But sufficient lands will be leased back to the company to guarantee it thirty years' bauxite supply, with an option to extend for a further ten years, computed at the current rate of extraction and with the condition that this rate be maintained.[49]

This agreement evidently follows the model for state majority participation in extractive industries that emerged toward the end of the 1960s. In this model — of which the Chilean and Zambian 51 percent nationalization agreements of 1969 are the clearest examples[50] — the government acquires a 51 percent share in the equity of the enterprise in return for deferred payments bearing a commercial interest rate; it also makes some additional fiscal concessions and leaves the transnational corporation in actual managerial control of the enterprise. In the Jamaica-Kaiser agreement, the government's payments for the mining facilities will exceed its equity income from the new enterprise for the first eight years of the agreement, the former beginning at 18.5 percent of the purchase price (10 percent principal plus 8.5 percent interest) and declining to just under 12 percent in the ninth year, while the latter is guaranteed at 12 percent of the purchase price. The government's payments for the lands, which begin at 17 percent per annum, will also exceed its rental income from the lands, for the rate for the leasehold is fixed at 7 percent and applies only to the land actually leased back to the company for mining operations. The government has also given up at least 1 percent of the production levy. In return for these payments and concessions, the government has not acquired firm control over either the mining facilities or the bauxite reserves. The mining facilities remain under Kaiser's operational control, and bauxite supplies are guaranteed for up to forty years — that is, for a substantial period of time after the payments for the government's majority share and for the lands will have been completed.

This agreement, however, established the pattern for Jamaican state involvement with the other bauxite-alumina companies. In December 1974, a similar agreement was reached with Revere for the acquisition of its mining facilities. Revere will continue to be full owner of its alumina plant, which will be expanded in capacity from 230,000 to 571,000 tons per year, with assistance from a consortium of Japanese aluminum companies that will purchase some 224,000 tons per year of the increased annual output. Final approval of the expansion will await the results of a feasibility survey, but should the outcome be positive and construction of the additional facilities begin before the end of 1975, the government will allow a rebate of J$5 per ton in the production levy for the five-year period 1974-78, a concession that it was stated would cost the government a total of J$10 million over these years.[51] In February 1975, the government began its negotiations with Reynolds for participation in bauxite mining and acquisition of lands.[52]

Another important development during 1974 toward greater state involvement in the Caribbean bauxite industry lay in the area of direct government-to-government joint ventures in aluminum smelting and alumina plants. Between May and June 1974, the governments of Jamaica, Trinidad and Tobago, and Guyana announced agreement in principle for joint construction and ownership by all three governments of two aluminum smelters, each with an annual capacity of 200,000 tons. One smelter is to be built in Trinidad and Tobago; its government is responsible for providing the electric power, whose production will be based on Trinidad's natural gas. The Trinidad and Tobago government will hold 34 percent of the equity in the plant; each of the other two governments will hold 33 percent and will be responsible for providing one-half of the required alumina supplies. The other smelter is to be built in Guyana; the Guyanese government will own 52 percent of the equity and will be responsible for the provision of power; the other two governments will each own 24 percent. It is planned that transportation facilities for the plants will also be owned by the three countries. According to reports, the projected completion date for the Trinidad smelter is 1979; completion of the Guyana smelter is slated for 1981.[53]

In the latter part of 1974, Jamaica and Mexico agreed to cooperate in the establishment of an international, intergovernmental industrial complex that would be vertically integrated from bauxite mining through to aluminum smelting. Under this project, a smelter with a capacity of 120,000 tons per year is to be built in Mexico at an estimated cost of $190 million, with the Mexican government as the largest shareholder and the Jamaican government as the second largest, with a 29 percent share. The smelter is to be linked with a 600,000-tons-per-year-capacity alumina plant to be built in Jamaica at a cost of $200 million; the Jamaican government will have a 51 percent share in the plant, the Mexican government will have the next largest share, and Kaiser Aluminum will be a minority shareholder. A minimum of 1.3 million tons per year of bauxite will be provided to the alumina plant by a new Jamaican mining company to be formed with the government as a 51 percent shareholder and Kaiser Aluminum as a minority shareholder. Kaiser will also provide 200,000 tons per year of its own bauxite to the plant.[54] The agreement also envisages further backward linkages in the form of a 60,000-tons-per-year caustic soda plant to be established in Jamaica by the government to furnish that material to the alumina plant; Mexico is committed to supplying the necessary salt as the raw material for the caustic soda production.[55]

The International Bauxite Association

The bauxite tax increases unilaterally imposed by Caribbean producers in 1974 took place against the background of the formation of the International Bauxite Association (IBA) in March of that year. The tax increases were not imposed collectively through joint resolution of the producing countries acting within the framework of IBA, as was the case with the tax and price increases imposed by the oil-exporting countries belonging to OPEC. Rather, the formation of IBA at the same time that the tax increases were being imposed provided either the fact or the appearance of political coverage and possibly support by other bauxite-exporting countries for those governments that were taking the initiative, especially Jamaica. Such political coverage was needed especially from bauxite-exporting countries outside of the Caribbean, and in particular from Australia and Guinea, the two non-Caribbean countries with considerable actual or (in the case of Guinea) potential production. It was important to the Caribbean countries that they be able to impress upon the aluminum companies the impossibility of playing off these other producers against the Caribbean by threatening to increase bauxite and alumina off-take elsewhere in order to pressure the Caribbean. It is difficult to say to what extent the formation of IBA was a critical contributing factor to the apparent success of the Caribbean tax increases. A preliminary judgment would be that, in conjunction with all the other factors prevailing in 1974, the formation of IBA as a background event probably did help to soften the companies' attitude toward Caribbean demands and increase their estimates of the possible risks involved in an outright confrontation with the producing countries.

IBA had been a long time coming. From the middle and late 1960s politicians and academics in the Caribbean had made suggestions for such an organization.[56] In 1970 Prime Minister Burnham of Guyana had privately approached other bauxite-exporting countries along these lines, as part of the Guyana government's preparations for its confrontation with Alcan, but the response was negative. Bauxite was obviously a highly eligible candidate for some kind of country cartelization, inasmuch as, since the 1950s, the Caribbean countries had accounted for a high proportion of world exports and had been supplying about 80 percent of U.S. bauxite requirements and virtually all of Canada's. But until 1973, it seems, the political preconditions for collective action by the producing countries were absent. During the 1960s Jamaica, the largest Caribbean producer, had governments that followed "open door" policies to foreign capital and were anxious to avoid provoking even the appearance of confrontation with foreign companies. Moreover, during the 1960s the Jamaican strategy was to negotiate construction of new alumina plants by the companies, a strategy that appeared to promise substantial benefits in the form of additional tax revenues. It was unlikely that any attempt at forming an IBA-type organization could have succeeded without Jamaica's involvement and support; in any case, Surinam was still a colony of the Netherlands and therefore incapable of sovereign action, and Guyana's production was too small to carry any real leverage. Australia, which emerged as a major producer toward the end of the 1960s, had a generally conservative government.

In 1972 political changes in both Jamaica and Australia brought into office new governments speaking the rhetoric of economic nationalism and anxious to demonstrate their commitment to the assertion of national economic sovereignty, especially over natural resources. In early 1973 Jamaica sent a mission to Australia to sound out the receptivity of that country to the idea of an association of bauxite producers; the Prime Ministers of these two countries and of Guyana were able to discuss the question at the Commonwealth Prime Ministers' Conference in Ottawa in the summer of 1973, where Prime Minister Gough Whitlam of Australia gave a speech critical of transnational corporations in resource industries, called for associations of primary producing countries, and suggested that his country shared many of the problems of developing nations.[57] At the September nonaligned summit in Algiers, mutual contacts were made by Jamaica, Guyana, Guinea, and Yugoslavia, and the conference approved a resolution calling for organizations of primary producing countries. The stage had been set, and in late October 1973, Yugoslavia played host to a meeting of representatives of six bauxite-exporting countries: Jamaica, Guyana, Surinam, Guinea, Australia, and Yugoslavia itself. A preliminary draft of the text of an agreement between the governments establishing the International Bauxite Association was worked out, with approval set for a ministerial meeting in Conakry to be held in the early months of 1974.

But between the Belgrade meeting in October 1973 and the Conakry meeting in March 1974, the international political climate had changed dramatically. OPEC had quadrupled the price of oil in the last quarter of 1973, and the Arab oil-exporting countries had imposed production cutbacks and a total oil embargo on the United States and the Netherlands as part of the struggle against Israel. In response to these actions, a virtually hysterical campaign was mounted in the West, designed to portray the OPEC countries and the Arabs as reckless and irresponsible and bent on bringing the industrial world to its economic knees. In this context, the moves for the establishment of IBA were viewed as an ominous development by the Western countries, and an alarm began to be sounded that a possible new OPEC was in the making. The U.S. government officially expressed concern and announced an accelerated program for the development of domestic bauxite substitutes; some of the aluminum companies also announced plans to develop bauxite alternatives from materials found in the major industrial countries.[58] In response to this, the prospective IBA members felt constrained to adopt a posture which was reassuring, if not actually defensive. As the conference approached, the trade press reported that Australia was "believed to be anxious to make sure the interests of importing countries are taken into consideration.[59] And on the eve of his departure for Conakry, the Jamaican Mines Minister stated flatly that IBA is "not another OPEC" and that "bauxite is not a geopolitical tool."[60] The Conakry conference did succeed in securing governmental approval for the IBA agreement from the seven founding members (the Belgrade six plus Sierra Leone). Supreme authority for the organization was vested in a Council of Ministers, with an Executive Board consisting of two delegates from each member state as the executive authority, and a Secretariat, located in Jamaica, as the administrative and research arm. In addition, the Jamaicans reported:

> Among other things the Ministers at Conakry agreed with the objective of securing maximum national ownership and effective national control over their bauxite industries and of maximising national ownership of such industries.
>
> The official communiqué said the member nations "will endeavour to ensure that the operations or projected operations of multinational corporations in any member country will not be permitted to damage the interests of any other member country."
>
> The communiqué also said that the Ministers "expressed their intention on behalf of their peoples to secure fair and equitable returns from the exploitation of their bauxite resources in order to promote their social and economic development."[61]

Support for the principles of national ownership and control, fair and equitable returns, and preventing the aluminum companies from playing off one country against another was obviously of special importance to Jamaica, which entered into negotiations with the companies on the revenue and ownership questions immediately after the conference. Jamaica was thus able to present the companies with a picture of general support for its policies from other IBA countries. But it is important to point out that the Conakry conference did not commit the IBA countries to any specific collective action or collective policy as such. Moreover, it soon became evident that Australia, the largest bauxite-exporting country, was now intent on presenting an image of "responsibility" and moderation to the world. In his statement welcoming the formation of IBA, the Australian Overseas Trade Minister stated pointedly that "there was no question of the producers seeking to exploit the users.... it was essential to take a responsible approach in paying due regard to the interests of consuming countries" [emphasis added].[62] The Australian Minister also gave as a reason for his country's membership in the organization that "the Association is fully consistent with Australia's policy to assist developing countries to achieve a reasonable return for exports of their raw materials."[63] This suggested a perceptible shift from Prime Minister Whitlam's posture of the previous August at the Commonwealth Prime Ministers' Conference: what had begun as an Australian desire to find common cause with developing countries against the power of the transnationals seemed to have become an aspect of Australia's external aid policy toward developing countries! This posture appears to have continued at the meeting of the IBA Council of Ministers held in Guyana in November 1974; it was reported that the meeting would be considering the possibility of adopting a common pricing policy for bauxite, but the Australian Minister reportedly did not think that this was feasible. [64]

The Australian attitude demonstrates the extent to which its economic nationalism is limited by a perceived need to maintain good relations with its traditional trading partners and investment sources in the industrialized world. But, in addition, Australia had a particular concern to reassure Japan, which absorbs a large part of Australian raw materials production. Japan depends on Australia for a growing share of its raw materials requirements in resources such as bauxite, iron ore, and nickel, and had of course been badly hit by the OPEC-imposed rise in oil prices. Australia was intent on indicating that it would not "do an OPEC" on Japan — indeed, on a visit to Japan in October 1973, Prime Minister Whitlam of Australia had made it a point to stress that the two countries

have a common interest in each other's prosperity. As great trading partners, we have a very high degree of interdependence.... We recognise that economic disruptions in Japan would affect Australia as well as Japan and we have no intention of causing this to happen. We have no wish to interrupt the supplies of minerals from Australia to Japan.... We recognise the remarkable interdependence of the two economies and will continue to make reasonable quantities of materials available at prices which reflect the value of the materials to both countries. [65]

With such an objective, it does not seem that Australia would consider it feasible for its bauxite export policy to be shackled by the need to maintain a common and collective IBA policy. Yet such a common and collective policy is an essential precondition of a successful producers' cartel. Furthermore, there are two substantial differences in the economic situations of Australia and of the other major bauxite producers that have profound implications for Australia's propensity for involvement in collective and militant action. Bauxite is the most important foreign exchange earner and the most important domestic industry for countries like Jamaica, Surinam, Guyana, and Guinea. In addition, these countries are underdeveloped and dependent, lack substantial industrialization, and (in the main) have high unemployment rates. Their governments therefore pin a large part of their hopes for economic development on improving the contribution of bauxite to the national economy. Australia's position is radically different: bauxite is relatively unimportant as an industry and a source of foreign exchange, and the Australian economy, though it is dependent in a real sense, has a developed structure with a large manufacturing industry and low unemployment rates. For Australia, it is general economic policy that determines bauxite policy, rather than the other way around, as it is in the Caribbean and Guinea. Evidently, this means that Australia will be far less motivated to seek to maximize its returns from bauxite as such, since, on the one hand, the relative benefits from such maximization to the general economy are much smaller than in the Caribbean and in Guinea, and, on the other, the perceived costs may be significantly higher in terms of damage to Australian external economic relations with its foreign trading partners. Thus, a preliminary evaluation suggests that Australian membership in IBA constitutes a source of weakness rather than of strength as far as collective and militant action is concerned. But whereas an organization confined exclusively to Third World countries may be more capable of cartel-like behavior, it is not certain that this would yield durable gains without Australian support, for that country's large production and enormous reserves make it possible for the aluminum companies to substitute production there for production in the Caribbean and in Guinea, at least in the medium term.

In any case, as 1974 drew to a close, it became clear that the other IBA countries were not interested in further militant actions that might bring them into conflict with the aluminum companies, and that the companies, for their part, did not regard the measures taken by the Caribbean IBA countries as meriting outright confrontation. Again, the position of Jamaica, the largest Third World bauxite-producing country, was critical here. Despite what, in retrospect, appear to be merely formal protests, the companies paid the amounts due under the new production levy promptly and without any real opposition. The companies obviously had room to maneuver, since the tight aluminum markets of 1974 allowed them to pass on the increased taxes easily in the form of higher aluminum prices. Moreover, the price increases needed to recoup the new taxes were relatively small, because of the very low ratio of bauxite costs to the total cost of aluminum production and the

selling price of primary aluminum. Just over 4 long dry tons of
bauxite are required to produce 1 short ton of primary aluminum;
a 500 percent increase in bauxite taxes from, say, $2 to $12 per
long dry ton implies an increase in aluminum production costs of
just over $40, which represents a mere 6 percent increase in the
aluminum selling price (based on a price of $0.33 per pound). In
addition, it is possible that the U.S. aluminum companies could write
off at least part of the additional levies against their U.S. taxes through
tax-credit arrangements. Thus, although the new taxes were huge in
relation to the previous tax take of producing governments, they did
not constitute a serious threat to the companies' profitability.

Moreover, in the latter part of 1974, the aluminum companies
in Jamaica also entered voluntarily into the next stage of negotiations with the government over the terms of state participation
in bauxite mining and state acquisition of the vast acreages of
company-owned land. By December the government had reached
an amicable agreement with Kaiser for the acquisition of 51 percent of the company's bauxite-mining enterprise, the largest producer of bauxite ore in Jamaica. Indeed, the atmosphere of confrontation that emerged in May-June 1974 was dissipated within a
few weeks; and at the IBA Executive Board meeting in Kingston in
November, Prime Minister Manley of Jamaica is reported to have
"invited the international bauxite and aluminum companies to see
in the establishment of the I.B.A. not a threat but as [sic] an avenue
for cooperation and mutual benefit."[66] Around the same time, it
was announced that Jamaica's Central Bank had been in the process
of buying shares of two of the major aluminum companies (Kaiser
and Reynolds) on the New York stock market, to hold as part of the
country's external assets. This form of recycling of what we may
call Jamaica's "bauxidollars" implies that Jamaica would acquire
an official stake in the companies' stock values and, through that,
their actual and expected profitability. Perhaps for this reason
executives of the companies concerned expressed great pleasure
at the Jamaican purchases; the President of Kaiser Aluminum
said that these transactions "should improve and strengthen relationships and understanding of mutual problems and opportunities."[67]

In addition to the absence of real country-company confrontation,
another notable feature of the 1974 Caribbean bauxite offensive and
the formation of IBA was the absence of confrontation or tension
between the producer governments and the consumer governments.
Caribbean bauxite goes overwhelmingly to the United States and
Canada, so it is these countries that are principally affected by the

balance-of-payments implications. However, the additional foreign-exchange costs of imported bauxite for these countries are
relatively small; the Jamaican increases, for example, involved
a net increase of around $160 million per year in the country's
foreign exchange take, and if identical arrangements were to be
applied throughout the whole Caribbean, the total incremental foreign exchange cost of Caribbean bauxite to the importing countries
would be less than $350 million per year. Even in the extreme
case where all the additional foreign exchange costs are borne by
the United States and Canada, this is an insignificant amount in
relation to their balance of payments; moreover, these countries
will recoup at least part of the additional costs in the form of
higher prices for exported aluminum. The fact is that during the
whole 1974 Caribbean tax offensive, there was no hostile comment
(that this writer is aware of) from government sources in either
the United States or Canada. This stands in stark contrast to the
hysterical anti-OPEC and anti-Arab campaign of both press and
government provoked by the OPEC price offensive and selective
oil embargo imposed by the Organization of Arab Petroleum Exporting Countries (OAPEC) in 1973. Partly, the difference in reaction is
due to the fact that oil is an absolutely vital commodity to the industrial
economies, and the foreign exchange implications of the OPEC offensive are massive, involving amounts running over $50 billion a
year. But partly, too, the difference must be that the Caribbean
action did not carry the kind of geopolitical implications generated
by the actions of OPEC and OAPEC. The Caribbean tax offensive
took place in a context in which the continued assurance and stability of supplies of the raw materials concerned to the United
States, Canada, and other importing countries was never called
into question. In addition, the actions raised no doubts that the
Caribbean countries concerned would remain generally within the
U.S. sphere of influence. Indeed, it is clear that strenuous efforts
were made to reassure the North American governments on just
these very points. In March 1974 Prime Minister Manley of Jamaica visited Washington and Ottawa, where it was reported that
he had cordial discussions on the bauxite question with Secretary
of State Kissinger and Prime Minister Trudeau.[68] The visit came
immediately after the formation of IBA, and just before the Jamaican government began negotiations with the aluminum companies on its new tax proposals. The timing was strategic, since
it presumably gave Mr. Manley the opportunity to assure Mr. Kissinger and Mr. Trudeau that IBA should not be regarded as a po-

tential new OPEC, to inform them of the Jamaican government's position on bauxite revenues, and to secure an understanding of his government's position in its coming negotiation with the U.S. and Canadian companies. Mr. Manley's speeches and those of other Jamaican leaders repeatedly stressed that the matter was purely a question of gaining additional revenues and foreign exchange to offset the impact of the oil price rises and asserting the nation's sovereignty.

V. SOME CONCLUSIONS: SHORT-RUN PROSPECTS FOR CORPORATE IMPERIALISM AND THE STATE IN THE CARIBBEAN BAUXITE INDUSTRY

We have noted that, unlike in the case of OPEC, the bauxite producers' association does not yet constitute an effective cartel, and the actions taken by the producing governments in 1974 were not such as to lead to open confrontation either with the companies or with the consumer governments. Given all this, what preliminary conclusions can we come to regarding the division of the industry's surpluses between the companies and producer governments, and their respective roles in the system of power relations that previously characterized the international aluminum industry?

First, a note of warning needs to be sounded on the revenue question. We have observed that the aluminum companies offered only weak resistance to the 1974 tax increases on bauxite; on the other hand, there is some evidence that Caribbean governments may have very little room left to increase their take from bauxite before it equals or exceeds the cost to the companies of producing alumina from alternative materials found in abundance in the major consuming countries. The U.S. Bureau of Mines and a number of the major aluminum companies have for many years been conducting research and experimentation on the feasibility of extracting alumina from various clays found in the United States and in France. Published results of U.S. Bureau of Mines research in 1964-66 suggested that alumina could be produced more cheaply from clay when the cost of bauxite exceeds some $14 a ton.[69] At that time, Jamaican bauxite was costing the companies approximately $3 per ton in direct production costs plus approximately $2 in taxes,[70] making a total of about $5 per ton — obviously well

151

below the hypothetical cost that would make extracting alumina from clay more attractive. Since the tax take is now in the area of $16 for Jamaica, the relative cheapness of using bauxite as a raw material must have been virtually eliminated. It is true that since 1964 inflationary trends must have pushed up the production costs of using clay, but bauxite production costs would have increased as well; moreover, it is quite possible that further technological advances in the use of clay since then have had cost-reducing effects. So far there is no evidence of a large-scale shift to alternative materials by the companies as a result of the Caribbean tax increases. However, a small shift in that direction has begun: in 1974 Alcoa and the French company Pechiney Ugine Kuhlmann together commissioned the construction of an alumina plant using clay as a raw material, to be located in Marseilles. Thus it may well be that the Caribbean countries are at or very near to the limit of their capacity to increase their take before widespread substitution of alternative materials, at least for incremental alumina production, is provoked.

On the other hand, there is no question but that the role of governments in the Caribbean bauxite industry is in a process of structural change. A new stage has been entered in which the governments will play a more active role than in the past in investment, ownership, decision making, taxation, and pricing. In fact, the old pattern was breached and the new stage initiated in 1970-71, when Guyana decided to set its own terms unilaterally for state participation in the Alcan subsidiary (Demba) and to nationalize the enterprise when Alcan rejected these terms. With Jamaica's decision in May 1974 to impose its taxation proposals on the companies like a sovereign state, instead of working toward a mutually agreed settlement as in the past, the new pattern can be said to have been clearly established. Jamaican state participation in the bauxite-producing companies and proposed joint ventures in aluminum smelting by Jamaica, Trinidad and Tobago, and Guyana, and by Jamaica and Mexico also indicate the trend toward growing state involvement.

One should be careful, however, in interpreting where the parameters of this development lie and precisely what its direction is. One cannot yet say that the growing role of governments in the industry is in opposition to the role played by the major transnational aluminum companies. So far, there is no indication that the governments have either the capacity or the inclination to attempt to challenge the dominant role of the aluminum companies in the international industry in production, processing, marketing, or technology. (The Guyanese nationalization has a limited significance in this respect, since it affected mainly cal- cined bauxite, which is not a central product in the international bauxite-aluminum industry.) The joint ventures proposed by gov- ernments in the Caribbean and Mexico take place essentially at the margin of the industry, and it is more than likely that the aluminum companies will be involved either as minority equity holders or as suppliers of technology, or both. The 1974 Caribbean tax measures imply a much increased cash flow to the Caribbean states from the international industry, but this takes place not so much (if at all) at the expense of the companies but at the expense of the consum- ers of primary aluminum and aluminum products. In a sense, the new tax measures integrate the Caribbean states far more deeply into the corporate oligopoly system that dominates the international aluminum industry. The aluminum companies are now the most important tax-collection agencies underpinning the process of national income creation in countries like Jamaica and Surinam. More than ever before, these countries are utterly de- pendent on the market power and economic performance of the major transnational aluminum companies, for it is the companies' dominant position in the industry which guarantees the level of aluminum prices and the stable and uninterrupted flow of produc- tion, shipments, and circulation of capital which underlies the steady and substantial stream of revenues to the states concerned. In that sense, although the Caribbean tax offensive has improved the financial position of these states, in structural terms they have become even more firmly an adjunct of the corporate system in the industry. (None of the other measures for state participation and joint country ventures announced in 1974 are inconsistent with this.) Thus, talk by Caribbean leaders of using IBA as an instru- ment of "cooperation" with the aluminum companies, and stock purchases by Caribbean governments in the equity of the parent aluminum companies, which are welcomed by the company execu- tives, should not be regarded as mere rhetoric. They speak of the real possibility of the emergence of a new partnership and alliance between Caribbean governments and the major aluminum companies within the existing structure.

Last, let us consider the domestic politicoeconomic context within which the Caribbean bauxite offensive took place. It should be noted that the changes in the treatment of bauxite initiated by the governments are not, to any significant extent, part of a general

process of economic reorganization directed at reducing external
dependence, generating a self-centered economy, and gearing economic life to the satisfaction of the material needs of the broad
mass of the population. The real context is quite to the contrary.
The governments have been impelled to act because the policies
of the transnational companies resulted in a period of bauxite-
induced expansion followed by one of relative stagnation; that is,
because the model of dependent growth based on bauxite was no
longer working. Difficulties in pursuing the model led to open or
incipient politicoeconomic crisis; the struggle by the governments to wrest more surpluses from the international industry
represents an attempt to resolve the crisis — that is, to permit
the model of dependent (and inherently unequal) growth to continue.
This is not to say that there have been no changes whatsoever in
the model as a result of the events of 1974. If it is true that, for
countries like Jamaica and Surinam, the governments are now
more than ever dependent on the corporate system in the industry
for their tax revenues, it is also true that the process of income
creation in these countries is now more than ever dependent on
the public expenditure financed by these revenues. In effect, we
are witnessing the development of <u>rentier states</u> attached to the
international aluminum industry and of "appendage economies"
based on these rentier states. This process also implies a structural shift in the role of the public sector vis-à-vis the private
sector in these economies. The public sector undertakes the burden of employment creation and provides the money demand, the
credit, and the foreign exchange necessary to allow the private
sector to continue its model of accumulation. Jamaican government policy after the new bauxite tax revenues started to flow in
the second half of 1974 demonstrates this clearly. Associated
with this is a structural shift in the importance and role of the
state bureaucracy vis-à-vis the private capitalist class. In effect,
the state bureaucracy is admitted to a position of parity in the administration and management of the economy, in return for its
contribution of the critical inputs needed to permit the model to
function. Thus, the government acquires equity in a number of
locally owned enterprises, which gives it places on the boards of
directors and, theoretically, a voice in policymaking. At the same
time, representatives of the private sector are incorporated into
a number of quasi-governmental positions in statutory organizations and other institutions that are the agencies of governmental
involvement in the economy. In this way, the distinction between

the private and public sectors becomes increasingly blurred; the government speaks of assuming the role of directing the economy in the public interest, but this is not real direction, since the type of investments, the composition of output, the distribution of income, and the nature of dependency remain essentially the same. (The foregoing applies specifically to the Jamaican case.)

It may well turn out, therefore, that the 1974 Caribbean bauxite offensive represents a structural adjustment in the industry, a process of change within an overall context of continuity. It is evident that the past pattern of almost completely subordinated and passive states has been breached, probably irreparably. Governments will play a more active, assertive, and initiating role in the industry than in the past. But it hardly follows that this role will be such as to transform the industry into an instrument of self-centered economic development for the Caribbean and the reorientation of economic life for the satisfaction of the needs of the population. Such a role has so far been frustrated by the system of corporate imperialism, which has made the industry rather an instrument for the dependent underdevelopment of the Caribbean. But the evidence so far is that the governments have been attacking not so much the system of corporate imperialism in the world aluminum industry as their own place within that system. What may in fact be taking place is a process of redefining the relationship between companies and governments — a redefinition that involves the formation of a new alliance between the corporate managers of the transnational aluminum companies and the buro-political managers of the Caribbean bauxite-producing states. This may well imply a greater incorporation of these states and social groups into the system of corporate imperialism, and their greater commitment to that system.

Even if such an alliance is in the process of formation, however, it will not necessarily prove to be a durable one. It could easily turn out to be short-lived and largely dependent on the special configuration of circumstances that prevailed in the 1973-74 period. Real conflicts between the companies and the governments could easily break out. For example, if a serious recession were to affect the aluminum industry, each group could try to shift the burden of adjustment onto the other; strong disagreements could emerge on such questions as price levels, production rates, and the distribution of production among countries.[71] Another source of conflict is almost certain to be the question of the use of alternative aluminum materials, for the possibility of a substantial

155

shift by the companies to nonbauxitic materials, at least for incremental aluminum production, must now be considered a very real one. Finally, there is no question but that Caribbean states will come under severe pressure from their populations for substantial changes in the economic systems. The new company-state relationships do not significantly move toward resolving the internal socioeconomic contradictions characterizing the region, but rather seem to involve the reproduction of such contradictions on a higher and more developed level. Continuing contradictions are bound to place severe long-term strains on whatever company-state alliances emerge from the present process. In that sense, the 1974 Caribbean bauxite offensive can be regarded, at best, as unfinished business.

Notes

1. For technical descriptions of the industry, see Stamper (1973) and Bracewell (1962). Except where otherwise stated, dollars in this essay are United States dollars.
2. Reno (1963).
3. Murphy (1967).
4. For descriptions of the early history of the U.S. aluminum industry, see Wallace (1937) and U.S., Department of Commerce (1955); some aspects of post-Second-World-War developments are treated in Girvan (1971b, chap. 2).
5. Huggins (1965, p. 46).
6. The analysis in this section draws heavily on Girvan (1971c).
7. See, for example, Best (1968) and Beckford (1972).
8. Girvan (1971b, p. 42).
9. Girvan (1970).
10. Rosane (1969, Appendix IV).
11. Singh (1969, p. 12).
12. Brewster (1971, pp. 205-6).
13. See Jefferson (1972) and Girvan (1971b).
14. Jefferson (1971, p. 214).
15. See below, p. 134.
16. See Best (1968).
17. The analysis of the Haitian experience draws heavily on Garrity (1975).
18. Wells (1968, pp. 15-16), cited by Garrity (1975).
19. Garrity (1975).
20. See, for example, U.S., Bureau of Mines, Minerals Yearbook, 1929 (Washington, D.C., 1929), chapters on "Aluminum" and "Bauxite"; Bracewell (1962, p. 192).
21. U.S., Bureau of Mines, Minerals Yearbook, 1939 (Washington, D.C., 1939). Metric tons are used in the case of Surinam.
22. Information on the 1949 terms is taken from U.S., Bureau of Mines, Mineral Trade Notes, 1949, Vol. 29, No. 9, p. 3; and Alcoa, Annual Report, 1949.

23. "Dutch Guiana Bauxite During 1925," Engineering and Mining Journal-Press, February 27, 1926, p. 381.

24. Details of the Brokopondo agreement are to be found in a Surinam government paper of the same name, dated January 15, 1958.

25. See Girvan (1971b, pp. 61-74). Long dry tons are used in the case of Jamaica.

26. Ibid.

27. "Jamaica Gets More From Bauxite," Daily Gleaner (Kingston), June 15, 1971, p. 1; U.S., Bureau of Mines, Minerals Yearbook, 1971 (Washington, D.C., 1971), the chapter on "Bauxite."

28. Huggins (1965, pp. 124-27).

29. "£102 mn. bauxite-alumina exports by 1975," Daily Gleaner, November 24, 1967, p. 1. The terms of the agreement for the biggest of the three plants — the Alpart plant — can be found in Jamaica, Ministry of Trade and Industry, Ministry Paper No. 2, 1967 (Kingston, 1967).

30. Statement to the House of Representatives, May 15, 1974.

31. For example, the companies financed virtually the entire construction costs of the plants with loan rather than equity capital, which resulted in huge tax-deductible interest payments. They were also permitted a tax-deductible depletion allowance of 12 percent of the value of gross income (sales).

32. U.S., Senate (1973, pp. 61, 62, 64).

33. The Demerara Bauxite Company (Demba) was the principal bauxite-producing company. It was actually owned by Alcoa until 1928, when it was transferred to Alcan together with most of Alcoa's subsidiary companies outside of the United States.

34. See British Guiana Lands and Mines Department, Annual Report (various years).

35. See Girvan (1967).

36. See Girvan (1971c).

37. See British Guiana, Combined Court (1917).

38. A more detailed analysis of the nationalization of Demba is given in the following essay and in Grant (1973).

39. Guyana Bauxite Company, Annual Report, 1972.

40. Guyana Bauxite Company, Annual Report, 1973. For comment, see DeCastro (1974).

41. For details, see the statement by Prime Minister Manley to the Jamaican House of Representatives, May 15, 1974, and the statement by the aluminum companies, May 16, 1974, both published as a supplement to the Caribbean Monthly Bulletin (University of Puerto Rico), May 1974.

42. "Aluminum Producers Buy Time on Bauxite," Business Week, June 22, 1974; "Companies Seek Arbitration on Tax Dispute," Daily Gleaner, May 22, 1974, p. 34; "NY journal: Bauxite Companies Appear 'Locked in Jamaica,'" Daily Gleaner, June 19, 1974; "Aluminum Prices Start a Rocket Ride," Business Week, July 13, 1974, p. 23.

43. "Surinam Bauxite Levy Now," Metal Bulletin, November 29, 1974, p. 24.

44. "Le message du président a vie de la Republique," Le nouvelliste (Port-au-Prince), December 3, 1974; "L'heureuse conclusion de negociacions avec la Reynolds," Le nouvelliste, December 6, 1974.

45. "Dominican Tax Law Doubted," Journal of Commerce, July 16, 1974.

46. "Reynolds Take Over Begins" Jamaica Weekly Gleaner, February 6, 1974, p. 11; "Guyana Moves to Get More from Reynolds," Jamaica Weekly Gleaner, July 16, 1974, p. 24; "Reynolds Bauxite Unit to Be Nationalized by Guyana This

Year," Wall Street Journal, July 16, 1974; "Reynolds Metals Co. Won't Pay Guyana Steep Tax Increase Enacted on Bauxite," Wall Street Journal, October 4, 1974; "Guyana Clamps Down on Reynolds Exports," Daily Gleaner, October 16, 1974, p. 17; "Guyana, Reynolds, Heading for Clash," Jamaica Weekly Gleaner, October 30, 1974, p. 12.

47. Actually, the amount of the unpaid production levy was $6.5 million, and in theory this was the amount deducted from the $14.5 million. But Guyana agreed to waive its claims on $2 million back taxes, which had already been claimed by the government and paid by the company early in 1974, but which was being separately adjudicated. See "Guyana Nationalizes Reynolds," Jamaica Weekly Gleaner, January 8, 1975, p. 22.

48. See Prime Minister Manley's statement of May 15, 1974; also "Manley Sets Out Pattern for Bauxite Talks," Daily Gleaner, May 31, 1974, p. 1.

49. "Jamaica-Kaiser Pact," Metal Bulletin, November 26, 1974, p. 23; "A Note on Bauxite," Jamaica Weekly Gleaner, January 1, 1975, p. 25; "Kaiser Proud to Be Partner With Govt. — Coyne," Jamaica Weekly Gleaner, January 15, 1975, p. 4.

50. Semonin (1971); see also essays 2 and 4 in this volume.

51. "Jamaica-Revere Partnership," Jamaica Weekly Gleaner, January 1, 1975, p. 1. This agreement never came to fruition, however, as Revere closed down its plant in August 1975.

52. "Govt., Reynolds Start Phase 2 of Negotiations," Jamaica Weekly Gleaner, February 12, 1975, p. 6.

53. "Bauxite Smelters for Trinidad, Guyana," Jamaica Daily News, June 9, 1974, p. 1; "Smelters for Trinidad, Guyana," Jamaica Weekly Gleaner, June 18, 1974, p. 8; "Caribbean Cooperation," Financial Times, June 28, 1974, p. 5.

54. Caribbean Monthly Bulletin, October-November 1974, pp. 4-5; "Second Mexican Smelter," Metal Bulletin, November 29, 1974, p. 24; "Jamaican-Mexican Industrial Complex Set," Jamaica Weekly Gleaner, December 4, 1975, p. 3.

55. "Jamaican-Mexican Industrial Complex Set," Jamaica Weekly Gleaner, December 4, 1975.

56. See Girvan (1967); "Manley Lauded for Role in IBA Formation," Jamaica Weekly Gleaner, March 20, 1974, p. 37.

57. "Whitlam on 'Multi-nationals' That Threaten Us," Third World (London), October 1973.

58. "Meeting of Aluminum-Ore Producer Nations to Be Watched for Signs of Arab-Like Pact," Wall Street Journal, January 10, 1974, p. 2; "Whatever Happened to the Big Bauxite Crisis?" Wall Street Journal, January 24, 1974, p. 12; "Bauxite Talks Stirring Concern Among Consumers," Jamaica Weekly Gleaner, March 8, 1974; "Reynolds Working on Substitute," Jamaica Weekly Gleaner, March 8, 1974; "Breakthrough for PUK Alumina Process," Metal Bulletin, February 14, 1974, p. 31.

59. "Bauxite Pact Talks Soon," Financial Times, February 12, 1974.

60. "Bauxite Countries to Form Assn.," Jamaica Weekly Gleaner, March 6, 1974, p. 1.

61. Ibid.; also "Manley Lauded for Role in IBA Formation," pp. 19, 37.

62. "Bauxite Pact Welcomed," Financial Times, March 12, 1974.

63. Ibid.

64. "World Bauxite Producers Not Out for War," West Africa, November 11, 1974. In the same article, it was also reported that "Dr. Jim Cairns, Australia's

deputy Prime Minister, and Minister for Overseas Trade... did not think that IBA could become as effective as the OPEC organization, because bauxite was widely distributed and the bauxite-producing states did not have the same degree of monopoly over their commodity as the oil producing states had." The November meeting admitted the Dominican Republic, Haiti, and Ghana to membership in IBA.

65. Australian Information Service, Australia Japan Keynote Speech by Australian Prime Minister (Tokyo: Australian Embassy, October 1973), p. 1.

66. "PM Sees IBA as Avenue for Co-operation," Jamaica Weekly Gleaner, November 6, 1974, p. 25.

67. "Govt. Buying Reynolds, Kaiser, Shares," Daily Gleaner, October 29, 1974, p. 1.

68. "Manley Holds Cordial Talks with Kissinger," Jamaica Weekly Gleaner, March 20, 1974, p. 28; "Kissinger in Bauxite Talks," Financial Times, March 15, 1974; "Bauxite Talks a Success — Manley," Jamaica Weekly Gleaner, March 20, 1974, p. 33.

69. See U.S., Bureau of Mines, A Cost Estimate of the Bayer Process for Producing Alumina, RI 6730 (Washington, D.C., 1966); Methods for Producing Alumina from Clay, RI 6431. See also U.S., Bureau of Mines, RI 6927, 5997, 6133, 6229, 6290, 6573, 7299, 7068.

70. See Girvan (1971b, pp. 44, 53, 67).

71. This was written in early 1975; by the latter part of that year, conflicts of this kind had already begun to surface in Jamaica. In August the Revere alumina plant was closed down completely by the parent company as a result of alleged economic and financial difficulties. In November, one of Alcan's two alumina plants was closed for two weeks, and the Alcoa alumina plant was shut down for some eight weeks in February/March 1976. In both instances, the companies cited labor unrest as the cause of their decisions for closure, but the employees claimed increased employer provocation and noncooperation since the imposition of the production levy and the recession in the U.S. aluminum industry. The government experienced shortfalls in its estimates of revenue from the bauxite production levy for the financial year 1975-76, and in March 1976 indicated its willingness to reduce the levy on individual companies that made an acceptable case for such relief.

BAUXITE NATIONALIZATION IN GUYANA

4

> You cannot be an independent country and be an economic satel-
> lite, not merely of another nation, but of a private corporation.
>
> — Prime Minister Forbes Burnham
> of Guyana

When the government of Guyana nationalized the foreign-owned
Demerara Bauxite Company (Demba) in July 1971,[1] the event was
something of a historical landmark on a number of levels. The
bauxite mining and processing operation taken over by Guyana is
a major factor in the economic life of the country: it is the largest
single generator of foreign exchange, of government revenue,[2] and
of (relatively) highly paid employment. The nationalization thus
constituted a decided and dramatic change in the economic policy
of the Burnham government, which until then had been considered
to be generally favorable to foreign capital.[3] Indeed, within the
wider Commonwealth Caribbean region, the Guyanese bauxite nationalization was regarded as a radical — and, to some, ominous[4] —
departure from the policy of accommodation to external capital
which had been a bulwark of postwar and postindependence economic policy in the region.

The Guyanese action also sent a shock wave rippling through the
international aluminum industry. Demba was a subsidiary of Alcan
Aluminium, Limited, one of the two largest transnational aluminum corporations with operations in well over thirty countries;
Demba was the largest bauxite operation in the Alcan family and
represented "a raw material foundation on which much of Alcan's
international superstructure is erected."[5] Most of the bauxite for
the international aluminum industry is taken from underdeveloped
countries in the tropical zone,[6] and the transnationals which dom-

160

inate the industry had traditionally enjoyed "good relations" with host governments — a euphemism for the passive acquiescence of these governments to relationships that were frankly exploitive.[7] The Guyanese bauxite nationalization was not only a major setback to the raw materials position of Alcan, it also generated anxieties in the international industry about the "reliability" of the principal sources of bauxite supplies and created the specter of radical changes in the attitude of the governments concerned toward the terms of supply of bauxite to the aluminum industry.

Although at the time the Guyanese move appeared as an isolated action — almost an aberration — subsequent events have shown it to be a historical precursor to changes in economic policies both in the Commonwealth Caribbean generally and in the international bauxite-aluminum industry. Public or at least national ownership, either in whole or in part, has virtually become part of the conventional economics in the region as far as the major export industries and public utilities are concerned. In 1974 the formation of an association of bauxite-exporting countries, and Jamaica's action in imposing an eightfold increase in its bauxite taxes, signaled a generalized change in the terms on which the bauxite-producing states will henceforth participate in the international aluminum industry.[8]

I. THE HISTORY, 1916-69

The Demerara Bauxite Company was incorporated in British Guiana in 1916 to hold and work a significant number of bauxite concessions that had been acquired by the Aluminum Company of America (Alcoa) in the British colony over the previous three years. Bauxite had been discovered along the banks of the Demerara River by the Geological Survey Department of the colony in 1910. Efforts to interest British and European companies in exploiting the deposits met with no success, and in 1913 the discovery came to the attention of Arthur Vining Davis, President of Alcoa. Davis sent an aide to British Guiana to capture as much bauxite as possible as quickly as possible, under the guise of buying land for a citrus plantation. By 1916 Alcoa, through its agents, had secured the bulk of the rich British Guiana deposits accessible to river transport on the Demerara.

Alcoa's interest lay in securing a reliable and high-grade source of bauxite to feed its aluminum production in the United States. The

company had been formed in 1888 to work the Hall patent for the electrolytic reduction of aluminum, and since that time it had become
vertically integrated through the building of an alumina plant at
East St. Louis and the acquisition of bauxite mines in Georgia and
Arkansas. By World War I, the company was seeking foreign
sources of bauxite, mainly in British and in Dutch Guiana, in order
to augment its domestic reserves and to preempt foreign bauxite
from competing aluminum companies.[9]

From the outset, there was a conflict between the British Guiana
authorities and Alcoa. The possibility of marrying Guyana's hydroelectric resources and its bauxite for the development of a
profitable and beneficial aluminum industry was the major concern
of civil service officers, especially Sir John Harrison, the Director
of Geological Surveys. At that time, however, few officials, if any,
made any distinction between the interests of the colony and those
of the British Empire, so the concern was expressed in terms of
protecting and preserving the "Imperial asset" for "Imperial" interest. Almost certainly for this reason Alcoa incorporated the
Demerara Bauxite Company locally in British Guiana in 1916 and
went to great pains to show that its directors, officers, and parent
company were British. Also in deference to Imperial sensibilities,
it promised to build an alumina plant to process British Guiana
bauxite "on British soil."

Notwithstanding its legal personality and its promise, Demba
became a vital part of the Alcoa system, while remaining divorced
from the Guyanese economy and Guyanese interests. Its bauxite
was fed into Alcoa's North American plants. The opportunity to
keep the promise in a manner consistent with Alcoa's interests
came when the company incorporated Aluminium, Limited, in
Canada in 1928, transferring to this company its vast hydroelectric
facilities and concessions in Canada, as well as most of its foreign
properties, including Demba. By forming Aluminium, Limited,[10]
as a legally separate and independent company, Alcoa's owners
were able to participate in foreign cartels, something which the
United States law prevented Alcoa itself from doing. The promise
to British Guiana was kept by building an alumina plant on British
soil — at Arvida on Canada, next to the smelter powered by Alcan's
hydrostations.[11]

From 1928 through 1950 Guyana's bauxite was the raw material
foundation for the burgeoning power and position of Alcan as an
aluminum company. This role was especially marked during the
period of World War II, when the Allied governments lent $173

million to Alcan for the expansion of its facilities in order to supply aluminum to the arms industries. By far the bulk of the bauxite for this expanded production came from Demba. Guyana's bauxite therefore contributed markedly to the victory of the Anglo-
American power system over the German-Japanese one; more
specifically, it was the base for Alcan's asset growth from $45
million in 1928 to $423 million in 1950, and for the growth of its
aluminum production from virtually zero to over 400,000 tons per
year. What this meant for Guyana was that the country's natural
resources were wed to the industrialization of the North American
economy and to the accumulation of the power and wealth of the
Davis and Mellon families. In the meantime, Guyana remained
underdeveloped and the Guyanese poor and economically impotent.

In the 1950s, a second phase in the Alcan strategy for Guyana
unfolded: calcined bauxite. Calcined bauxite is used mainly in the
steel and other metal industries, for the production of refractory
firebricks used to line furnaces. It is produced by the superheating
of bauxite that has a very low iron content, and in value is much
greater than metal grade bauxite but much lower than alumina, its
main competitor as a refractory material. In the 1950s and 1960s,
Alcan developed an important calcined bauxite operation at Demba.
A relatively small alumina plant was also built in the late 1950s to
use some of the accumulated bauxite waste of the last fifty years,
and exports of dried bauxite were maintained in order to feed the
Arvida alumina plant. Progressively, Alcan relied less and less
on Guyana as a source of material for its growing aluminum production.

What happened was that Alcan was shifting to new bauxite countries. In the 1950s and 1960s Jamaica was the chosen one — two
alumina plants were built with a combined capacity of over one
million tons per year. In the 1970s Guinea and Australia will be
the major sources of the company's incremental supplies. While
Guyana's rich surface deposits were progressively depleted as a
result of decades of mining, and costs increased, large surface
deposits became available in these other countries.

There was also a shrewd element of political strategy underlying Alcan's policy. In the 1950s British Guiana became what is
known in the language of international companies as a "poor investment risk." In 1953 the nationalist-Marxist People's Progressive Party was voted overwhelmingly into office under a new constitution. Within six months, the British threw the party out of
office, abrogated the new constitution, and installed a nominated

government. Subsequently, the movement split into essentially two factions, one East Indian (the People's Progressive Party, or PPP, led by Dr. Cheddi Jagan) and one African (the People's National Congress, or PNC, led by Mr. Forbes Burnham), and serious racial violence occurred in the 1960s.[12] It was therefore in Alcan's interest to depend as little as possible on Guyana. At the same time, Alcan had an investment and an organization in place, and bauxite concessions, so that it had an interest in maximizing its profits from the Guyana operation. By developing calcined bauxite in Guyana, Alcan was concentrating on a product which was profitable — but upon which the company's worldwide processing and fabricating facilities does not depend, as they do on bauxite and alumina production. In this way the development of the Guyanese bauxite industry was planned so as to minimize Alcan's investment risk and at the same time promote its profits. As a direct result, Guyana continued to be excluded from high-valued aluminum production and relegated to a relatively small alumina production. Since the value of a ton of bauxite rises from about G$18 as dried ore to G$65 as alumina and about G$250 as aluminum ingot,[13] the overwhelming bulk of the value added in the transformation of Guyana's raw materials took place outside of the country. Consider that during 1917-69 Demba shipped nearly 50 million tons of dried bauxite, just over 2 million tons of alumina, and no metal, and one begins to comprehend the enormous export of incomes from Guyana to North America over the period. The potential to use the country's bauxite as a base for the development of chemical, metallurgical, and hydroelectric industries was completely unrealized; rather than developing the Guyanese economy, the terms of Demba's operations reinforced the pattern of underdevelopment that had been the continuing legacy of specialization in sugar cane production under the infamous plantation system.[14]

Even such value as was created by the production and minor processing of bauxite within the country was distributed iniquitously. For 1917-69, of the industry's total exports, which were worth over G$1,200 million,[15] the government's revenue from royalties and export duties amounted to G$21.1 million, or 1.6 percent; even adding income tax, the government's total revenue from the company in the 1963-68 period amounted to only 3.4 percent of the value of exports.[16] The take of the country as a whole — that is, with taxes, labor incomes, and other local payments added to taxes — normally amounted to just over one-third of the value of the company's exports.[17] The company's small tax payments bear eloquent testimony to Alcan's power and maneuverability as a large, oligopolistic, vertically integrated transnational enterprise. The "prices" for Demba's "sales" to its parent Alcan were fixed by the latter so as to minimize the corporation's overall tax burden, and as a direct result Guyana experienced some of the lowest prices and taxes per ton recorded in the Caribbean.[18] Moreover, when the company decided to build its small alumina plant in Guyana (opened in 1961), it secured so-called pioneer industry tax concessions from the colonial administration — although it had by then been operating in the country for some forty years. The result was that for the first ten years of the plant's operation it paid virtually no taxes at all.[19]

Indeed, one of the most striking features of Demba's operations in British Guiana was the power and influence it wielded in the body politic. From 1917 clear up until the late 1950s, the British colonial administration accommodated to the company's demands when it was not giving it active support. The reasons are not difficult to find: Demba was producing a material of strategic military as well as economic significance to the West; furthermore — and no less important — it was a dollar earner for the sterling area. But even the nationalist politicians felt constrained to acknowledge the company's power. It has been pointed out that on three different occasions between the early 1950s and 1964 Dr. Jagan asserted as a matter of policy that he had no intention of nationalizing bauxite[20]; and one of the first actions of Mr. Burnham's government in 1965 was to sign a relatively favorable agreement with Demba regularizing the company's tax status. Given that both leaders were ideologically opposed to foreign capital in general and had every reason to believe that Demba in particular was exploiting the country, these gestures should be taken as a grudging acknowledgment of the leverage represented by Alcan's influence with the metropolitan powers and its control over markets, technology, and capital in the aluminum industry. The split in the national movement also weakened the bargaining position of both the Jagan and the Burnham governments, as "both Alcan and Reynolds turned the inability of the Guyana Government to ensure political stability in the 1950s and the early 1960s to good account."[21]

While governmental dissatisfaction with Demba involved the issues of taxation and processing, it was in the mining community of some 30,000 people that the company had a tangible and daily impact on the lives of ordinary Guyanese. Isolated as a physical and social enclave some sixty miles up the Demerara River from the capital city,[22] the town of Mackenzie was quite literally created by Demba to service its production operations, and it became the classic case of the company town in the Caribbean.[23] Demba was not only the all-powerful employer, it also operated the hospital, the residential, educational, and recreational facilities, the police department, and even the local government.[24] Separate and superior facilities were provided for the "staff" personnel, who were predominantly white and North American,[25] so there was a complete identity between the occupational hierarchy within the company and the social structure of the company town, with white foreigners at the top disposing of virtually absolute power over the daily lives of the mass of black Guyanese. The leader of ASCRIA, the foremost black nationalist movement in Guyana,[26] incisively summed up the attitude of the majority of bauxite workers to Demba:

they [the workers] have, until recently, been bound to live in the most stratified community in Guyana, with its South African and U.S.A. idea of neighbourhood living and of white supremacy. The physical arrangements were such also that the whole imperialist machinery could be clearly seen; the extraction of the ore, the processing and added value, the shipping away of wealth, the importation of raw chemicals, the small group of expatriate decision-makers, the tokenism, the social gaps, the misery of the poorer districts, the hill top luxury of the white population, the buying out of leaders, the divide and rule tactics, the process of exploitation which they could feel in their skin.[27]

Hostility toward the work situation and the company was an intrinsic feature of the culture of the Guyanese in the mining community, and wildcat strikes were frequent.[28] The relatively well paid[29] and stable employment offered by the company was zealously sought and jealously protected by the workers, but few who had had the experience could regard it as anything other than a necessary evil.

As the company completed a half-century of operations in Guyana, its officers spoke of its record as a "good corporate citizen" and its "continuing dialogue"[30] with the government. But this represented more the mythology of its public relations effort than the reality in the hearts and minds of Guyanese; to the extent that its relationship with the government was free from dispute, the reason was far more Demba's and Alcan's considerable power than genuine governmental satisfaction. In fact, Demba's fifty years had laid the basis for a rare consensus within a Guyanese community normally split by socioeconomic and racial antagonisms — a consensus that the company's operations, on both the economic and the social level, were incompatible with the aspirations of an independent Guyana.

II. PRELUDE TO NEGOTIATIONS, 1970

In April 1970, the ruling People's National Congress adopted a resolution at its annual convention calling on the government, by itself or in association with cooperatives, to hold a minimum of 51 percent of the equity in enterprises exploiting Guyana's forest and mining resources. This resolution was used by the government as its mandate to seek a majority holding in Demba, and negotiations began in December of that year. Nevertheless, since party and government leaders were the same and the resolution itself was obviously sponsored by the government, one must identify the factors that were ultimately to take the ruling regime in Guyana into a course of open confrontation with Alcan.

We have already seen that both sections of the national movement shared a common anti-imperialist ideology and identified foreign capital ownership in the bauxite and sugar industries as one of the chief manifestations of Guyana's colonial condition. Mr. Burnham's tactics apparently required that he make an accommodation with foreign capital before the granting of constitutional independence, and agreements were made with both Demba and the smaller Reynolds Guyana Mines in 1965.[31] In 1966 Prime Minister Burnham met with Alcan President Nathanael Davis, and the two issued a joint statement in which Alcan committed itself to erect a smelter in Guyana provided cheap electricity were made available. But the policy of accommodation yielded no benefits; the smelter never materialized, Demba engaged in virtually no expansion, and, largely as a result, Guyana's economy stagnated. At the same time, the euphoria of independence dissipated; the population, like that of the entire Commonwealth Caribbean, showed growing signs of disaffection with the failure of changes in constitutional status to bring an end to foreign white economic domination and local black economic dispossession. Black power movements hostile to the black governments in Jamaica and Trinidad emerged; in Guyana, where black nationalism had been directed primarily against East Indians, an incipient antigovernment hostility could be discerned.

Under these pressures, the regime moved to resurrect the anti-imperialist stream in the nationalist ideology; Guyana, after all, had very little to lose since new foreign capital investment was at a trickle. In February 1970, Guyana was declared a cooperative republic — "republic" because the English monarchy was replaced by a presidential system; "cooperative" because the institution of the cooperative was adopted by the government as the vehicle for socioeconomic revolution — in the words of the official slogan, "To make the small man a real man." It was inevitable that a sharp contradiction would emerge between the idea of the cooperative republic and the reality of continuing foreign domination of the country's major industries, and it is in this context that the regime decided to adopt the principle of majority local ownership in the forest and mining industries.[32]

The period between April and December 1970 was marked by thorough technical preparations for the negotiations with Alcan. A team was assembled which drew upon the most experienced and expert officers in government service in the fields of geology, economics, taxation, statistics, and accounting. In addition, two West Indian academics who had done work in the economics and political sociology of bauxite were utilized as advisers.[33] The team was given a relatively free hand by the government in discussing, evaluating, and recommending various alternative strategies for participation. And although the companies were ready to begin negotiations from April, the government's seriousness was indicated by its willingness to wait for months while its technical officers prepared themselves and gained the knowledge and expertise necessary for the negotiations.

As the months passed the initial apprehensiveness of these men at the enormity of the task handed them by the politicians was replaced by an attitude of growing confidence and excitement at the prospect of accepting responsibility for a nationally controlled bauxite industry. From an evaluation of participation agreements in Chile and Zambia, a number of things became clear to these officers and to the government. One was that transnational mining companies in these countries conceded a government majority interest in return for certain significant government concessions. First, the companies retained control over the operation by means of management contracts and minority shareholders rights which allowed them to name personnel to the top managerial posts in the enterprise and gave them vetoes over important decisions relating to finance and production policies. Second, the companies secured a superior financial position as a result of government participation by getting the government to cut taxes and controls over profits remittances, by securing expansion financed by the government or third parties, and by securing a favorable valuation of the assets to be acquired and the means of payment for these assets. For example, by securing a valuation of their assets at market valuation, with payment over a relatively short period of time at a commercial rate of interest, government participation could be made financially favorable to companies and, by the same token, unfavorable to government.[34]

Thus, the government of Guyana became convinced that an agreement containing the control and the financial aspects of the Chilean and Zambian models would be both technically unsound and politically dangerous. This conviction was to underlie the most important of the points subsequently stated to be nonnegotiable by the government in the Demba talks.[35]

But having decided this, the next difficulty logically to be considered was this: suppose the company, faced with government nonnegotiables on the most important points, decided not to agree. Suppose it pulled out, wrote off Guyana, or simply refused to agree to the government's position. Then Guyana would be faced with the task of running the industry on its own, either because the company had pulled out or because the government would have to impose a solution. In other words, the government would have to be prepared to nationalize, as part of its preparedness for participation. Otherwise, the government would be negotiating from a position of weakness and the negotiations could hardly be taken seriously.

In effect then, what took place in the months preceding the negotiations was the emergence and growth of the psychological preparedness for nationalization by politicians and technicians alike. Inevitably, this led to the identification and preparation of the physical steps necessary for the implementation of any decision to nationalize. From very early in the exercise, a preliminary evaluation had been made of Guyana's capacity to market and attract personnel independently. One thing that became evident from this exercise was the conviction that the world had sufficient need for the products of the Guyana bauxite industry outside of the Alcan system, and sufficient expertise, to make an independent industry commercially viable. The second was that, in spite of this, there could be no absolute certainty that Guyana would be able to maintain its exports, especially in the short run, at a level sufficient to avoid serious dislocation. Beyond a certain point, therefore, the decision to nationalize would have to be a step into the uncertain, and one that could be made only if both government and people had the confidence to manage and make sacrifices.

It was around this point that the most agonizing arguments took place at the technical level. Ultimately the question was resolved by the politicians, for the simplest of political reasons: "I prefer," remarked the Prime Minister, "to take on Alcan rather than the people of Guyana," and, on another occasion, "Comrade, it is better to die on your feet than to live on your knees."

Thus, by the time negotiations began in December 1970 there were few in the government who did not recognize that the government might be faced with the possibility of applying the ultimate sanction — nationalization — although at the time it could not publicly embrace the possibility as it was committed then to the principle of negotiating. In following up on this, serious studies began to be prepared on the implications of a government takeover for working capital, foreign exchange, supplies, and marketing, as well as the legislative implications. Preparations for negotiation therefore created a dynamic of their own, and they generated a further contradiction: if the government were prepared for the political and economic difficulties associated with an imposed nationalization, why bother to negotiate for part national ownership at all? The rationale was that a negotiated participation that secured the agreement of the company should confer many of the benefits of full nationalization without many of the attendant difficulties; but, as it turned out, the contradiction was resolved in a different way as a result of Alcan's refusal to agree to Guyana's abrupt change in the rules by which the company-country game was traditionally played.

III. THE NEGOTIATIONS FOR GUYANA'S PARTICIPATION: DECEMBER 1970 TO FEBRUARY 1971

The government's chief aim was to maneuver Alcan into a position where it had to accept Guyana's principal and basic terms for participation in Demba. First, the government, through private correspondence with the company, secured agreement that meetings would be held beginning December 7 to discuss the principle of government participation. This having been established, the government then wrote the company setting out the nonnegotiable principles guiding its proposed participation; simultaneously, the

Prime Minister spoke to the nation announcing Alcan's agreement to hold discussions and setting out with considerable persuasiveness the government's terms for participation. The famous nonnegotiables established by the government were:

1. The government's participation shall be a majority.

2. Participation will be by means of purchase of a share of the assets of the company.

3. The valuation of the assets for the purpose of acquiring such a majority share shall be the book value of the company's assets for income tax purposes at December 31, 1969, plus any additions during 1970 not by reappraisal or revaluation.

4. The payment for the government's participation shall be out of the government's share of the future aftertax profits of the undertaking.

5. The government's majority shall carry with it the effective control which inheres in a majority holding.

6. Regardless of the date of any agreement that might be arrived at between the government and the company, the effective date of acquisition shall be deemed January 1, 1971.[36]

An analysis of these nonnegotiables will show that the government's aim was to acquire its majority share while at the same time preempting in its own favor certain features that in the Zambian and Chilean agreements had been modeled to defeat substantially the very purpose of the majority holding. By referring to "effective control," the government was in effect saying to Alcan, "No management contract, no minority shareholders' rights which will paralyze our decision-making powers as the majority shareholders." By specifying book value for income tax purposes, the government was saying, "No valuation at replacement cost or market value" which could result in the government's paying two or three times the income tax value — a difference amounting to hundreds of millions of dollars. By specifying payment out of the government's share of the future profits, the government was saying two things. First, that as a result of participation, its financial position should not be made worse off. This was a direct lesson from the Chilean and Zambian experience; there payment was made through government bonds issued when the price of copper was very high and the government's share of profits was at the outset more than enough to cover the payments, but subsequently, the price of copper fell and the governments faced the prospect of paying more than they were receiving. Second, by tying payment to future profits the government was providing an inducement to

Alcan to cooperate, as a minority shareholder, in ensuring that future profits were in fact made.

The nonnegotiable points, however, left a considerable area open for bargaining and concessions on both sides. The government's share could be fixed at anywhere between the theoretical limits of 99 and 51 percent as a result of negotiations. The proportion of the government's share in future profits after tax to be allocated to payment for the assets was negotiable. Although the government insisted on effective control, the area and extent of Alcan involvement in management and decision making was negotiable. And since the question of the marketing of Demba's products was not mentioned as nonnegotiable, the way was left open for Alcan to negotiate long-term purchase contracts for these products as part of the agreement.

Alcan was caught unawares by the government's action. It did not expect to be faced with nonnegotiables; it was shocked at the content of the terms specified; and it was alarmed at the degree of politicization with which the government had invested the issue through the Prime Minister's broadcast to the nation. It expected negotiations; it was faced with a fait accompli. The company was in a quandary: it had already agreed to attend talks on government participation, but it did not wish its attendance to imply agreement to the government's terms. The company therefore issued a statement that it would still meet with the government representatives as planned, but for the purpose of "seeking clarification of the points raised." At the same time, it regretted "that the government of Guyana has, by what appears to be a unilateral decision, decided on a radical change in the arrangements under which [Demba] has operated in Guyana"; it assured its shareholders, employees, and customers that their interests would be safeguarded; and it concluded pointedly that "if supplies of metal-grade bauxite and alumina are affected, Alcan believes that alternative sources of supplies can be arranged."[37] The message to Guyana was plain: we will talk, but do not take that to mean that we agree to your terms; furthermore, we are prepared to do without your bauxite if necessary. The Guyana-Alcan confrontation had begun.

If the reaction from Alcan was quick and to the point, so was that from the Guyanese nation. From all quarters came overwhelming support for the principle of state control of bauxite in general and of Demba in particular, and also for the terms proposed by the government. The support included the mineworkers' union and even the conservative business community; the only divergences from the government's position came from Opposition leader Dr. Jagan and Dr. Clive Thomas, a prominent university economist,[38] both of whom argued that the government should carry out full instead of partial nationalization. The consensus generated was virtually unprecedented in Guyana's history. The government was able to face Alcan with a nation unanimous in its support for state control of Demba and was further able to point to the threat from the Left: it could tell Alcan that its position was "likely to be criticised, if at all, only for its moderation."[39]

The atmosphere of confrontation was tangible as the talks opened in the boardroom of the Guyana Development Corporation. On one side sat the large government negotiating team: led by the Minister of Mines, it included senior government officers in the government departments concerned with geology, mining, economic development, taxation, banking, and law, as well as special advisers drawn from academia; the mayor of the mining town and the president of the mineworkers' union sat in as observers. On the other side were senior officials from the Alcan head office in Montreal and from the subsidiary, Demba. In a very real sense, the attitudes in evidence around the negotiating table reflected in microcosm the confrontation taking place everywhere between the Third World and the world of metropolitan capitalism. At best, relations between the two sides were formal and cool; not infrequently, overt skepticism, distrust, and even outright hostility were expressed on either side. At any rate, the die had already been cast before the talks began. The government never succeeded in securing Alcan's agreement to its terms, and in effect substantive negotiations for government participation in Demba never started, although the meetings continued for over two months. The President of Alcan[40] let the proverbial cat out of the bag when he blurted out in one of the opening sessions that, for Alcan to agree to Guyana's terms, it would take "a helluva lot" of return concessions on Guyana's part. What "a helluva lot" meant in concrete terms became evident when Alcan submitted a counterproposal of its own in the early stages of the talks.

The company proposed that Alcan and the Guyana government should form a partnership, to which Alcan would contribute the Demerara Bauxite Company, partly in the form of equity and partly as a loan. The government would be required to contribute G$50 million to the partnership, probably raised from the World Bank, which would be used to finance an expansion of calcined bauxite production. As an additional stipulation, this expansion would be the only expansion carried out by the company for a period of five years. Alcan's loan to the partnership (i.e., part of Demba's assets) would be repaid as a first charge on the new company's cash generation. Finally, the new company would be administered by a chief executive officer who would in effect have all managerial and administrative powers vested in his person and who would be nominated by Alcan.

The proposal, which was originally submitted in December 1970, was modified somewhat as the talks dragged on into February 1971. At the outset, Alcan proposed that the company would be capitalized at approximately G$100 million, 51 percent owned by Alcan and 49 percent by the government. The government's G$49 million equity would be provided by the World Bank loan and Alcan's G$51 million by the contribution of Demba. The remainder of the value of Demba — approximately G$49 million — would be contributed as a loan to the new company, repayable by annual installments at a commercial rate of interest. In February, this was modified as follows:

1. The company would be capitalized at G$100 (one hundred Guyana dollars), 51 percent to Guyana and 49 percent to Alcan.

2. The entire amount of Demba's assets would be contributed as a loan.

3. Interest and redemption payments on this loan, payable to Alcan, would be a first charge on the company's cash generation.

4. The company and its shareholders would not be subject to any Guyana tax of any kind — that is, income, corporation, property, withholding, import or export duty, royalty, or any impost — nor any exchange control restriction with respect to interest, dividends, or fees for its shareholders.

5. The company's profits, after meeting a small amount of fixed capital additions and repayment and interest charges on its debts, would be allocated 70 percent to the government and 30 percent to Alcan.[41]

The logic of the Alcan proposals was impeccable from its own standpoint. It would recover its investment in Demba (in the modified proposal, all G$100 million of it) in cash, at a commercial rate of interest, as a first charge on the new company's cash flow. At the same time, it would retain permanently a half-share in an enterprise that would have been expanded at the government's expense, this expansion to take place in a product offering no competitive threat to its alumina and aluminum operations worldwide. Alcan would also retain operating control over the enterprise. The

net result would be that Alcan would secure an increased cash
flow from its Guyana operations, with no new capital infusions on
its part, and it would retain control. State participation would be
turned to the company's benefit, just as in Zambia and Chile. By
the same token, the proposals could not but prove unacceptable to
the government. They meant that Guyana would have to incur an
increase of G$50 million in the national public debt as a condition
of its participation in the bauxite industry; also, its money would
be used for an expansion program designed and engineered by
Alcan and agreed to before the government had had the opportunity
to evaluate various options from the inside, as a member of the
partnership: The government could not, if it wished, involve the
enterprise in an alumina expansion or initiate aluminum production at least for the first five years; also, it would have little, if
any, control over the enterprise. Compulsory retirement of the
Alcan loan and compulsory distribution of profits would entirely
strip the new enterprise of all sources of self-financing. Since
the new enterprise would pay no taxes of any kind, Alcan's 30 percent share of dividable profits would amount to the same as if it
had about 50 percent of profits after taxes, so that the 70-30 split
of profits was illusory and, moreover, linked to a complete abro-
gation of the government's sovereign rights over the largest sector
of the economy. The government, in other words, would be required to incur real liabilities and make concrete concessions in
return for benefits that were at best uncertain and at worst non-
existent.

An impasse had been reached, and neither side would budge.
The government could not back down from its position without
losing enormous face in the eyes of the Guyanese public. Alcan,
for its part, was probably concerned that to agree either to the
manner or to the content of the Guyanese demands would create a
dramatic precedent that other host nations would almost certainly
wish to follow. Alcan was almost surely under strong pressure
from the other aluminum companies to resist the Guyanese demands for the same reason. The company was evidently prepared
for whatever dislocations a Guyanese nationalization might entail,
for it felt secure in the flexibility and the resources that only a
transnational corporation can count on. Its diversified raw materials position, with access to bauxite in Jamaica, Guinea, Brazil,
Australia, and Malaysia; its stocks; its contacts with other aluminum companies that also have access to raw materials; its accessibility to the metropolitan governments; the depressed state

of the aluminum market; and Guyana's probable reliance on Alcan as a market for Demba's products even if nationalization were to take place — all these factors must have helped convince the company that the loss from a Guyanese nationalization would be a small price to pay for the maintenance of the legitimacy of the existing pattern of company-country arrangements in the international bauxite-aluminum industry. The Alcan tactic was therefore to keep on meeting and talking with the government indefinitely, without agreeing to any of the government's terms. Evidently this was not an appealing timetable to a government under political pressures, and in his speech of February 23, 1971, marking the first anniversary of the cooperative republic, Prime Minister Burnham made the nationalization announcement to an expectant nation with the following words:

It seems to me that there is no alternative to us saying "thus far and no further." ... We have offered peace and reason and been met with unreason. We have offered partnership and have been threatened with continued domination. Our choice is between being men and being mice....

Today we declare the first major and concrete act of economic independence, the taking over of the Demerara Bauxite Company at Mackenzie.... Comrades! By nationalizing Demba we are asserting our manhood as a nation, our confidence in ourselves, in our people, because it is the ordinary man, the worker — manual or intellectual — who can conceive and make the things that support a nation.... In nationalizing Demba, I place the fate of our nation in the hands of the people. If you, the people, will take as natural the wrath of the former masters because we refuse to give up what is rightfully ours, if you trust your own strength, our strength and our creative genius, we shall succeed.[42]

The nation was electrified; the Prime Minister was universally acclaimed. The business community, the radical intellectuals, and the Opposition PPP all supported the government. For the first time in recent history, Dr. Jagan and Mr. Burnham were at one. At Mackenzie, the bauxite workers sang triumphantly as they danced in the streets to the music of steel bands: "Nationalization bill go pass, Backra man sa eat long grass."[43] A dream had come true: David had spat in the face of Goliath, for Guyana was to take on Alcan, and economic independence was to be secured.

As it turned out, the euphoria was not to last longer than a few weeks.

IV. THE NATIONAL AND INTERNATIONAL POLITICS
OF NATIONALIZATION: FEBRUARY-JULY 1971

Speaking one day after the Prime Minister's nationalization announcement, a university professor acclaimed the government's decision as "truly one of the most momentous in the history of this country. To all of us who have been engaged in perpetual struggle against foreign economic domination of our society, the declaration moves us a little closer to eventual victory." But he also warned that "total victory against foreign economic domination depends heavily on the extent to which the people of this country are involved in that struggle. An economic revolution has to be fought for, and won, by the people. If it is confined simply to a struggle between the leaders of the government and foreign company executives, then victories will not be easily forthcoming; and even those we do achieve may be just as easily reversed, when the interests of foreign capital begin to plot against the country."[44]

In the following months, these words were to prove remarkably prophetic.[45] Although the decision to nationalize Demba was unanimously supported within Guyana and appeared to arouse an unprecedented national consensus, the paradox was that it generated — or, rather, brought to the surface — stresses and strains within the society that were soon to shatter the facade of national unity. The government, appearing at first as the nation's champion against an exploitive transnational corporation, was slowly but inexorably driven back into a defensive position internally as a result of domestic political pressures. This, in turn, was to weaken its ability to stand up to the subtle pressures Alcan was able to mobilize against it, on both the external and the internal fronts.

The first problem arose in connection with the passage of legislation to enable nationalization. In order to provide that payments for nationalized assets be made out of the future profits of the enterprise, the government proposed to amend the Guyana Constitution to specify that compensation should be "reasonable" rather than "prompt and adequate." Constitutional amendments require a two-thirds majority in the Parliament, and this meant that the support of the parliamentary Opposition — Dr. Jagan's PPP — was necessary. Although Dr. Jagan had previously been vociferous in his calls for the full nationalization of Demba, he now claimed to detect a Machiavellian conspiracy in which the nationalization was in reality part of a devious American plan to secure Guyana's bauxite. In Dr. Jagan's alleged scenario, the United States was no longer certain of being able to control Alcan because of rising economic nationalism in Canada, and the management of the nationalized Demba would be turned over to the smaller U.S.-owned Reynolds Guyana Mines, thereby placing it under direct American control.[46] Dr. Jagan therefore claimed to be reluctant to support the nationalization bill unless the takeover of both Demba and Reynolds Guyana Mines was specifically stipulated.

It soon became evident that Dr. Jagan's real intention was to wring certain domestic political concessions from the government. In the end, he did support the government's nationalization bill, in return for commitments from Prime Minister Burnham to terminate a variety of discriminatory and repressive practices directed against the PPP and its followers.[47] Greater involvement of the PPP in the decision-making process was also provided for. The agreement — the so-called Burnham-Jagan "Peace Plan" — was greeted in many quarters with even greater excitement than the nationalization decision itself. It raised hopes for the gradual dissolution of the distrust and antagonism between Guyana's two principal racial groups, represented in the two major political parties, and for a new era of national — that is, interracial — unity and peace. Unfortunately, events were rather to bear out those cynics, including the majority of the followers of both parties, who doubted the sincerity and good faith of one or the other side and who never believed that the peace would last for any significant period.[48] To all intents and purposes, the participation of the PPP ended with the passage of the nationalization bill by the National Assembly; to the large East Indian community that comprises at least one-half of the Guyana population, the nationalization never became more than a purely PNC-African affair, with little if any relevance to them. It is obvious that this would seriously limit the ability of the government to call on the nation as a whole to put up with whatever dislocations and hardships a continual confrontation with Alcan might entail, and its freedom to maneuver was to that extent limited from the outset.

The active pressures against the government, however, were to come from the bauxite workers themselves, overwhelmingly African and traditionally followers of the ruling party. In fact the decision to nationalize Demba brought to the surface very real and deep anxieties among the workers relating to their working terms and conditions under state ownership. It was feared that rates of remuneration would be cut to bring them into line with those in government departments and statutory corporations, which were considerably lower than the rates in Demba. The workers harbored deep doubts about the ability of the government to find the management and the marketing outlets necessary to keep the plant operating. They were worried about their job security. Allegations about financial corruption and malpractices in government departments and enterprises were rife. And there was the fear that employment in a government-owned plant would become a matter of political patronage.[49] The Demba management played skillfully on these anxieties; it encouraged and promoted them quietly through its daily contact with the workers in the plant, and especially it cast quiet doubts on the government's ability to keep the plant in operation independently of the Alcan connection.[50] The company knew that the government was relying heavily on the support of the bauxite workers; by the same token, if this support could be eroded, the government's bargaining power in the negotiations over compensation would be weakened. At the same time, Alcan maintained a public face of cordiality and graciousness toward the government: it announced its readiness to cooperate in effecting an "orderly handing over" to government ownership. In doing so the company dampened public hostility toward it and made it more difficult for the government to arouse support by portraying Alcan as the archenemy of Guyana.

The government attempted to allay the workers' anxieties in a number of ways: it incorporated into the nationalization law a clause stipulating that no employee would suffer an adverse change in his employment conditions as a result of nationalization; it advertised loudly its arrangements for management and marketing; and it gave repeated assurances that there would be no political interference in the operation of the company after the government takeover. The limited success of these attempts to reassure the workers became evident when two issues appeared to crystallize their anxieties. The first concerned a wage dispute with Demba that had been pending since the previous year (1970). The dispute was under arbitration at the time of the government's February 1971 decision to nationalize Demba; by April the workers had formulated a concrete demand that the arbitration be completed and whatever award made be paid out, before the government actually took over the company. Failing satisfactory assurances on this point, the workers went on strike in support of this demand.[51] There is little doubt that, in the eyes of the strikers, it was the government that had the power to meet their demands, and their strike was directed primarily against the government rather than the company. Their insistence on completion and payment of the award can only be explained in terms of doubts on their part as to the ability or the good faith of the government to ensure that payment be made after the government takeover. As it happened, the government elected to resist this demand, and even the lesser demand that the Prime Minister visit the mining town in person to reassure the workers. Instead, it decided to break the strike by a "well-known colonial method": riot police used teargas against the strikers and arrested twenty-one of them, including the leaders.[52] Subsequently, the strikers went back to work, but it is difficult to believe that the resumption was anything but a sullen one. The apparently formidable alliance between the government and the bauxite workers had been breached. This caused further stresses in the government's relationship with the working class movement as a whole, represented by the Trades Union Congress, and also with the radical wing of the ruling PNC, represented by ASCRIA, both of whom opposed the use of force against the strikers. Added to the existing breach in national unity represented by the African-Indian cleavage, these divisions, by the beginning of May 1971, put the government in a weak, virtually isolated position internally at the same time that major international pressures were being mobilized against it.

Alcan's main objective at this point was to secure a reasonably favorable settlement on the terms of the government's compensation for the nationalization of Demba. This was important not only for its direct financial significance but also because the settlement would serve as a precedent in any future nationalizations in the industry. Alcan could bring powerful leverage to bear on Guyana in a number of ways. There was always the threat — never openly stated — that the company could strangle the new enterprise at birth by cutting off its markets, either directly through litigation over the ownership of bauxite shipments, or indirectly by lining up support from other aluminum companies. But there were other sources of leverage that could be activated immediately. One of these concerned the accumulated pension funds of Demba's employees in the RILA (Retirement Income and Life Assurance) scheme, which were kept with the Royal Trust Company in Canada. The government wished these funds to be repatriated to the credit of the new state enterprise, since they would represent a useful source of financing. A large number of bauxite workers also wanted to withdraw their accumulated funds from the scheme when Demba ceased to exist juridically and was replaced by the new Guybau — yet another indication of lack of confidence in the ability or integrity of a government-appointed management. Alcan, however, maintained — dishonestly, as it turned out[53] — that it had no legal power to have the RILA funds transferred to Guyana, and this attitude caused considerable embarrassment to the government, since it appeared incapable of protecting the workers' interests. The RILA issue thus appeared as another, though perhaps subsidiary, issue in the bauxite workers' strike in April. It was soon to become evident that Alcan was using the RILA issue as a bargaining ploy in its negotiations with the government on the compensation issue.

Meanwhile, other pressures were subtly brought to bear on the government. These involved parties other than Alcan and were designed to threaten the government where it hurt most — in the financial area. One of the two foreign commercial banks in Guyana, when approached by the government for credit facilities for the new Guybau, replied that the government and the industry would be required to submit themselves to "objective" tests of economic viability. This response was interpreted as meaning that the bank concerned "would not take a decision before the government accounted for its political actions both with respect to nationalization and the miniaturising process."[54] Even more ominously, the United States government indicated clearly that it was greatly interested in seeing Guyana reach an amicable agreement with Alcan regarding compensation. The American interest arose partly out of the wish to protect the smaller U.S.-owned Reynolds Guyana Mines, but also out of the wider implications of the Guyana nationalization as a precedent, especially in the rest of the Caribbean. The U.S. attitude was made known through the medium of the World Bank: it abstained from voting on a Guyanese application for a sea defense loan of $5.4 million in June 1971. In explaining the U.S. decision, a U.S. Treasury Undersecretary made it plain that the decision was linked to the compensation issue:

The World Bank has a long-established policy of not lending to countries that have expropriated foreign private investments unless there is evidence that satisfactory progress is being made toward settlement of the expropriation dispute.... [In the Guyana-Alcan case] the United States did not believe that sufficient facts were at hand to permit the judgement as to the existence of reasonable efforts towards fair compensation.... In these circumstances, we felt obliged to register our position by abstaining on the loan....

The official ended in terms reminiscent of a slightly annoyed father scolding a wayward child:

> Developing countries must therefore tread very lightly in using expropriation of foreign investment as a means of responding to domestic political pressures. If they do so, and thereby discourage the flow of private investment, those who suffer in the end are the very ones they want to help.
>
> Such actions are not only harmful in development terms; they may also be self-defeating in terms of the long-run domestic impact in the country involved.[55]

As vesting day (the day fixed for the actual government takeover of Demba) approached on July 15, the government therefore found itself under pressure from Alcan, the foreign commercial banks, and the powerful U.S. government, while the bauxite workers were restless and uncertain over the issue of their RILA funds. To have assumed management of the operation against such a constellation of external pressures together with a hostile work force was inconceivable. The government therefore compromised on the principle of compensation on the basis of book value with payment out of the enterprises's future profits. It agreed to pay a total of G$107 million (US$53 million) in installments over twenty years with interest effectively at 4.5 percent.[56] This amount was higher than the book value of Demba's assets, the payments were not linked to the enterprise's future profits, and, as some critics pointed out, the annual interest payment alone would absorb approximately one-half of Guybau's normal profit flow. In return, Alcan agreed to repatriate the RILA funds, an amount estimated to be between G$9 million and G$12 million. Alcan was clearly satisfied with the settlement, describing its terms as "within the guidelines" the company had set and pointing out that the amount of G$107 million was "somewhat higher" than the book value of Demba's assets.[57] Other powerful interests joined in approving the settlement: the U.S. State Department, the World Bank, and the Canadian Ambassador in Washington all "expressed delight at the amicable resolution of the dispute."[58] The Guyana government had secured the nonhostility of the West — but it had had to pay a price for it.

Accordingly, the atmosphere in Guyana on vesting day was considerably less euphoric than on Republic Day, five months earlier, when the Prime Minister's nationalization speech had been delivered. Hardly any workers joined with government leaders as they began a march in the mining town to celebrate the takeover; the atmosphere in the bauxite area was described euphemistically as one of "solemnity and sobriety."[59] A newspaper columnist in a

generally sympathetic article nevertheless pointed out that the new
nationalized company was relying on a British firm as its marketing agent, an American firm as its purchasing agent, and an
American bank (Chase Manhattan) to provide G$8 million initial
working capital. The Guyana government, commented the columnist, could not be said to "be engaging in a confrontation with western imperialism by nationalizing Demba."[60] Others were more
blunt in their judgment: the radical monthly Ratoon newspaper
analyzed the compensation settlement under the banner headline:
"The Great Bauxite Robbery"; another article discussed Guybau's
links with British and American companies under the banner headline: "Bauxite Recolonized."[61] The contrasting attitudes of the U.S.
State Department and the Ratoon newspaper constituted a dramatic
turnabout from the picture of national unity and support for the government against the hostility of international capitalism that had
emerged only a few short months before.

* * *

The Guyanese bauxite nationalization, then, represented a disengagement from the international capitalist economic order that
was at best limited, and an internal economic decolonization that
was at best only partial. But the episode throws a number of factors into stark relief. First, it shows how the interest of a national
government in seeking to utilize natural resources for national development can conflict violently with the perspectives and strategies of a global company. Second, it shows how the exercise of
a nation's sovereign right to nationalize, in the absence of agreement with a foreign company, can be effectively limited by the
pressures the company can mobilize in its defense, irrespective
of the merits of the government's case. The company's ability to
mobilize such pressures arises out of the importance of the
general principle of "prompt and adequate compensation" to
the capital-exporting community, and the fact that the individual
episodes are never viewed exclusively in terms of their intrinsic
characteristics but also in terms of their wider implications as
precedent setters. Third, it demonstrates the vulnerability of a
government in the face of these pressures when the internal polity
is fragmented and critical sectors of the national population harbor
doubts about the competence or the integrity of the regime.

In spite of its limitations, the nationalization constituted an
important initial step in what is now a general movement for

a restructuring of the terms on which governments in the bauxite-producing countries participate in the international bauxite-aluminum industry. In the Commonwealth Caribbean, Guyana's action made a critical contribution to legitimizing the idea of state ownership in resource industries, a policy which has now been followed by Trinidad and Tobago in relation to its oil industry and which is proposed by the present Jamaican government for bauxite mining. In that sense the nationalization signaled the initiation of a new wave of economic nationalism that is now sweeping the region from one end to the other.

Notes

1. By a dramatic coincidence, the nationalization was effected on the same day (July 15, 1971) as the expropriation of the U.S. copper companies by the government of President Allende in Chile.

2. Demba generated about one-third of Guyana's commodity exports and about 10 percent of the government's total revenue.

3. Mr. Burnham had been considered to be more friendly to the West than his predecessor, Dr. Cheddi Jagan, now Opposition leader, who claims to be a communist.

4. The Daily Gleaner, the largest and probably the most influential daily newspaper in Jamaica and the Commonwealth Caribbean, editorialized that Guyana's action constituted "a big and dangerous step into the unknown" (December 3, 1970, p. 12).

5. In the words of an Alcan official. See Rosane (1969, p. 2).

6. Principally the Caribbean, West Africa, and Australia. The Caribbean alone supplies nearly 90 percent of the raw material for the U.S. aluminum industry.

7. See essay 3 in this volume.

8. Jamaica's action was followed in some measure by Surinam, Haiti, and Guyana itself with respect to the operations of Reynolds Guyana Mines (see essay 3).

9. A more detailed account of the company's early history in Guyana can be found in Girvan (1971a). An excellent account of Alcoa's early history as a monopoly is given in Muller (1968, chaps. II-IV).

10. The name was changed to Alcan Aluminium, Ltd., in the 1960s. The Aluminum Company of Canada is the principal operating subsidiary of Alcan Aluminium and was the parent company of Demba.

11. See Huggins (1965, p. 35).

12. Dr. Jagan's PPP was reelected to office in 1957 and again in 1961; but in the 1964 elections held under proportional representation, Mr. Burnham was brought to power.

13. In 1970 prices. Actually, over a great part of the period of Demba's operation its bauxite exports were valued at $4-$5 per ton. In the above values, G$1 = US$0.50.

14. On the plantation system, see Beckford (1972).

15. Singh (1969, p. 11). Demba's share in this total was G$905 million.

16. Ibid., p. 12.

17. See, for example, Rosane (1969, Appendix IV). For instance, out of a total sales value of G$86 million in 1968, the company returned only G$30 million to the Guyanese economy.

18. Girvan (1967, p. 8).

19. The concessions comprised mainly a five-year tax holiday followed by substantial investment allowances.

20. Kwayana (1972, p. iii).

21. Grant (1973, p. 258).

22. Until a few years ago, the mining town was not even linked properly to the rest of Guyana by road, and transport was mainly by company-owned launch up and down the Demerara River.

23. See Grant (1971).

24. Up until 1967, there was no formal local government apparatus and Demba quite literally ran the town; in that year local government was formed but it was widely known that the salaries of the officials were paid by Demba through the channel of subsidies to the town council.

25. For a vivid picture, see Grant (1971) and St. Pierre (1969, pp. 20-25).

26. African Society for Cultural Relations with Independent Africa, which has a strong following in the mining community.

27. Kwayana (1972, p. 3). Demba workers could also feel the exploitation in their lungs, since both at work and in their homes they were constantly subjected to bauxite dust emanating from the plant.

28. St. Pierre (1969).

29. A company official put it well when he wrote that "Demba wage levels may not seem munificent to the northern observer" but "must be viewed against Guyana's per capita national income" of US$215 in 1965 (Rosane [1969, p. 7]).

30. Ibid.

31. I.e., one year before independence, which was granted in 1966.

32. The omission of the sugar industry from this policy was notable. Sources close to the government explained that continued British ownership was a guarantee of accessibility to external markets and that the industry was a money-loser anyway, while independent political observers tended to advance the explanation that government involvement in the sugar industry would confer no political benefits on the regime since the sugar workers are primarily East Indian and supporters of the Opposition PPP. The sugar industry was finally nationalized in May 1976.

33. Of which the present writer was one, for the period May 1970 to February 1971. This implies a more than usual lack of detachment in the analysis of that period, which follows.

34. For an analysis of the Zambian case, see Semonin (1971); for the Chilean case, see Griffin (1969, chap. IV).

35. The nonnegotiables are listed below.

36. See Guyana (1971).

37. Press statement by Alcan, November 30, 1970.

38. Dr. Thomas is Professor of Economics at the University of Guyana. See Thomas (1970).

39. From the speech by Hon. Hubert Jack, Minister of Mines, at the opening session of the talks.

40. I.e., of the Aluminum Company of Canada, parent company of Demba and principal operating subsidiary of Alcan Aluminium, Ltd. The gentleman concerned was at the time an executive vice-president of Alcan Aluminium and has since become president and chief executive officer of that company.

41. See Burnham (1971). The 70-30 proposal was probably designed to bear a superficial resemblance to Guyana's starting negotiating position of taking a 70 percent share in Demba.

42. Guyana (1971).

43. Kwayana (1972, p. 36). ("Backra man" means "white man.")

44. Thomas (1971, p. 1).

45. Mr. Moses Bhagwan, a lawyer and former chairman of the PPP-linked Progressive Youth Organization, also sounded a note of skepticism in saying that the proposed nationalization "may become the revolutionary point of departure if the leadership of the PNC so wish it to be, and follow through with a series of political initiatives that reflect an appreciation that we are a poverty-stricken, crisis-ridden divided nation," but "a genuine socialist transformation of society is not generated out of isolated acts of radicalism, but through a profound programme aimed at national reconstruction.... There is no evidence to suggest that the decision to nationalise the bauxite company at Linden was conceived in the context of such a programme" (Guyana Graphic, February 28, 1971, p. 3).

46. See Dr. Jagan's speech in the National Assembly on the bauxite nationalisation bill, February 27, 1971; also "PPP: Nationalise Reynolds Too!" Guyana Graphic, February 26, 1971, p. 1.

47. "'Burnham and Jagan Agree on 'Peace Plan,'" Guyana Graphic, March 2, 1971, p. 1.

48. At the time, a PNC working-class activist was reported as saying, "Don't worry with all that r—— in the House [National Assembly] this evening. Them chaps not serious. The Kabaka [Prime Minister Burnham] is a smart man, you know"; while a PPP supporter asked, "Why has it taken so long for Dr. Jagan's points to be accepted?" (Ricky Singh, "The Burnham-Jagan Peace Plan," Sunday Graphic, March 7, 1971, p. 5.)

49. Kwayana (1972, pp. 11-12).

50. Ibid.

51. For a detailed account and analysis of the strike, see Kwayana (1972).

52. The most likely explanation of the government's attitude was that it did not wish to legitimize the leadership of the strike leaders, perceived as "militants," who were opposed to the existing leadership of the bauxite workers' union, which was in turn a close political ally of the governing party.

53. "Rila: Alcan Has Authority — Jack," Guyana Graphic, July 10, 1971, p. 1. See also Grant (1973, pp. 262-63).

54. Grant (1973, p. 264). "Miniaturising" refers to the government's policy to "miniaturise" the foreign-owned commercial banking sector by developing the Guyana National Cooperative Bank at the expense of the foreign-owned commercial banks.

55. "US Treasury Official Explains Abstention on Loan Proposal," Guyana Graphic, July 10, 1971, p. 5. The official concerned was Treasury Undersecretary Charles E. Walker, reported in testimony before the Subcommittee on International Finance of the House Banking and Currency Committee on July 6. For an analysis, see Grant (1973, pp. 265-68).

56. Interest was actually set at 6 percent, but the government's withholding

tax was estimated to take one-quarter of this. See Ricky Singh, "Take-Over at Linden Today," Guyana Graphic, July 15, 1971, p. 1.

57. "Settlement 'Within Our Guidelines,'" Guyana Graphic, July 15, 1971, p. 1. Alcan President Nathanael V. Davis was also quoted as saying that the insurance value of Demba's assets was G$85 million.

58. "Delight over Guyana Accord on Demba," Trinidad Express, July 19, 1971, back page. The newspaper was quoting from a Reuters report.

59. Ibid., quoting the Guyana Sunday Graphic writer Ulric Mentus.

60. Ricky Singh, "Foreign Aid and Guybau," Guyana Graphic, July 15, 1971, p. 11.

61. Ratoon, August 1971, No. 5, front page.

TOWARD A MINERALS POLICY FOR THE THIRD WORLD

5

I. THIRD WORLD MINERALS IN THE INTERNATIONAL POLITICAL ECONOMY

Perhaps more than any other area, the minerals sector[1] symbolizes the exploitative relationships that exist between the Third World and the developed capitalist (center) countries. The mineral resources of the Third World play an absolutely essential and strategic role in the economies of the center countries. In petroleum, gold, diamonds, and the ores of steel, aluminum, copper, antimony, chrome, cobalt, manganese, lead, zinc, tin, and natural phosphates, the Third World produces a significant share — sometimes the bulk — of total capitalist world production, the majority of which is consumed by the center countries. And in many instances, the Third World's share of production is growing as the dependence of the center countries on imported materials increases.[2] Within the broad category of primary products, the mineral commodities exported by the Third World are more strategic than their agricultural exports because (1) the center countries have achieved a high degree of self-sufficiency in food but have become progressively dependent on imported mineral materials; (2) mineral resources are nonrenewable; and (3) they provide essential inputs into manufacturing industry, which is the basis of the growth dynamic of the advanced countries. Thus, it is largely through their mineral exports that the Third World supports the high incomes and continuous growth of the advanced countries.

The instruments of integrating Third World mineral resources with manufacturing industry in the center have historically been the large, monopolistic transnational corporations, which have engaged in direct investment in the Third World for extraction of the required raw materials for export to processing facilities in the

188

center. At the same time, and as a result, this pattern of exploitation has given rise to deformed, dependent economic structures in the Third World, and the systematic divorce of resource use from the satisfaction of the basic material needs of the people in these countries.[3]

It was not always so. In the precapitalist period, the peoples of what is now the Third World used mineral commodities and substances for a wide variety of purposes. Copper and iron were used for agricultural implements and weaponry, gold and silver for currency and jewelry, crude petroleum as an inflammant. The level of material and technological development was low, but there was an organic equilibrium among needs, wants, productive activities, and the pattern of resource use.

That equilibrium was permanently smashed by the capitalist expansion of Western Europe, followed by that of the United States and Japan. The pattern was established by the Spanish plunder of the gold and silver of the Aztec and Inca empires in America in the sixteenth and seventeenth centuries. In the centuries that followed, Africa and then Asia were also to feel the merciless effects of the looting of human labor and natural resources in the interests of primitive capital accumulation in Western Europe. Such primitive capital accumulation, which took the form of money capital in the hands of a merchant class, played a critical role in catalyzing the transition from commercial capitalism to industrial capitalism in Europe.

It was in the age of industrial capitalism that a direct linkage was established between mineral production in the peripheral areas of the world and the industrial systems of the developed capitalist countries. In the middle and late nineteenth century, Western Europe's main interest in the peripheral areas was as a source of cheap agricultural raw materials which would keep down the cost of wage goods at home, thereby stabilizing labor costs. The energy and metallurgical industries — the two principal users of mineral products — were based on domestic resources, principally coal, iron ore, and other metalliferous ores, hydroelectric power, and petroleum. But by the end of the nineteenth century the situation was changing rapidly. Depletion of domestic nonrenewable resources, rapid growth of the energy and metallurgical industries, and the new technology of large-scale production all stimulated a quickly growing interest in overseas supplies of mineral materials. Another factor was the emergence of large, vertically integrated monopolistic corporations in the center countries, which came to engage in worldwide searches and struggles for raw materials in order to secure and bolster their monopoly position.

The petroleum industry itself was both the forerunner and the largest single manifestation of this development. The Royal Dutch-Shell Oil Company was formed in 1907 by a merger of Dutch and British interests exploiting the oil of the Far East. Britain organized the Anglo-Persian Oil Company in 1914 to exploit Persian oil, as the British navy decided to shift from coal to fuel oil. American oil monopolies moved aggressively into Latin America by the second decade of the twentieth century, and in the 1920s and 1930s the principal U.S. and European companies fought spirited and sometimes bitter battles for oil resources and concessions in Latin America and the Middle East.[4] The lead of the oil companies was followed by other companies engaged in the basic industries, such as copper, aluminum, and steel, all of which established overseas raw materials production in the period after the First World War. Moreover, in the 1930s Japan came on the scene as a major imperialistic competitor for the raw materials of the peripheral areas, beginning with Manchuria and other areas in the Pacific. It would be no exaggeration to say that the lust for mineral resources has been a major factor in interimperialist rivalries in the periphery, including those leading to the two world wars in the present century.

Since the Second World War, there has been a rapid intensification of the dependence of the advanced capitalist countries on the mineral resources of the Third World. Apart from the high and virtually unprecedented economic expansion of the capitalist bloc in this period, two specific factors have contributed to this development. The United States emerged out of the ashes of the war in 1945 as the dominant economic power, and the United States is relatively much more self-sufficient in mineral raw materials than the other advanced capitalist countries. However, during the 1950s and 1960s, Western Europe and Japan grew rapidly relative to the United States, and these latter two are highly dependent on imported raw materials. At the same time, the United States has itself become progressively transformed into a country whose economy depends largely on imports for supplies of a number of its critical industrial inputs. Already, imports provide a major part of U.S. supplies of petroleum and the ores of aluminum, lead, mercury, platinum, tin, titanium, zinc, chromium, cobalt, columbium, manganese, nickel, and tungsten. Estimates based on present trends indicate that this dependence is likely to become much more pronounced over the remainder of this century.[5]

These developments pose two contradictory implications for the countries of the Third World. On the one hand, the situation is pregnant with possibilities for intensified interimperialist rivalries for the resources of the periphery, as the increasingly mineral-short center countries strive to secure reliable access to the critical materials they need. At the same time, we can also expect intensified efforts to bypass the periphery entirely by the use of two strategies. First, the application of technology for the development of substitutes, such as nuclear power to substitute for oil and aluminous clay to substitute for bauxite. The second strategy is the mining of the seabed; it was recently estimated, for example, that the proportion of world demand in 1980 that could be supplied by fifty seabed mining operations amounts to 10 percent in the case of manganese, 66 percent for nickel, and 39 percent for cobalt.[6] On the other hand, to the extent that the share of the Third World in mineral production continues to grow, it will be able to exert a growing leverage over the center countries as regards the terms on which these commodities are supplied. Increased conflict, therefore, both among the center countries and between the center and the periphery, is one broad possible alternative for the international political economy of minerals over the next twenty-five years or so. The other broad alternative is that the center countries will be able to dilute their rivalries and secure sufficient cooperation to present a united front to the periphery and ultimately will be able to cement a new set of alliances with the ruling groups in the periphery which will secure an adequate and reliable flow of raw materials in return for a greater share of mineral-industry surpluses conceded to these ruling groups.[7] Again, the petroleum industry represents both the forerunner of these developments and the symbol of the two broad alternatives. And what happens in the case of oil will probably establish the pattern for all mineral commodities for some time to come.

II. MINERALS IN THE THIRD WORLD: THE PROBLEMS DEFINED

From the point of view of the Third World, we can identify at least eight outstanding problems relating to the political economy of minerals which result from the legacy of imperialistic exploi-

191

tation and for which a coherent policy needs to be devised.

1. The first problem is that our knowledge of the actual and potentially productive resources in the underdeveloped countries is itself underdeveloped. Our present knowledge of resource availabilities is the product of the uneven, haphazard, and socially irrational pattern of imperialist interest and exploitation in the periphery. Historically, central capitalism has shown a marked and understandable preference for (a) countries whose resources are nearest and most accessible to the markets of the center, such as the Caribbean, the Middle East, and the coastal regions of Africa and Latin America; and (b) countries that have virtually opened themselves up to the rape of international capital, such as Canada and Australia, and more recently Brazil and Indonesia. Thus, large areas of Africa, Latin America, and Asia have not yet been subjected to systematic and comprehensive geological exploration, and we lack anything approaching a complete inventory of the mineral resources of the Third World.

2. A second and closely related problem is the completely irrational and uneven development of mineral production among countries of the periphery. It is often observed that some of the richest oil-exporting states are those with the smallest populations: the United Arab Emirates, Abu Dhabi, Kuwait, Saudi Arabia, and Libya. It is usually forgotten that this pattern is to a large extent the result of deliberate political decisions by imperialism, both to "balkanize" the Arab world and to allocate oil production to states without the potential strength and ambitiousness represented by large populations. Thus Amin has made the point that if Arab oil income were divided by the total Arab population, the average per capita level would be far more modest.[8] The oil pattern has its equivalents in other minerals. Thus in the 1950s Jamaica was chosen for large-scale bauxite production in preference to Guyana, the Dominican Republic, and Haiti at least partly because of political considerations; and it is obvious that the large proportion of mineral production supplied by Canada, Australia, and South Africa is to a large extent the result of political decisions by imperialism. A more rational pattern would be based on greater balance in mineral production spatially, geographically, and demographically.

3. The third problem is that mineral production has been one of the principal means by which the center countries have drained off surplus from the economies of the periphery. Surplus drainage is far more visible in this sector than in agricultural production

because mineral production is usually capital intensive and therefore gives rise to large profits as a share of total sales. Thus the
gross outflow of investment income from the periphery to the center
now runs at some $7 billion a year, to which should be added royal-
ties and fees amounting to perhaps as much as another $1 billion; and
the majority of this is related to investment in minerals (including
oil).[9] Surplus drainage is also intensified by transnational firms
through such methods as biased transfer pricing (overvaluing imports and undervaluing exports), charging subsidiaries extortionate
fees for technology and management, and pressuring governments
to finance infrastructural works and to give generous tax concessions.

4. Closely related to surplus drainage is the low returned value
(actual monetary payments to the local economy) from mineral exports by the periphery to the center. Returned value from the
bauxite industries to the Caribbean and West Africa, for example,
has until recently amounted to only between one-third and one-half
of the value of exports. This is typical of the situation in other
mineral industries,[10] such as iron ore and copper (only in recent
years have the oil-exporting countries increased their share in
total export value to well over 50 percent). Returned value is low
because the surplus, which forms a large part of total export sales,
accrues to the foreign companies, and most of the inputs are imported. Returned value comprises mainly wages, which represent
a small proportion of total costs, and taxes, which are often low
because of the weak bargaining position of the governments and the
transfer-price manipulations of the transnational companies.

5. In addition to surplus drainage and low returned value, there
are other, less obvious diseconomies in the present pattern. One
of these is the extremely low national value added based on mineral
production in Third World countries, which results from the fact
that the bulk of the processing, refining, and manufacturing based
on the mineral commodities is carried out in the industrial center
countries. A classic example is provided by the bauxite-aluminum
industry, where the bulk of the value added is generated in aluminum smelting and fabrication. Since these processes are located
almost entirely in the industrial center countries, the bauxite-
producing countries, which are relegated to bauxite mining and the
production of alumina (the intermediate product), receive something like only 6 percent of the value of fabricated aluminum products derived from their raw material. This general pattern also
applies to petroleum, iron ore, and other mineral commodities.

193

6. A similar though not identical diseconomy is the almost complete lack of backward and forward linkages based on mineral production in the periphery. Industries producing inputs for mining and mineral processing, and utilizing mineral commodities as inputs, are conspicuous by their absence. It is astonishing, for example, that after fifty years of large-scale mining activity in the periphery, not a single Third World country can point to a major industry manufacturing mining equipment and machinery, which could have formed the basis of indigenous capital-goods industries. We have already pointed out that mineral commodities are strategic inputs into the energy and metallurgical industries, which form the basis of mature industrial systems. Yet these industries have failed to emerge in the periphery in spite of the existence of considerable resource potential there.

Lack of backward and forward linkages, and low national value added, are merely the reflections of the fact that mineral production in the periphery is structurally integrated with industrial production in the center. Hence, the linkages and value added take place in the center: that, indeed, is the very reason for mineral production in the Third World. It is even possible to see this clearly within the structure of the large, vertically integrated corporations based in the center countries, which extract raw materials from the periphery and themselves transform these materials into finished products in the center, thus to a large extent internalizing the value added and the linkages within the firm itself.

7. An important problem in many Third World countries is the high degree of expatriate staffing in the mineral industries, especially in technical and managerial posts. This is especially marked in many oil-producing countries and in mining operations in Africa and the Caribbean. Basically, this situation reflects deliberate policy by the transnational firms engaged in the industries, since local labor could be trained to perform these tasks without any great difficulty.[11] A policy of expatriate staffing is one strategy used by the firms to blunt demands for greater national control over decision making and for nationalization, since it enables the firms to point to the alleged incapacity of the host country to operate the industry on its own. Obviously, expatriate staffing implies a large leakage out of the local income stream created by the mineral industry; more importantly, it underdevelops the national capability to operate and develop the mineral industry in the national interest.

8. Finally, and as a general point, the Third World countries

lack control over decision making and development strategy with
regard to their mineral industries and mineral resources. Lack
of control flows from a number of factors, and it is important to
be aware of all of them, since attacking the most obvious while
leaving the more subtle ones untouched will not solve the problem.
The more obvious factors are (a) expatriate staffing; (b) foreign
ownership; and (c) foreign management (since ownership can be
nationalized but management left in foreign hands). But lack of
control is also due to (d) technological dependence, which implies
that production possibilities are defined in terms of the technology
in use by the international capitalist system and especially in the
center countries; (e) market dependence and unequal market power
in the international trading system, which imply unfavorable terms
of trade for mineral exports; and finally (f) participation in the
international capitalist system, which implies that the Third World
countries are submitted to an international division of labor imposed upon the world by that system and by the structure of relative
prices which it uses. All of these factors have to be dealt with
comprehensively by any policy for minerals in the Third World.

III. ELEMENTS OF A MINERALS POLICY
FOR THE THIRD WORLD

A minerals policy can only be properly developed in the context
of a general strategy in Third World countries for economic liber-
ation, self-reliance, and satisfaction of the basic material needs
of the population, especially rural and urban workers, underem-
ployed, and unemployed. Such a strategy must of necessity be based
on a correct diagnosis of the basic physiognomy of dependent underdevelopment. One way to characterize the problem is to picture
the peripheral economy as a system distinguished by the absence
of a capital-goods sector linked organically to the production of
mass consumer goods for the masses of the population, as is the
case in the economic system typical of the center countries.[12] Instead, the peripheral economy is dominated by an export sector
oriented toward the center, and it imports mainly luxury consumer
goods for the local elite. Hence, even when local manufacturing
production of consumer goods is initiated, it is geared to elite consumption, and even when capital-goods manufacturing is developed,
it is geared to a consumer-goods industry which is itself oriented
to elite consumption.

195

An alternative way of viewing essentially the same phenomenon is to characterize underdevelopment as consisting essentially of two disparities in the economic system: (1) the disparity between the structure of resource use (production) and the structure of demand; and (2) the disparity between the structure of demand and the structure of the real material needs of the mass of the population.[13] Whichever approach is adopted, it is evident that an economic strategy for the simultaneous resolution of the problems of material poverty and dependent underdevelopment should have as its central characteristic the utilization of indigenous materials as the basic inputs into a producer goods sector that supplies the inputs for a consumer goods sector which, in turn, produces commodities for the satisfaction of the basic material necessities of the mass of the population.

It will readily be seen that mineral resources (together with agricultural resources, of course) have an absolutely strategic role to play in such a strategy. Thomas has identified a relatively small number of basic materials that are the main inputs into any mature industrial system — be it of the capitalist centers or of the Soviet Union or China. These materials are iron and steel, aluminum, textiles (natural and synthetic), paper, plastics, rubber, glass, leather, cement, and industrial chemicals.[14] We are immediately struck by the fact that the raw substances for these basic materials are found in great abundance in the Third World as a whole (though with our present underdeveloped geological knowledge the distribution of specific minerals is of course geographically uneven). Indeed, this is perfectly consistent with the previous analysis, since it is precisely the access to Third World resources which has facilitated the consolidation of mature industrial systems in the central capitalist countries. What policy instruments should therefore be deployed by the Third World to ensure that its resources are adapted to a strategy of self-reliance and need alleviation? We would suggest the following short list, without pretending that it is in any way exhaustive.

1. Mineral-resource strategies must take their orientation and meaning in the context of a general disengagement from the international capitalist system, a rejection of the international division of labor imposed by the system and the structure of relative prices which goes with it, and a development strategy that takes the needs of the mass of the population as the objective of economic growth rather than its derivative.

2. Localization of staff and the full and integral nationalization

of ownership and management is an absolutely necessary condition — though not a sufficient one — for halting surplus drainage and for reorienting mineral resource use in the service of the general economic strategy.

3. Mineral exports to the center will have to be gradually and progressively phased out. Minerals are nonrenewable resources, and every ton of petroleum and mineral ore exported to the center represents that much less indigenous resources available for present or future use as an input into the local productive system for the satisfaction of the people's needs. The center countries will have to learn to eliminate wasteful consumption and adapt their economies and their consumption patterns to locally available resources.

4. Organizations of producer countries are an important means of increasing market power in the international system and improving the terms of trade and the returns to mineral exports to the center, and they should be used wherever possible. But they should be regarded as a transitional strategy rather than as a permanent one, to be employed in the interim period while exports to the center are being phased out and mineral production is being oriented toward domestic use. For it should be pointed out that there is a sense in which the very success of producer organizations presumes greater integration with the center; in addition, the effect of producer organizations is ultimately limited by (1) the development of substitutes in the center countries; (2) the mining of the seabed by the center countries; and (3) the use of the resources of countries such as Australia and Canada which have powerful cultural and ethnic links with the center countries.

5. Policies for local geological exploration must be pushed vigorously, so that the countries of the Third World can begin to develop a fuller and more balanced inventory of their available mineral resources.

6. A serious and concentrated effort for indigenous technological research and development must be made, with the objective of finding new and improved ways and means of utilizing local mineral resources in each country in the local productive system for the satisfaction of mass needs. This also implies that consumption patterns should be adapted to locally available resources and technology, instead of being standardized and homogenized across the entire world economy by the transnational corporations as instruments of the international capitalist system.

7. A more rational balance will have to be found between, on the

one hand, specialization of particular national spaces in the large-scale production of particular mineral commodities and, on the other, the proportional development of all branches of the economy, including mineral production, both within countries and among them in the Third World.

8. Structural integration of the economies of different national spaces should be pursued in the context of the general strategy. This should not be confused with current "regional integration" schemes, which consist largely of integrating the elite markets of different Third World countries so that they can be better exploited by the transnational corporations. The kind of integration required has as its objective the broadening of the resource base and the market to make more feasible the initiation of basic producer goods activities oriented toward local demand, and to facilitate the overall disengagement from the international capitalist order.

9. Direct state-to-state transactions among Third World states have the potential of bypassing the transnational corporations and facilitating structural integration among Third World countries at the expense of integration with the center. This also depends, however, on the way in which these transactions are used and the overall context within which they are developed.

Notes

1. Petroleum is included as part of the minerals sector here.

2. See, for example, Pierre Jalee, The Pillage of the Third World (New York, 1968), and The Third World in the World Economy (New York, 1969).

3. See, for example, essay 1 in the present volume.

4. H. O'Connor, The Empire of Oil (New York, 1955); E. Penrose, The Large International Firm and Developing Countries: The Case of the International Petroleum Industry (London, 1968).

5. L. Gordon, Environment, Resources and Development in a Resource-Rich Industrialized Nation, paper prepared for UNCTAD Expert Group Meeting on Alternative Patterns Development, Geneva, May 1974, TAD/RD/ENV/R.11.

6. The Problem of Seabed Resources and the International Commons: A Note by the UNCTAD Secretariat, TAD/RD/ENV/R.4 (Geneva: UNCTAD).

7. N. Girvan, "Economic Nationalists vs. Multinational Corporations: Revolutionary or Evolutionary Change?" in Multinational Firms in Africa, ed. by S. Amin and C. Widstrand (Uppsala: Scandinavian Institute for African Studies, 1975).

8. Samir Amin, "Some Preliminary Notes on Oil and Afro-Arab Relations," IDEP, DIR/2654-rev. (mimeo).

9. United Nations, Multinational Corporations in World Development, ST/ECA/190 (New York, 1973), Tables 40, 42.

10. See, for example, R. Mikesell et al., Foreign Investment in the Petroleum

and Mineral Industries (Baltimore, 1971).

11. See, for example, Robert S. Browne and Norman Girvan, Africanization of Personnel in the Mining Industry of Selected African Nations (New York: The Black Economic Research Center, 1974).

12. Samir Amin, "The Theoretical Model of Capital Accumulation and of the Economic and Social Development of the World of Today," IDEP Series in Economic and Social Development, No. 1.

13. Clive Y. Thomas, "Industrialization and Transformation for Africa," in Amin and Widstrand, Multinational Firms in Africa; and Dependency and Transformation (New York, 1974).

14. Thomas, "Industrialization and Transformation."

EXPROPRIATION AND COMPENSATION FROM A THIRD WORLD PERSPECTIVE

6

I. SIGNIFICANCE OF THE COMPENSATION QUESTION

The question of compensation for expropriated[1] property takes us, in many respects, to the heart of the relationship between the developed capitalist countries and the Third World. On no other subject is the gulf between the two — in interests, perspectives, and position — potentially so great, nor so pregnant with passionate and violent conflict. The rules of international law, the principles of international economics, and the science of international politics can help clarify the issues involved and provide arguments for the claims of contending parties. But they cannot yield solutions that are "neutral" or free of value judgments and philosophical assumptions which reflect and affect the interests of contending parties in different degrees.

The question is one in which realpolitik has always been a dominant, if not decisive, factor. Current standards of compensation that are "internationally accepted" derive from concepts of private property peculiar to the capitalist countries of the North Atlantic. In the light of notions of property characteristic of the precolonial cultures of Asia, Africa, and Indo-America, the philosophical tenets of capitalist attitudes toward private property appear to be a special case in human society and a relatively recent phenomenon in human history. That these standards should have "internationally accepted" status only attests to Euro-American hegemony in the capitalist world. A unilateral expropriation, compensation for which is determined according to the Third World country's own internal standards rather than those made internationally, runs a high risk of being termed "theft," and how far it can be successfully accomplished depends on the balance of economic, political, and military forces in the given situation.

200

II. THINKING THE UNTHINKABLE: THE THIRD WORLD'S CASE FOR COMPENSATION

The question of compensation in international economic relations usually contemplates the case of the expropriation of a foreign company's (or individual's) assets in a Third World country. By contrast, the case for compensation of the peoples of the Third World for centuries of abuse by Euro-America is rarely argued. This is another illustration of the way in which current attitudes reflect the interests of the nations of the North Atlantic. A cursory examination of the evidence illustrates the point more lucidly. After World War I, Germany made reparations to the victorious Allies for the destruction of life and property, for which it was held responsible; after World War II, it paid the state of Israel in recognition of its responsibilities for the crimes visited upon the Jewish race. Yet who has compensated the African peoples for the millions seized and killed in the service of the European slave trade, or for the land, cattle, and minerals expropriated during European colonization and the millions who died in the process? What restitution have the aboriginal peoples of the Americas and Australasia received for the expropriation of their countries by the white settlers? And what recompense do the descendants of the Incas, the Aztecs, and the peoples of India now enjoy for the treasures looted from them by the European nations?

The point is of more than historical or psychological interest. It is not just that many of these acts of genocide and property deprivation are within living memory. It is rather that the immiserizing poverty and demoralizing economic impotence of Third World peoples today can in most cases be traced back to the destructive effects of the European impact and to the characteristics of the systems erected to service the European interest. It is true that by today's standards the level of material and technological development of Third World peoples were low at the time of the European impact. But the poverty of the ghetto, the slum, the Indian reservation, and the "native" reserve is immeasurably worse — qualitatively and probably quantitatively — than the poverty of the self-sufficient, self-regulating communities of the past.

Of the European slave trade in Africa, Rodney has said: "When one tries to measure the effect of European slave trading on the African continent, it is very essential to realise that one is measuring the effect of <u>social violence</u> rather than <u>trade</u> in any normal sense of the word."[2]

Some of the destructive effects identified are: (1) depopulation, concentrated in the most able-bodied and productive sections of the population, and at a time when population was a critical factor in the promotion of economic development; (2) the decline of agriculture and manufacturing industry; and (3) a general shift in social and state activity to slave raiding, kidnapping, and fratricidal wars. This infamous trade went on for over three hundred years and laid the basis for the underdevelopment of the bulk of black Africa. It was followed in the late nineteenth century by European colonization and settlement, the effects of which were particularly severe in East, Central, and Southern Africa. The traditional communal land rights of the African peoples, in existence for countless generations and sanctified by indigenous law, religion, and political and social organization, were ruthlessly expropriated by edict of the colonizing powers and their chartered companies.[3] On the rare occasions when such companies were required to yield their rights, they received generous compensation.[4] Large numbers of people were deliberately massacred in order to terrorize them into submission to the European conquest; cattle were stolen and slaughtered to make the indigenous people dependent on European employment. In the Congo, a thriving agricultural and industrial riverine culture supporting at least 20 million people was physically, economically, and culturally decimated by the primitive exploitation of the Leopoldian "system." It is estimated that at least 10 million died as a result of this system in the twenty-year period between 1891 and 1911,[5] more than the number of Jews killed in Hitler's concentration camps. Yet no compensation has even been considered, much less paid. Today, the Congolese state (Zaire) is paying the former Union Minière du Haut Katanga for "participation" in the copper mines.

The European impact on Indo-America was no less severe. The bustling and creative civilizations of the Incas and the Aztecs were smashed. Between 1503 and 1660 the Spanish shipped some 16.8 million kilos of silver and 181,000 kilos of gold from the area[6]; during the same period, the population of Latin America was reduced from 40 million to 12 million by the combination of slaughter, enslavement, disease, and malnutrition resulting from Spanish colonization.[7] As in Africa, indigenous communal lands were forcibly expropriated and parceled out to settlers. Indeed, this process of colonization by expropriation continues to this very day in the area, especially in the vast region of the Amazon jungle.

India, Indonesia, and China had more advanced material cultures

202

than Europe in the seventeenth century.[8] Conquest, plunder, forced labor, taxation, and enforced specialization in an export monoculture reversed the relative positions, and Asia was progressively reduced to underdevelopment. From India alone, the value of the wealth transferred by Britain has been variously estimated at between £ 500 million and £ 1,000 million.[9]

What bolsters the Third World's case for compensation is the consideration that this destruction of life, expropriation of resources, and the returns on investments in production and trade guaranteed by military force can also in large measure be held responsible for the present affluence of the developed world. For Adam Smith, the discovery of America and of the sea route to the East were "the two most important events in the history of mankind," to which Europe owed much of its prosperity.[10] The huge increase in the supply of specie resulting from the Iberian plunder of the New World benefited the other Western European nations, who developed their trade with Spain and Portugal in order to secure their share of the loot.[11] The profits and stimulus to production derived from the slave trade and slave-based tropical production in the Americas provided the basis for the industrial revolution in Britain and France,[12] and also in the United States.[13] Tribute exacted from India also made a significant contribution in the case of Britain. And once established, the consolidation and spread of the industrial revolution was enormously facilitated by the cheap food and raw materials secured from the colonies and quasicolonies. The current energy crisis is only the most dramatic recent manifestation of the extent to which the material welfare of the developed world is based upon the resources of the Third World. The effects of the process of underdevelopment, on the one hand, and development, on the other hand, have been reproduced and intensified over centuries by the implacability of what has been called "the march of compound interest."[14] Another celebrated economist, John Maynard Keynes, pointed out that:

Indeed, the booty brought back by Drake in the Golden Hind may fairly be considered the fountain and origin of British Foreign Investment. Elizabeth paid off out of her proceeds the whole of her foreign debt and invested a large part of the balance (about £42,000) in the Levant Company; largely out of the profits of the Levant Company there was formed the East India Company, the profits of which during the seventeenth and eighteenth centuries were the main foundation of England's foreign connections; and so on. In view of this, the following calculation may amuse the curious. At the present time (in round figures) our foreign investments probably yield us about 6-1/2 percent net after allowing for losses, of which we reinvest abroad about a half — say 3-1/4 percent. If this is, on average, a fair sample of what has been going on since 1580, the £42,000 invested by Elizabeth out of Drake's booty in 1580 would have accumulated by 1930 to approximately the actual aggregate of our present foreign investments, namely £4,200,000,000 — or, say, 100,000 times greater than the original investment.[15]

The clear significance of Keynes's observation is that the historical contribution of Third World peoples to the economic development of the North Atlantic countries has to be compounded over time to be calculated fully. Correspondingly, any compensation due the Third World peoples for past deprivations must be compounded at an appropriate interest rate, if it is to yield a value which is "fair" in present-day terms.

III. COMPENSATION FOR THE THIRD WORLD: A PRACTICAL ILLUSTRATION

To be sure, the actual derivation of a compensation formula for Third World peoples is fraught with challenging intellectual difficulties. Still more so would be the question of the actual implementation of such a formula. Nonetheless, the basic intellectual problems are no more intractable than those associated with the "normal" case of compensation for nationalized property. One might hazard a guess that if half the effort put into litigation and associated academic research on the latter subject were to be devoted to the former, a reasonably coherent and implementable set of principles could indeed be worked out. Our purpose here is not with such an exercise. But a practical illustration of an attempt to develop a compensation formula to meet a claim of this kind might be of some help to the "Western" reader, who may be somewhat taken aback at the abrupt inversion of the terms in which the compensation question is normally discussed.

Dealing with the case of Afro-Americans in the United States, Robert Browne concludes that a minimal reparational formula should include at least three elements:

1) a payment for unpaid slave labor prior to 1863;

2) a payment for the underpayment of blacks since 1863;

3) a payment to compensate the black man's being denied the opportunity to acquire a share of America's land and natural resources when they were widely available to white settlers.[16]

The first and second elements (including compound interest)

are designed to compensate the black community for the chronic nonpayment and underpayment for its labor and for the stock of income-earning capital which it would have accumulated over the years had its labor been compensated at market prices and had opportunites been provided for investment in the human resources of the black community comparable to the opportunities available for whites. The third element is for the compensation for one specific advantage which was available to the earliest immigrants to America (and blacks were among the earliest) but from which they were deliberately excluded.[17]

Indeed, one economist carried out an exercise to estimate what a payment under (1) above might be. Marketti set out to compute the value of "unpaid black equity" in the slave industry, estimating the income stream produced by the slaves for their owners and compound interest on this income up to the present at various alternative rates of interest. Slave prices were used as proxies for "the present value of the exploited net income stream" returned on slave capital at several points in time during the 1790-1860 period. From this data he derived an implicit net income flow, upon which interest is compounded. The crude decennial census figures were refined to allow for variable income-generating capacities within the slave population. The estimate of the current, compounded value of the labor exploited from black slaves during the 1790-1860 period falls within the range of $448 billion to $995 billion.[18]

Such exercises suggest that the actual computation of "historic debts" may not be as far-fetched an idea as it at first appears. To be sure, the application of the method to the case of nation-states would involve substantial elaboration and modification. One basic difficulty which will probably arise is that many of the claims for compensation will not be international but internal: for example, the case of Latin American peons against large landowners, or of South African blacks against the white settlers. In such cases, "compensation" means not only or even primarily cash payments, but also direct retransfers of the resources that were forcibly expropriated in the first place. Even in such cases, however, the former colonial power can be held ultimately responsible for the initial expropriation, so that there is still a case for international compensation as well.

This brings us to a second difficulty: that of laying claims against individual nation-states. Spain and Portugal are today puny, underdeveloped economies that are in no position to compensate their former colonies. Indeed, the classic colonial powers (Britain, France, Holland), although well developed, nonetheless have a smaller capability of carrying out any substantial compensation than the United States, which is itself not a classic colonial power. This illustrates the limitations of considering the question on the level of individual nation-states. As we pointed out earlier, citing Adam Smith, the whole of Western Europe profited from Iberian conquest of the New World. And the United States did benefit from European colonialism and imperialism; the bulk of the population, the funds, and the capital equipment for that country's early growth came from Europe at the height of imperialism, and the slaves came from Europe's quasicolonies. Hence, the claims should be regarded as claims by the underdeveloped peoples of today on the entire North Atlantic community — that is, Western Europe and the United States.

Indeed, the real difficulties in computing and implementing compensation for Third World peoples are not methodological at all. They are political. The international balance of power simply does not permit such claims to be even considered seriously, much less computed or implemented. Here, indeed, lies the real lesson of Germany's reparation payments to other Europeans and to the Jews after the two world wars, compared with the absence of reparations to Third World peoples. Part of the reason for this monumental inconsistency lies, of course, in simple racism: what is unacceptable when visited upon European peoples may be considered merely "unfortunate" — at times necessary — when the victims are the nonwhite races. But the real lesson in this for Third World peoples is that those who wished Germany to pay were in a position to force it to do so.

It is not the morality of the claim which resolves the compensation question, therefore, and still less the "legality" — whatever that means. Both the legality and the perceived morality have a curious habit of adapting themselves to what is politically necessary or expedient. It is, rather, the balance of international and internal power relations that underlines the resolution of the question, with the lawyers merely serving as the instruments of the interests involved. For this reason, it is unlikely that the Third World peoples will be in a position to place a bill of reparations before the North Atlantic countries in the immediate future. What it does mean, however, is that Third World peoples and their governments will tend to approach the question of compensation for the expropriated property of the capital-exporting countries —

which are mainly the North Atlantic countries — with a mixture of cynicism and pragmatism. When the Zambian government, at independence, decided to compensate the British South Africa Company for the revocation of the latter's charter over all the minerals in the country, it did so in the knowledge that the charter had originally been acquired through a combination of military conquest, trickery, and theft. But it also was aware that some compensation had to be paid if Zambia were to establish a "good name" for itself in the eyes of the powerful financial community in the City of London.[19] As long as Third World countries continue to be dependent on the capital and the markets of the developed world, the question of compensation will continue to be considered in the narrower context associated with the expropriation of foreign property by a Third World state. But the day might come when such compensation is merely entered as a credit against the historic debts owed to the peoples of the Third World.[20]

IV. THE EXPROPRIATION MOTIVE IN THE THIRD WORLD

Within the narrower context, let us now turn to consider standards of compensation that are fair and reasonable from the point of view of the expropriating country. If our consideration is not to be arbitrary, we need to formulate a set of criteria that will maintain equitable principles of compensation when applied to particular cases. A criterion which says, for instance, that the payment terms should not constitute a net burden on the foreign exchange position of the country will yield one result when applied to an export industry and a different result when applied to an industry catering to the domestic market. Therefore, we need to consider a typology of cases in which the expropriating situation may arise and to which the criteria of "fairness" should be applied. To facilitate the development of such a typology, we need to have as a background paradigmatic abstractions representing the two parties in the dispute — the transnational corporation and the Third World country. For a model picture of the transnational, multidivisional corporation which is integrated both vertically and horizontally across national frontiers, and which is governed by a centralized decision-making and planning apparatus, the reader is referred to essay 1 in this volume.

The basis of the abstraction of the Third World country is the isolation of a number of sectors of economic activity in which subsidiaries of transnational corporations are likely to be operating. These sectors may be categorized as (1) a plantation-agriculture sector; (2) a mineral-export sector; (3) a public utilities sector; and (4) a domestic manufacturing sector. There is also, of course, a government sector responsible for sustaining the level of national income and generating economic development, full employment, and equitable income distribution, as the national interest demands.

Each sector has certain typical technical characteristics of production and occupies a particular place in relation to the national economy. This relationship conditions the way in which the Third World government perceives the need to adapt the sector to the needs of national economic development, that is, the expropriation motive. At the same time, however, the subsidiaries in each sector will also exhibit certain characteristic forms of integration with their parent corporations. And this relationship, in turn, conditions the perception by the transnational corporation of its interests in the conflict with the Third World government.

1. The plantation-agriculture sector. In this sector, large areas of land are controlled by plantation enterprises, which employ large masses of relatively unskilled, low-paid labor in the production of a single crop, such as sugar or coffee, for export to metropolitan markets. Under these conditions, the agricultural sector tends to exhibit a rigid "export bias." Adjustments to changes in external marketing conditions take the form of changes in production levels rather than changes in the allocation of land and labor to different export crops or to domestic foodstuffs. The growth of domestic nonagricultural incomes and the induced growth of domestic food demand result in rising imports of food rather than growing domestic production. At the same time, the terms of trade for the plantation export tend to decline over time, eroding its purchasing power with respect to imports, including imported food. Some of the export revenue from the crop also leaks abroad both to pay foreign shareholders dividends and to pay for imported capital goods and materials. Because of their desire to be in a position to adjust production levels at will, the plantations keep substantial excess supplies of land in reserve; through their monopoly control over land, they also control labor supplies and arrange to keep reserve supplies of labor as well. Hence, underutilization of land and labor is endemic to the system. As monopsonistic buyers of labor, the plantations are in a position to keep wages low. Consequently, for the mass of the rural population, incomes are maintained at a subsistence level, choking the growth of the domestic

market for the products of manufacturing industry.[21]

The objective of the Third World government in this case is likely to be one, or both, of the following two broad alternatives. The first is to increase production of the plantation crop to secure the additional foreign exchange required for the development effort; the second is to adopt a more flexible system of resource use to service domestic demands for food and agricultural materials for industrial processing, thereby cutting back production of the plantation crop and perhaps initiating the production of new exports. In both cases, there will be a desire to increase employment and incomes, especially in the rural areas, by bringing idle land and labor into production and to nationalize the profits from agricultural production to secure them for use by the national economy in general and the government in particular. Cuban policy after the Revolution exhibited both objectives at different times: the first in 1959 and after 1963; the second from 1960 to 1963.

For the transnational corporation, the plantation represents a part of its raw materials base for a worldwide system which includes transport and facilities ancillary to transport (such as storage), refining, manufacturing of the end product, manufacturing of inputs (such as machinery and transport equipment), and marketing. An expropriation that seeks to maintain or increase the level of plantation production and to retain the transport, refining, and marketing links with the transnational corporation will obviously be less adverse to the firm than one that seeks either to shift exports to different markets and generate new external connections or to shift entirely to different export crops and domestic food.

2. The mineral-export sector. This sector produces strategic mineral resources (petroleum, bauxite, iron ore) for transport, refining, and so on, in metropolitan countries by other branches of the transnational corporation, as in the plantation case. Here, however, production is typically capital intensive. Thus large amounts of profits and depreciation funds are generated by the industry while relatively little labor is employed. To the government, therefore, this sector represents a crucial source of finance for the development effort — a source that is even more valuable because it is being realized in the form of foreign exchange. Additionally, mineral resources are frequently strategic inputs for industrialization. Accordingly, the government may naturally wish to use whatever natural resources the nation has as the basis for an industrial development effort. At this juncture, the conflict with the interests of the transnational corporation is likely to be sharpest

because the firm itself has a global production system based on the use of the mineral resource. In other words, the national economy and the corporate economy represent directly competing interests for the use of the resource as an industrial input.[22]

3. The public utilities sector. Activities such as electric power, railways, and communications have a different significance for both the Third World country and the transnational corporation. In this case, the output of the industry already forms a strategic input into the national economy. Thus the industry's price structure, growth rate, and direction of expansion are of vital importance to both the rate and direction of development of the national economy. Moreover, the nature of this sector's activities are frequently such that the public utility companies have de jure or de facto monopoly status. This situation has two immediate implications. First, the particular company concerned has overt or latent powers of monopoly pricing; and second, the company concerned represents to the government the only means of securing the desired commodity or service at the price level and expansion rate deemed necessary for national development.

To the transnational corporation, the operation of a subsidiary in the public utilities sector of a Third World country's economy represents a source of cash profits, since the output is sold on the local market to outside customers. Furthermore, the subsidiary is a captive customer for the sale of manufactured equipment and "technical services" of one kind or another from plants in other countries. Such "sales" by the transnational corporation to its own subsidiary can give rise to as much profit as that actually generated by the subsidiary itself. Thus, the attitude of the transnational corporation toward the expropriation will depend on the way in which the expropriation affects these two interests.

4. The domestic manufacturing sector. Manufacturing activities that produce a commodity such as steel, refined petroleum products, chemicals, or other strategic inputs for industry can be classified as "public utility" activities for the purposes of this discussion. Similar considerations apply to these manufacturing activities as to the public utility case. However, those industries engaged in the production of items that may be classified as nonessential in the production structure, such as consumer durables, are subject to slightly different considerations. The production of such items is likely to use components and technology imported from the parent corporations and is geared to satisfy demands of the more privileged groups in the society. Historically, such

industries have not been important as targets of expropriatory action by Third World governments, nor have they been a major source of company-country conflicts. The potential interest of Third World governments in such industries would arise from more general, comprehensive policies of national planning for resource allocation, including the allocation of foreign exchange. Hence, expropriation in these cases is normally associated only with full-fledged socialist regimes, in which social ownership and comprehensive central planning is a matter of ideological principle. [23] The potential interest of Third World governments in these industries might arise from a desire to utilize their surpluses and their foreign exchange payments to parent corporations for inputs and technology for purposes deemed to have higher benefits in terms of national economic priorities.

The interest of the parent corporation in its subsidiary, in this case, is in maintaining the subsidiary (1) as a source of cash profits; (2) as a captive customer for the components, technology, and "services" provided by other plants; and (3) as a means of controlling and enlarging its share of the global market for the end product. The exact nature of the expropriation, of course, will affect each of these interests in some particular way.

There is a tendency on the part of academic and other commentators from the North Atlantic to regard acts of expropriation by Third World governments as unfortunate and uninformed aberrations of government conduct. The words "rash," "irrational," "xenophobic," and "senseless" are often used to conjure up an image of a lunatic who runs amok and destroys the very source of his livelihood. The frequent implication is that therapy, in the form of sound economic advice from foreign experts, is necessary. Moreover, economic development textbooks are written to include discussions demonstrating the value of foreign capital to the development process of Third World countries, and expensive projects are mounted to show the ways in which the interests of transnational corporations and those of Third World governments may be harmonized.

Hopefully, the brief discussion above and the other essays in this volume have helped to show that conflict between the transnational corporation and the Third World government is to a large extent structurally inherent in the relationship,[24] arising from the divergence of the structure and perspectives of the transnational corporation from those of the national economy. Hymer suggests: "Multinational corporations are private institutions which organize one or a few industries across many countries. Its polar opposite is a public institution which organizes many industries across one region."[25]

Consequently, acts of expropriation must be seen as attempts to resolve structural conflicts by transferring ownership of natural resources and other assets from one party to the other through the assertion of the principle of national sovereignty. Such acts usually have an economic rationale which derives from the needs of economic development and the material improvement of people in Third World countries. The motives are not only to capture surpluses generated through the use of the nation's natural resources and through monopoly market situations, but also to secure control so that the industry in question can be organized effectively to support policies of full employment, income growth, and industrialization. Except for cases in which expropriations take place because of attachment to socialist or communist principles, such acts usually occur after periods of dispute and attempts at negotiated settlement. This period can last for decades and go through many phases.[26] Moreover, expropriation occurs only after the government in question has taken the psychological step of assuming responsibility for production and marketing, with confidence in its capabilities and in those of the nation. In this sense, expropriation must be viewed as an act of maturity rather than one of childishness.

V. COMPENSATION CRITERIA FOR THE THIRD WORLD

The "fair" amount and method of compensation from the point of view of the Third World government can now be evaluated in the context of the industry concerned and the specific motive for the government takeover. The elements of compensation arrangements are many and varied, and their total effect must be accounted for in assessing their financial significance. Traditionally, the characteristics of compensation arrangements have been discussed almost exclusively in terms of the method of valuing the assets concerned and the promptness of payment. These are undoubtedly key aspects of the question. But other elements of the compensation package can have an equally important influence on the total effect. A more complete listing would include the following five elements:

1) method of valuing the assets;
2) deductions to be made from the agreed value of the assets

for debts of various kinds due to the state;

3) the time schedule, currency, and interest rate adopted for deferred payments of the agreed net debt of the state to the parent corporation;

4) fiscal regulations applying on any remaining equity interest of the parent corporation and the corporation's net earnings therefrom;

5) other earnings by the parent corporation from the new enterprise resulting from the "sale" of services (e.g., marketing, management).

1. Valuation. A fairly large number of alternative valuation methods exist, but the ones most likely to be used as the basis for contending positions are the capitalized market value, the replacement value, the depreciated book value, and the sales value of real assets. The capitalized market value is based on the expected profitability of the operation as a going concern, with an appropriate time discount factor. The formula used will be a price/earnings ratio or some variant of it. Usually, some figure agreed upon as the normal or expected annual net profits of the operation will be multiplied by an agreed factor in computing the market value. In this method there is an implicit view of the government as an investor making a takeover bid for the business on a mythical stock exchange.[27] This method was used in the "Chileanization" agreements between the Frei administration in Chile and the United States copper companies.[28]

The principal problem with this method lies not with the practical difficulties of making reality conform to the myth, but rather with the validity of using the profits of the enterprise as a basis for valuation. In natural resource industries, a portion of the profits can be ascribed to the use of and control over the natural resource itself and not merely returns on invested capital. In other words, they contain an element of what economists call "economic rent" or "quasi rent." In most Third World countries, especially former colonies, the argument can be made that because formal ownership of the minerals is vested in the state, the economic rent should be excluded from the valuation. Similar valuation problems can arise both in the plantation-agriculture case, in which part of the profits is due to monopoly control of land, and in the public utilities case, in which part of the profits is due to monopoly status in the market.

A much more intractable problem in using profits as a valuation basis is that the amount of net profits of the business itself is to a

213

large degree subject to government influence. Merely by raising its tax rate by a certain amount, the government can, for example, halve the annual net profits of the operation and thereby halve the "market" value. Government power to regulate prices can also be used to the same end in the public utilities case. Therefore, the capitalized market value method has a frail foundation when the buying party can unilaterally and arbitrarily change the factors that determine the value itself.

The basis of the replacement value method is the amount that it would or will cost the firm to replace the fixed assets it has lost as a result of the expropriation. This method, therefore, may be relied upon to produce a result which is generally favorable to the parent corporation. Like the capitalized market value method, it involves the implicit principle that the firm should suffer as little as possible financially — and, if possible, not at all — as a result of expropriation.

Third World governments are more likely to favor a method such as the depreciated book value used for income tax purposes. This method was proposed by the Guyana government for its participation in the bauxite-producing subsidiary of the Alcan aluminum company.[29] The calculation of the amount of due compensation by this method is based on the actual historical cost of the assets involved less the amounts historically deducted and written off against income tax for depreciation. This amount will be much lower than the replacement cost since the current cost of capital goods is higher than in the past, and since the capital is purchased at market prices before deduction of depreciation. Moreover, the equity of this method is supported by the fact that it utilizes the value officially and formally recorded by the transnational corporation in its books for purposes of its prior dealings with government authorities. The government can reasonably argue that the firm cannot legitimately use one valuation for the purposes of tax payments and then seek to use another (much higher) valuation for purposes of compensation. The practical advantage of this method over the capitalized market value method or the replacement cost method is that it allows for little dispute over the exact figure that should be used.

A fourth method of valuation is based on an estimate of what the parent corporation would actually realize if it were to sell the physical assets concerned. The use of this method is almost certain to result in the lowest possible valuation. Machinery and equipment will have, at best, second-hand value on the market and, at worst, scrap value. Lands owned by plantations are usually very large in relation to local land supplies; therefore, placing this land on the market will steeply depress the price. Land containing mineral deposits cannot be mined without government permission, and mining leases cannot be sold by one lessee to another. Thus, ownership of the surface area becomes worthless once government permission to use the resources of the subsoil has been withdrawn. An equivalent situation holds for public utility companies operating as legal monopolies. Essentially, this "sale" value of the real assets amounts in large part to a forced sale value in which the party who is acquiring the assets — the government — is not only identical with the party who is forcing the sale but also the party who can virtually dictate its own terms.

Obviously, this method will arouse the bitterest opposition from the companies because it gives rise to the lowest possible valuation and involves the most drastic violation of the norms associated with the sanctity of private property. Yet it must be pointed out that this method is the logical result of the application of the principle of national sovereignty and the right of the sovereign state to nationalize. A decision to nationalize is, in effect, a decision to impose a forced sale. Once the validity of the sovereign right to nationalize is recognized, the properties of a forced sale may be attached realistically to the act of nationalization itself. To put it another way, a forced sale value is no more unfair to the company than the capitalized market value is unfair to the government. Both methods involve the application of norms that attach to only one of the parties: in the one case, the sovereignty of the state; in the other, the sanctity of private property. If we speak of the standard of compensation for Third World governments, then, we speak of the forced-sale value; anything more amounts to a concession involving the relaxation of the sovereignty principle.

2. Deductions. Once the valuation of the assets being expropriated has been settled, the next question concerns the determination of outstanding liabilities due the state from the corporation. Such liabilities have to be valued and deducted from the state's gross liability to determine its net liability. A preliminary list of such possible liabilities would include:

a) direct liabilities due the community for historical expropriation and exploitation;

b) unpaid taxes due to a variety of questionable financial practices;

c) economic rent due the state as represented by excess profits;

215

d) employee benefits owed or owable;

e) compensation for environmental damage.

a. Direct liabilities for historical exploitation. This involves cases in which the state can claim compensation from the particular company concerned as a result of charges arising out of section II of this paper. Some companies (though certainly not all) that are the targets of expropriatory actions owe their origins directly to colonial occupation and conquest. Such cases will be most frequent among mining, plantation, and trading enterprises in countries in Africa, Asia, and the Caribbean that are recently independent from the European colonial powers. We refer to those companies which secured their initial position through either force or fraud or a combination of both, and which then consolidated and used their position to generate profits over a long period of time that were sufficient not only to expand their capital stock in the country, but also to remit substantial profits home. In such cases, there will be a question as to what feasible moral basis there can be for compensating the company. Indeed, the legal basis for compensation will also be questionable, for what "law" and whose "law" sanctified colonization in the first place? It was reasoning of this kind which led the Zambian government to offer what was, in effect, only a token contribution as compensation for the canceling of the British South Africa Company's mineral "rights."[30] By and large, however, the terms upon which most European colonies achieved their constitutional independence and their generally weak international bargaining power have militated against their taking such a "radical" approach to the compensation question. Nonetheless, it is an approach that could appear with increasing frequency in the future.

b. Unpaid taxes. A more widespread and general category of deductible liabilities is that arising where a case can be made that the company has engaged in financial practices that have illegitimately deprived the state of taxes. A vertically integrated corporation which "sells" inputs and services to its subsidiary and "buys" its subsidiary's output in effect determines the book profits of its subsidiary — and therefore its tax payments — through its pricing policies for such transactions. It is now widely accepted that this is part of the normal accounting practices of transnational firms.[31] Thus, a company can assign an artificially low price to the "sales" of its subsidiary.[32] It can overprice capital equipment and materials supplied to the subsidiaries; it can charge an unjustifiably high price to the subsidiary for patents, technical services, and management. It can supply capital to the subsidiary in the form of loans — which yield interest payments treated as tax-deductible costs of the subsidiary — rather than in the form of equity capital — which yields taxable dividends.[33]

A special case of unpaid tax liabilities is that in which the company has claimed an immunity from certain tax or taxes, an immunity the government does not recognize. The best-known recent instance of this was the case of the International Petroleum Company in Peru.[34] The government recognized its liability for the company's assets expropriated in 1968, but claimed restitution from the company due as a result of its allegedly illegal exploitation of an oil field since 1924. The restitution claimed was many times in excess of the value of IPC's expropriated assets, so that in effect no compensation was paid to the company.

c. Economic rent. Another kind of deduction which arose in the Chilean copper expropriation of 1971 relates to economic "rent." In many, if not most, Third World countries, ownership of the products of subsoil is vested in the state, and the foreign companies exploit minerals on concession from the government. It can be argued that the companies are entitled to a fair return on their investment in mineral exploitation, but that all profits in excess of fair returns are economic "rents" which are properly the property of the state. The Allende government in Chile argued that the rate of return on the copper companies' Chilean operations was substantially in excess of the rate of return on their international operations. The "fair" rate of return was fixed at 12 percent on book value; profits in excess of this rate were computed retroactive to 1955. The sum of these excess profits was found to be far greater than the book value of the companies' properties.[35] Hence, as in Peru's expropriation of the IPC in 1968, the companies' debt to the state was found to be in excess of the state's debt to the companies, and no net compensation to the companies was effected.

d-e. Employee benefits; compensation for environmental damage. There may be other possible deductions in these areas. The company may be found to be in debt to its employees — or to the government on their behalf — on account of contributions to employee benefit funds and other responsibilities such as construction of employee housing. Such deductions were also made in the Chilean expropriation of 1971.[36] A relatively recent category of deduction arises out of the rapid growth of awareness of environmental questions: it relates to adjudged liabilities of the companies for pollution and other forms of environmental damage. This was raised in the case of Peru's recent (early 1974) decision to expropriate Cerro de Pasco's mining subsidiary in that country.[37]

3. Time schedule, currency, and interest rate of payments. Transnational corporations and the governments of capital-exporting countries tend to emphasize the "promptness" of payment as basic to fair compensation arrangements. The ideal against which all other arrangements are measured is immediate payments in the form of convertible currency. Such a standard strikes at the very heart of the motive for which expropriation is undertaken by the Third World government. Because the expropriation motive reflects the need to nationalize the surplus and foreign exchange generated by the subsidiary for national use, immediate payment in cash will be either financially impossible or, if possible, inconsistent with the purpose of the expropriation. The payment would deplete not only the cash resources of the government but also, and more importantly, the nation's foreign exchange reserves. Third World governments normally suffer from a chronic shortage of foreign exchange; such a shortage is itself, in fact, one of the characteristics of underdevelopment. It is difficult enough to make cash payments in the form of domestic currency. Possible means include government borrowing from the central bank, borrowing on the local capital market from private investors, and increases in taxation. When the cash is in the form of foreign exchange, the method adopted would have to provide means for facilitating the availability of the resources in the latter form. This will necessitate recourse to such measures as cutting imports, trying to expand exports, borrowing internationally, and running down existing exchange reserves, all of which impose severe additional burdens on an underdeveloped economy. Indeed, as our previous discussion has shown, it is precisely because of such strains that a Third World government resorts to expropriation in the first place.

The standards adopted for Third World governments, therefore, will be based broadly on the principle of ability to pay. In practice, this means that some form of deferred payment must be used and that the arrangement will relate both the amount and the form of payment to the position of the enterprise after nationalization. In other words, the annual payment of principal and interest must be low enough to permit the expected net aftertax profit of the enterprise to cover it and leave something for the enterprise or the government to use.[38] Moreover, whether or not payments are made in convertible currency will depend on the expected ability of the new enterprise to generate foreign exchange.

The dimensions of the problem can be appreciated more fully by the following example. Suppose that the net profits of an expropriated company normally amount to approximately 15 percent of the agreed value of assets. Paying a theoretical commercial interest rate of 7 percent would leave an annual flow amounting to 8 percent of assets. Thus, if all of the profits are used for amortization and interest payments, it will take roughly eight years to pay off the debt with nothing left behind for the government to use for other purposes. More realistically, a Third World government works with the following arithmetic. Using two-thirds of the net profit of the nationalized enterprise for developmental purposes would leave behind a flow amounting to 5 percent of the value of assets for debt servicing. If this residual amount is used entirely for amortization, it will take twenty years to pay for the assets on an interest-free basis; if interest is paid, it will take even longer. If the agreed value of the assets is lower, then it will take a shorter time to pay, but only because the principal involved is smaller.

Such calculations assume that the enterprise — after nationalization — will continue to earn the level of profits it earned prior to nationalization. There are, however, many possible circumstances that render any model founded upon such an assumption of little more than academic value. Suppose, for example, in the case of an export industry, that the transnational corporation and its home government boycott sales of the nationalized enterprise. Or suppose that whatever the industry, the flow of components and spare parts is cut off. Profit levels may then decline during a period of dislocation while markets, production, and supply sources are reorganized. Such a period may endure for years. Would it then be reasonable for the Third World government to agree on compensation terms that assume profit levels that are themselves disrupted by the aggressive actions of the transnational corporation and its home government? The answer can only be no. The Third World government is put in an impossible position: the transnational corporation and its home government concede the right to expropriate in principle, but insist on "prompt and adequate" compensation, which is impossible in practice. To put pressure on the Third World government, the transnational corporation and its home government impose economic sanctions, which make it difficult for the Third World government to provide for any compensation at all. This is then used as further evidence of the Third World government's "unreasonableness."

The result is that deferred payment arrangements by the Third

World government not only must be based on "ability to pay" but also must be made contingent on the maintenance of "good behavior" on the part of the transnational corporation and its government in those areas that affect the enterprise's ability to pay. For all industries, this means doing nothing to interfere with the normal flow of materials, components, and spares to the nationalized enterprise. For export industries, it means, in addition, doing nothing to disrupt the maintenance of the normal export markets of the enterprise. In the context of the vertically integrated transnational corporation this means the maintenance, for a transitional period at the minimum, of at least some of the transport, processing, supplying, and marketing links between the new enterprise and its former parent.

A further complication arises in applying the "ability to pay" principle to industries catering to the domestic market when part of the expropriation motive is to reduce the price of output in order to service the rest of the economy. This could be the case for public utilities, industries producing basic industrial inputs, and consumer goods industries producing items for mass consumption. Expropriation may take place here in order to reduce the profit rate. In such a case the validity of this motive must be recognized in evaluating the enterprise's ability to pay.

We can now apply these considerations broadly to the main types of industries found in the Third World country. In plantation-agriculture, the main form of capital is land. Since this asset is non-transportable, its price is subject to internal factors and the government is in the strongest position to impose a forced-sale value. Since this industry is also labor intensive, the share of profits in output is likely to be relatively low. This requires an extended period of deferred payment, which may be shortened to the extent that the agreed value of assets is lowered, and to the extent that the new enterprise is able to improve profits by raising production and prices. Both the amount of payment and the payment's international convertibility will be partly contingent on the maintenance of normalcy in the external relationships of the enterprise. This would permit arrangements that might include delivery of the output of the nationalized enterprise to the transnational corporation as part of the payment flow. Such a device permits payment to be made in kind and resolves part of the marketing problem for the Third World government, as well as part of the raw materials supply problem for the transnational corporation.

In mineral-export industries, production is usually capital intensive. Since machinery and equipment are more amenable to international pricing, there is a higher floor to the forced-sale value, but since profits form a high share of the value of output, ability to pay is generally favorable. Furthermore, since the distribution of mineral resources between countries is skewed, and since time is needed to discover new deposits and bring them into production, mineral exports are more amenable to oligopolistic pricing by producer nations, as witness the case of petroleum and copper. Hence, payment periods can be relatively short and convertibility relatively easy to guarantee. Chile paid for the 51 percent of Kennecott it acquired under the 1964 agreement in two years in U.S. dollars, largely as a result of bonanza prices for copper. Zambia is compensating expropriated interests over a period of eight years by 6 percent bonds which are guaranteed convertible into U.S. dollars. In slight contrast, Guyana proposed to acquire its share of the bauxite industry by paying out of the future profits of the new company, and in the final negotiated nationalization agreement, payment is to be made over a period of twenty years at an effective interest rate of 4.5 percent. This reflects a lower ability to pay, due to the lack of a "free" market in bauxite and alumina, the currently depressed state of the aluminum industry, and the lack of oligopolistic pricing by bauxite-producing countries.

In both domestic manufacturing and public utilities, production is likely to be more capital intensive than in plantation-agriculture and less so than in mineral exports. The general level of the forced-sale value will occupy a corresponding position. However, since a favorable ability to pay in this case implies a price structure that is considered too high in the context of the national economy, it may well have to be revised downward. This implies a fairly long period of deferred payment. Since the industries cater to the home market, they do not directly generate foreign exchange and, hence, the convertibility of payments cannot normally be guaranteed. The transnational corporation, in other words, experiences a degree of exchange risk that is no greater and no smaller than the risk it experienced as the full owner of the subsidiary when it realized surplus in the form of domestic currency.

4. Fiscal regulations applying to any remaining equity interest of the transnational corporation and its earnings from such equity interest. When the government acquires only a controlling interest — for example, 51 percent — of the transnational corporation's subsidiary, the parent retains ownership of an equity interest in the operation. In such cases, the parent may seek to negotiate the

sale of various services to the new mixed company, such as management, marketing, technical services, and purchasing. In these instances, therefore, the net financial effect of nationalization — in reality, partial nationalization — is a result not only of the compensation arrangements for the majority share acquired by the Third World government, but also of the financial characteristics of the arrangements governing the transnational corporation's minority interests and its sales of services to the new company.

In some outstanding recent cases — Chile in 1964, Zambia in 1969, and Guyana in 1971 — transnational corporations sought fiscal concessions on their minority interest as the price of their agreement to the government's acquisition of a majority interest. Among the concessions sought were drastic tax cuts — or exemptions from taxes altogether — and freedom from exchange control and other restrictions. Such concessions may be given by the Third World government to secure an agreement by the transnational corporation to undertake expansion of the enterprise using government money or funds provided by third parties. The objective of such an agreement is to ensure that the total of compensation payments and earnings from the transnational corporation's minority equity are not only maintained but also increased relative to its previous earnings as full owner of its former subsidiary.[39] When tax rates are reduced, the Third World government, in effect, is induced to accept dividends on its equity interest (for which it is obliged to pay) partly in lieu of tax receipts, for which of course it does not pay and to which it is entitled as of right. When expansion is to be undertaken, the Third World government must either put up the money itself or secure the funds from international financial institutions under government guarantee. Such arrangements, therefore, while having the appearance of harmonizing the interests of the Third World governments and the transnational corporations, will probably be approached with growing caution by Third World governments in the future.[40]

5. Other earnings by the parent corporation. The provision of a variety of services to the new company also represents an important form of earnings to the transnational corporation, since payment for these is usually put on a percentage-of-gross-revenue basis. Under such conditions, the receipts of the transnational corporation for such services do not bear a direct relationship to the actual value of the services provided. On the other hand, as managing and marketing agent on a commission basis, the transnational corporation does have an incentive to maximize produc-

tion, sales, and prices. Yet the transnational corporation's incentive to maximize profits through minimizing costs may be weaker, as its only interest in so doing would be to maximize the return on its equity interest.

The value of such arrangements to the transnational corporations, however, goes beyond its financial implications. These arrangements offer means by which the parent corporation may retain various kinds of control over an enterprise that is nominally controlled by the Third World government. Such arrangements thus have the advantage for the transnational corporation of conceding the form of government control without the substance. The arrangements are also made to appear advantageous to the Third World government by securing the parent corporation's provision of a variety of skills without which, theoretically, the goals of the expropriatory action cannot be attained. Ideally, these governments should be in a position to retain only those links that are absolutely essential for the maintenance of production and profits, and only for as long as they are necessary. Transnational corporations tend to argue that if they are to provide the external links that minimize the risks inherent in deferred payment arrangements, the links must be provided in forms that are sufficiently comprehensive and long term to retain control for the transnational corporation.

The overall result is that transnational corporations are often willing to concede majority holdings to the government, and to provide external links to the new enterprise, only on terms that are at variance with both the financial and the control motives of the Third World government. As with the standards of compensation for full expropriation, the inherent structural differences between the perspectives of the two parties tend to be very wide.

VI. CONCLUSION

The considerations we have been discussing are summarized in schematic form in Table 12. The various aspects of compensation arrangements are outlined in the rows of the table with the alternatives ranked in the order of their degree of advantage or likelihood for the Third World government. The four main types of industry selected for this analysis are placed in the columns. The table is filled in by a general assessment of the extent to which any compensation feature corresponds to the interests of the Third

Table 12

Ranking of Compensation Alternatives

	Plantation-agriculture	Mineral-export	Public utility	Domestic manufacturing
Valuation				
Forced-sale value	Preferable	Preferable	Preferable	Preferable
Depreciated book value	Possible	Possible	Possible	Possible
Replacement cost	—	—	—	—
Capitalized market value	—	—	—	—
Deductions				
On account of:				
Historical expropriation, etc.	Possible	Possible	—	—
Unpaid taxes	Possible	Possible	Possible	Possible
Economic rent	Probable	Probable	—	—
Employee benefits	Possible	Possible	Possible	Possible
Environmental damage	Improbable	Probable	Possible	Possible
Timing of payment				
Long term	Preferable	Preferable	Preferable	Preferable
Short term	Improbable	Possible	Improbable	Improbable
Immediate	—	—	—	—
Interest Rate				
Zero	Preferable	Preferable	Preferable	Preferable
Nominal	Possible	Probable	Possible	Improbable
Commercial	Improbable	Possible	Improbable	Improbable
Currency of Payment				
National	Preferable	Preferable	Preferable	Preferable
Convertible	Possible	Possible	Improbable	Improbable
Fiscal and exchange burden				
Greater	Preferable	Preferable	Preferable	Preferable
Same as before	Probable	Probable	Probable	Probable
Lower	Improbable	Improbable	Improbable	Improbable
Provision of services				
Selective, at Third World govt. discretion, at "market" value	Preferable	Preferable	Preferable	Preferable
Total, long term, on percentage basis	Improbable	Improbable	Improbable	Improbable

World government as the expropriating party. The most advantageous arrangement for the Third World government is labeled "preferable." Beyond this, however, some slight differences in the positions of different industries emerge. Of the industries distinguished, mineral exports are likely to be the most financially capable for the purposes of compensation. They are, however, more likely to be adjudged liable to the state for past historical expropriation and for economic rent. Public utilities and domestic manufacturing may be the least capable financially because of the sensitivity of the remainder of the economy to their price structure. They are also less capable of paying in convertible currency than are plantation-agriculture and mineral-export industries, but they are also less likely to be adjudged liable for past expropriation and for economic rent. In all cases, the concessions sought by the transnational corporations with regard to fiscal and exchange burden and provision of services are not likely to be consistent with the motives for which Third World governments seek full or part nationalization.

This analysis has endeavored to reveal a number of points to bear in mind in evaluating compensation arrangements from the viewpoint of the Third World governments that carry out expropriations. First, countries whose peoples have been the victims of centuries of decimation, plunder, and exploitation are bound to approach the question of compensating foreign interests with a great deal of cynicism. That they contemplate compensation at all may be only in deference to international realpolitik. Second, the economic motives for expropriation imply certain specific financial and control aspects of the compensation arrangements that are consistent with such motives. These will vary from industry to industry, but as a general rule they will differ profoundly from what is considered "fair" by the transnational corporations. Finally, this profound difference stems from the wide divergences in structure, perspectives, objectives, and, ultimately, philosophy between the Third World countries and the transnational corporations.

Notes

1. No distinction is drawn in this article among "confiscation," "expropriation," and "nationalization" as separate methods of divesting foreign interests in property. "Expropriation" is used throughout the article in its generic sense — that is, state acquisition of a private foreign property interest for public use. The state action may either totally or partially deprive the alien owners of title

or control. This usage of "expropriation" is intended to avoid the ambiguous normative differences that these terms have been used to represent. For an excellent discussion of these normative distinctions, see S. Friedman, Expropriation in International Law (1953).

2. W. Rodney, How Europe Underdeveloped Africa (London and Dar-es-Salaam: Bogle-L'Overture and Tanzania Publishing House, 1972), p. 104. (Emphasis added.)

3. The literature on this subject is voluminous. A vivid account by a conscience-stricken contemporary Englishman is given by E. Morel, The Black Man's Burden (New York: Monthly Review Press, 1969) (first published in 1920).

4. M. Crowder, in West Africa Under Colonial Rule (London: Hutchinson, 1968), remarks: "Perhaps the most scandalous example of expatriation of profits earned in a West African country was the £2.25 million received by the Niger Company, and its successor the U.A.C., between 1906-44, from government mining revenue in compensation for the revocation of the Royal Niger Company's Charter" (p. 303).

5. Morel, The Black Man's Burden, p. 109.

6. O. Sunkel and P. Paz, El subdesarrollo Latinoamericano y la teoría del desarrollo (Mexico, 1970), p. 290.

7. K. Griffin, Underdevelopment in Spanish America (Oxford, 1969), p. 47, citing C. Clark, Population Growth and Land Use (1964). Griffin (pp. 19-50) provides a good summary of the destructive effects of the European impact on Third World peoples.

8. Ibid., pp. 34-41. "Europe's subsequent ability to dominate the rest of the world depended not upon her cultural superiority or economic strength but upon two technological breakthroughs: the construction of large ocean-going sailing vessels and the development of gunpowder and naval cannon" (p. 34).

9. P. Baran, The Political Economy of Growth (New York: Monthly Review Press, 1957), p. 145.

10. Adam Smith, The Wealth of Nations (New York: The Modern Library, 1937), p. 590. The celebrated economist went on to note that "to the natives, however, both of the East and West Indies, all the commercial benefits which can have resulted from those events have been sunk and lost in the dreadful misfortunes which they have occasioned" (p. 590).

11. Ibid., pp. 557-606.

12. E. Williams, Capitalism and Slavery (1944).

13. See, for example, W. North, The Economic Growth of the United States (1961).

14. W. Rostow, The Stages of Economic Growth: A Non-Communist Manifesto (1960).

15. John Maynard Keynes, The Applied Theory of Money (1930), pp. 156-57, cited in Griffin, Underdevelopment in Spanish America, p. 36.

16. Robert S. Browne, "The Economic Basis for Reparations to Black America," The Review of Black Political Economy, Vol. II, No. 2, pp. 67-77.

17. Ibid., p. 77. It is pointed out that this reparations concept "has focused exclusively on the compensation necessary to cover the costs bequeathed by slavery to persons now alive. The objective is to restore the Black community to the economic position it would have had had it not been subjected to slavery and discrimination. No effort is being made to compensate it for the historical costs borne by its now deceased slave ancestors in the form of reduced consump-

tion, loss of freedom, brutality, etc. Such costs approach infinity and are not calculable in monetary terms."

18. Ibid. See also J. Marketti, "Black Equity in the Slave Industry," The Review of Black Political Economy, Vol. II, No. 2, pp. 43-66.

19. M. Faber, "The Recovery of the Mineral Rights," in Towards Economic Independence, by M. Faber and J. Potter (1971), pp. 40-61.

20. This has, of course, already happened on a microeconomic basis, in the case of Peru's expropriation of the International Petroleum Company in 1968 and Chile's expropriation of the Anaconda and Kennecott subsidiaries in 1971. See D. Furbish, "Days of Revindication and National Dignity: Petroleum Expropriations in Peru and Bolivia," and R. Lillich, "International Law and the Chilean Nationalizations: The Valuation of the Copper Companies," in The Valuation of Nationalized Property in International Law, ed. by R. Lillich, Vol. 2 (Charlottesville: University of Virginia Press, 1973).

21. See generally G. Beckford, Persistent Poverty (1972, chaps. 6, 7).

22. The Caribbean bauxite industry illustrates this point. See essays 3 and 4 in this volume. An application of the expropriative motive in this situation can be found in N. Girvan, "Why We Need to Nationalize Bauxite and How," Readings in the Political Economy of the Caribbean, ed. by N. Girvan and O. Jefferson (1971).

23. An example of the kind of problem that can arise in this situation is provided in the following statement by Ernesto "Ché" Guevara, made while he was Minister of Industry in Cuba: "Coca-Cola was one of the most popular drinks in Cuba, but today it tastes like cough syrup. It has seven, eight, or nine — I don't remember how many — ingredients, some of which are secret. This was one of those secrets held by American factories: ingredients arrive with the label 'xz-29' and all the Cuban technician has to know is that he must put a certain amount into the mechanism in which the components are mixed, and out comes the ordinary Coca-Cola with the taste we all know. It was necessary to do much investigation and a substitute has been found, but sometimes we have to eliminate an ingredient that we can't get and can't make" (E. Boorstein, The Economic Transformation of Cuba [1968], p. 104).

24. Extended discussions of such structural conflict can be found in Beckford, Persistent Poverty (1972); R. Mikesell, Foreign Investor-Host Country Relations (1971); see also essay 1 in this volume. Mikesell's book contains a mine of information on petroleum and other resource industries and is characterized by its emphasis on the harmonization of country-company conflicts.

25. S. Hymer, "The Multinational Corporation and the Law of Uneven Development," in Economics and World Order from the 1970s to the 1990s, ed. by J. Bhagwati (New York: Collier-Macmillan, 1972).

26. See the many articles in Mikesell, Foreign Investor-Host Country Relations.

27. An actual takeover bid is usually prohibited by the fact that subsidiaries in Third World countries are usually wholly owned by their parent multinational corporations and their stock is not traded.

28. See R. Saez, Chile y el cobre: perspectivas de una nueva política (1965), for the method used to value the 51 percent of Kennecott's subsidiary acquired in 1964. Corporación del Cobre, Agreed Nationalization (1969), discusses the formula which was to have been used for the acquisition of the remaining 49 percent of Anaconda's subsidiary (the first 51 percent was acquired at book value).

29. See Hon. L. F. S. Burnham, S.C., Prime Minister of Guyana, "Control of Our Natural Resources," Address to the Nation, February 1971. This method was also used by the Zambian government for the acquisition of its 51 percent share in its copper mines and by a number of OPEC governments for their "participation" agreements with the oil companies.

30. The Zambian government contributed £2 million, which was matched by an equal contribution from the British government; the company seems to have wanted up to £50 million at the outset. It should be borne in mind, however, that what the government acquired was the right to receive the royalties paid by the copper industry, and not assets as such. Faber, "The Recovery of the Mineral Rights."

31. Indeed, it is such practices that create the opportunities for some countries to specialize in being "offshore tax havens."

32. See, for example, the case of Jamaican bauxite, Girvan (1971b, pp. 72-73).

33. This was one of the complaints of the Zambian government arising out of the operation of the 51 percent "Zambianization" agreement of 1969. See statement by President Kaunda, Lusaka, August 31, 1973.

34. See Furbish, "Days of Revindication," pp. 62-64.

35. It should be noted that, according to Chilean calculations, the allowed rate of return of 12 percent, though smaller than the companies' rate of return in Chile, was higher than the rate of return on their international operations. See Corporación del Cobre, mimeographed document (2 pp.), Santiago, July 12, 1972.

36. Lillich (1973, pp. 123-24).

37. See Financial Times (London), January 2, 1974, p. 8.

38. This was also used in the case of Guyanese bauxite. See essay 4 in this volume.

39. See P. Semonin, "Nationalization and Management in Zambia," New World Quarterly, Vol. 5, No. 3, 1971, 1; K. Griffin, Underdevelopment in Spanish America, chap. 6; see also essay 2, page 84.

40. It was as a result of such caution that the Guyana-Alcan negotiations broke down.

BIBLIOGRAPHY

Adams, Nassau. "An Analysis of Food Consumption and Food Import Trends in Jamaica, 1950-1963." Social and Economic Studies, March 1968.

Amin, S., and Widstrand, C. (eds.). Multinational Firms in Africa. Uppsala: Scandinavian Institute for African Studies, 1975.

Barber, A. "Emerging New World Power: The World Corporation." War/ Peace Report, October 1968, p. 7.

Beckford, George. Persistent Poverty. Mona and New York, 1972.

Best, Lloyd. "A Model of Pure Plantation Economy." Social and Economic Studies, September 1968.

Bracewell, Smith. Bauxite, Alumina and Aluminium. London, 1962.

Brewster, Havelock. "Planning and Economic Development in Guyana." In Readings in the Political Economy of the Caribbean, ed. by N. Girvan and O. Jefferson. Kingston, 1971.

Brewster, Havelock, and Thomas, Clive. The Dynamics of West Indian Economic Integration. Mona: Institute of Social and Economic Research, University of the West Indies, 1967.

British Guiana, Combined Court, Reports and Correspondence Relative to Bauxite in British Guiana, 1910 to 1917. Georgetown, 1917.

Brooke, Michael Z., and Remmers, H. Lee. The Strategy of Multinational Enterprise. New York, 1970.

Browne, Robert S., and Girvan, Norman. Africanization of Personnel in the Mining Industry of Selected African Nations. New York: The Black Economic Research Center, 1974.

Burnham, L. F. S. "Control of Our Natural Resources." Address to the nation by the Prime Minister of Guyana on Republic Day, February 23, 1971. Georgetown, 1971.

Chandler, Alfred D. Strategy and Structure. New York, 1966.

Chile, Departamento del Cobre. El cobre en Chile. Santiago, 1969.

_____, Senado. Cobre: antecedentes económicos y estadísticos relacionados con la gran minería. Santiago, 1969.

Comisión Económica para América Latina. Antecedentes sobre el desarrollo de la economía chilena. Santiago, 1953.

Cordova, Armando. "Notas sobre el desarrollo económico venezolano." Caracas, 1963. (Mimeo.)

Corporación del Cobre. Agreed Nationalization. Santiago, 1969.

DeCastro, Steve. "A Review of Guybau's Annual Report for 1973." Caribbean Monthly Bulletin (Puerto Rico), August 1974.

Demas, William. The Economics of Development in Small Countries with Spe-

Bibliography

cial Reference to the Caribbean. Montreal, 1965.

Encina, Fernando. Nuestra inferioridad económica. Santiago, 1911.

Faber, M., and Potter, J. Towards Economic Independence. Cambridge: Cambridge University Press, 1971.

Garrity, Monique P. "The Multinational Corporation in Extractive Industry: The Case of Reynolds' Haitian Mines." In Working Papers in Haitian Society and Culture. New Haven: Yale Antilles Research Program, 1975, pp. 183-289.

Girvan, Norman. The Caribbean Bauxite Industry. Mona, 1967.

_____. "The Case for State Participation in the Surinam Bauxite Industry." Paramaribo, 1970. (Mimeo.)

_____. "The Denationalization of Caribbean Bauxite: Alcoa in Guyana." New World Quarterly, Vol. 5, No. 3, 1971a.

_____. Foreign Capital and Economic Underdevelopment in Jamaica. Mona: Institute of Social and Economic Research, University of the West Indies, 1971b.

_____. "Making the Rules of the Game: Company-Country Agreements in the Bauxite Industry." Social and Economic Studies, December 1971c.

_____. "Why We Need to Nationalize Bauxite and How." Readings in the Political Economy of the Caribbean, ed. by N. Girvan and O. Jefferson. Kingston, 1971d.

_____. Copper in Chile: A Study in Conflict Between Corporate and National Economy. Mona: Institute of Social and Economic Research, University of the West Indies, 1972.

Girvan, Norman, and Jefferson, Owen. "Corporate vs. Caribbean Integration." New World Quarterly, 1968.

Grant, Cedric. "Company Towns in the Caribbean." Caribbean Studies, April 1971.

_____. "Political Sequence to Alcan Nationalization in Guyana — The International Aspects." Social and Economic Studies, Vol. 22, No. 2, June 1973.

Griffin, Keith. Underdevelopment in Spanish America. London, 1969.

Harewood, Ainsworth. "The Oil Industry of Trinidad and Tobago." Unpublished master's thesis, McGill University, 1969.

Hartshorn, J. Oil Companies and Governments. London, 1967.

Hiriart, Luis. Braden: historia de una mina. Santiago, 1964.

Huggins, H. D. Aluminium in Changing Communities. London and Mona, 1965.

Hymer, Stephen. "The Multinational Corporation and the Law of Uneven Development." In Economics and World Order from the 1970s to the 1990s, ed. by J. Bhagwati. New York, 1972.

Jefferson, O. "Measuring Economic Progress in Jamaica." In Readings in the Political Economy of the Caribbean, ed. by N. Girvan and O. Jefferson. Kingston, 1971.

_____. The Post-War Economic Development of Jamaica. Jamaica, 1972.

Kwayana, Eusi. The Bauxite Strike and the Old Politics. Georgetown, 1972.

Lenin, V. I. Imperialism, the Highest Stage of Capitalism. 1917.

Leoncio. "Chile: The Working Class Road to Socialism." Race Today, October 1974.

Lewis, Vaughan. "Comment on Multinational Corporations and Dependent Underdevelopment in Mineral-Export Economies." Social and Economic Studies, December 1970.

Lieuwen, Edwin. Petroleum in Venezuela. Berkeley, 1954.

Lillich, Richard B. (ed.). The Valuation of Nationalized Property in International Law. Vol. 2. Charlottesville: Virginia University Press, 1973.

Machiavello, Santiago. El problema de la industria del cobre en Chile y sus proyecciones económicas y sociales. Santiago, 1923.

Malave, Hector. Petroleo y desarrollo económico en Venezuela. Caracas, 1962.

Mamalakis, Marcos. "Contribution of Copper to Chilean Economic Development, 1920-67." In Foreign Investment in the Petroleum and Mineral Industries, ed. by R. F. Mikesell et al. Baltimore, 1971.

Marcosson, Isaac. Anaconda. New York, 1957.

Mikesell, R. F., et al. (eds.). Foreign Investment in the Petroleum and Mineral Industries. Baltimore, 1971.

Molina, Sergio. El proceso de cambio en Chile. Santiago, 1972.

Moran, Theodore. "Transnational Strategies and Defense by Multinational Corporations: Spreading the Risk and Raising the Cost for Nationalization in Natural Resources." International Organization, Vol. 27, No. 2, Spring 1973.

_____. El Cobre Es Chileno: The Multinational Corporation and the Politics of Dependence, the Case of Copper in Chile. Princeton, 1974.

Muller, Charlotte. Light Metals Monopoly. New York, 1968.

Muñoz, Oscar. La crisis del desarrollo económico chileno: características principales. CEPLAN Doc. No. 16. Santiago, 1972.

Murphy, C. J. V. "The Mellons of Pittsburgh." Fortune, October, November, and December 1967.

O'Connor, Harvey. The Empire of Oil. New York, 1955.

_____. The Guggenheims. New York, 1937.

Penrose, Edith. The Large International Firm and Developing Countries: The Case of the International Petroleum Industry. London, 1968.

Petras, James F., and Laporte, Robert, Jr. "Can We Do Business with Radical Nationalists? Chile: No," Foreign Policy, No. 7, Summer 1972.

Pinto, Aníbal. Chile: un caso de desarrollo frustrado. Santiago, 1962.

_____. Chile: una economía difícil. Mexico, 1964.

Quandt, William B. "Can We Do Business with Radical Nationalists? Algeria: Yes." Foreign Policy, No. 7, Summer 1972.

Radice, H. (ed.). International Firms and Modern Imperialism. London: Penguin, 1975.

Reno, Phillip. "Aluminium Profits and Caribbean People." Monthly Review, October 1963.

Reynolds, Clark W. "Development Problems of an Export Economy: The Case of Chile and Copper." In Essays on the Chilean Economy, ed. by M. Mamalakis and C. Reynolds. New Haven, 1965.

Rosane, Robert. "The Role of Demerara Bauxite Company Limited in Guyana over Fifty-Three Years." Georgetown, 1969. (Mimeo.)

Saez, Raúl. Chile y el cobre: perspectivas de una nueva política. Santiago, 1965.

Seers, Dudley. "The Mechanisms of an Open Petroleum Economy." Social and Economic Studies, June 1964.

Semonin, Paul. "Nationalization and Management in Zambia." New World Quarterly, Vol. 5, No. 4, 1971.

Singh, Sobharam. "Government Policy and Involvement in the Mining Industry." Georgetown, 1969. (Mimeo.)

Stamper, John W. "Aluminum." Washington: U.S. Bureau of Mines, 1973. (Mimeo.)

Stopford, John M., and Wells, Louis T., Jr. Managing the Multinational Enterprise. New York, 1972.

Bibliography

St. Pierre, Maurice. Industrial Unrest in a Guyanese Mining Community. Georgetown: Critchlow Labour College, 1969.

Sunkel, Osvaldo. "National Development Policy and Dependence in Latin America." Journal of Development Studies, October 1969.

Thomas, Clive. Meaningful Participation: Its Meaning and Scope. Ratoon Pamphlet No. 1. Georgetown, October 1970.

_____. "Bauxite and Nationalization." Ratoon, No. 2, February 1971.

Trinidad and Tobago. Second Five-Year Plan, 1963-1967. Port-of-Spain, 1964.

_____. Third Five-Year Plan, 1968-1972. Port-of-Spain, 1968.

Tugendhat, Christopher. The Multinationals. London, 1973.

United Nations. Multinational Corporations in World Development. New York, 1973.

_____. Economic and Social Council, Commission on Transnational Corporations. Areas of Concern Which Could Be Used as a Basis for Preliminary Work for a Code of Conduct to Be Observed by Transnational Corporations. E/C/10/1, 2, April 14, 1975.

_____. Report on the First Session (17-18 March 1975). Official Records, 59th sess.

Universidad de Chile, Departamento de Economía, Sede occidente. Comentarios sobre la situación económica. 2nd Semester, 1972. Publication No. 4. Santiago, 1972.

U.S., Congress, Senate, Committee on Foreign Relations, Subcommittee on Multinational Corporations. Hearings, Overseas Private Investment Corporation (OPIC), 93rd Cong., 1st sess., July 1973.

_____, Department of Commerce. Materials Survey — Aluminum. Washington, D.C., 1955.

_____, Department of the Interior. Materials Survey — Copper. Washington, D.C., 1952.

Venezuela, Ministerio de Minas e Hidrocarburos. Petroleo y otros datos estadísticos, 1966.

Vera, Mario. La política económica del cobre en Chile. Santiago, 1962.

Vuscovitch, Pedro. Speech to CIAP Subcommittee, April 1972.

Wallace, Donald. Market Control in the Aluminium Industry. Cambridge: Harvard University Press, 1937.

Wells, Louis T., Jr. The Evolution of Concession Agreements. Economic Development Report No. 117. Development Advisory Service, Harvard University, 1968.

Williamson, Harold; Andrew, Ralph; and Daum, Arnold. The American Petroleum Industry. Vol. 1: The Age of Illumination, 1859-1899. Northwestern, 1959.

Williamson, Harold; Andrew, Ralph; Daum, Arnold; and Elose, R. The American Petroleum Industry. Vol. II: The Age of Energy, 1899-1959. Northwestern, 1963.

INDEX

Note: Works and authors cited only in the Notes or Bibliography do not appear in this index.

Index

Index

Index

manufacturing
  domestic, 210-211
  growth of output in, 47-48
market
  oligopolistic control of, 14
marketing, state control of in Chile,
    53
Marketti, J., 205
Marowijne River, 129
mechanization, 39
Mellon family, 99, 163
Mexico, 15, 18, 80, 152
  Jamaica and, 142-143
  and oil, 16
mineral-export economy
  corporate imperialism in, 11-51
  dependency of, 12
  rate of expansion of, 46-47
  states with, 11
  underdevelopment of, 12
mineral industry
  in national economy, 43-44, 209-
    210
  wage rates in, 45
mineral resources, Third World
  capitalist dependence on, 190
  domestic use of, 197
  interimperialist rivalries over,
    190
  inventory of, 192
  political economy of, 191-195
  precapitalist, 189
  strategies, 196-198
  surplus drainage, 192-193
  uneven development of, 192
monopoly capitalism, 13-16, 58
Moran, Theodore, 67, 68, 79

National Bank of Haiti, 126
national economic system
  aspiration to establish, in Chile,
    53
  conflict with transnational corpo-
    ration, 41
  mineral industry as basis of, 12
nationalism, economic, 4-5
nationalization, 49-50. See also
    Compensation; Expropriation
  agreements, 140-143
  in Guyana, 174
  in Jamaica, 138-139

in Chile, 53, 87, 171
  compensation for, 180
  in Guyana, 153, 170-172
  international politics of, 177-184
  preparedness for, 169
  of resource industries, 4
  state right to, 183, 215
  strategy against, 194
  Zambian, 171
nationalized enterprise
  boycott of, 218
  equity interest in, 221-222
  maintenance of normalcy in, 220
  services to, by transnational cor-
    poration, 7, 222-223
national sovereignty, principle of,
    212
natural resources. See also Raw
    materials
  accessibility rights, 111-112
  industries, Third World, 5, 6-7
  reduction of, 43
  state sovereignty over, 8, 144-145
  utilization of nonrenewable, 5-6
neomercantilism, 17
nickel, 191
Nigeria, 7
nitrate industry (Chile), 60, 81
Nixon, Richard, 90, 91
Norway, 107
nuclear power, 191
Nuevo Trato, 65-68, 72, 76, 82

OAPEC. See Organization of Arab
    Petroleum Exporting Countries,
    150
oil, 16
OPEC. See Organization of Petro-
    leum Exporting Countries
OPIC. See Overseas Private In-
    vestment Corporation
ore
  reserve depletion, 17-18
  U.S. imports, 190
Organization of Arab Petroleum
    Exporting Countries, 150
Organization of Petroleum Export-
    ing Countries (OPEC), 3, 4, 8,
    49, 137, 145, 150
output determination, 27-30
output/export equilibrium, 27

Index

ABOUT THE AUTHOR

Director of the Caribbean Centre for Corporate Research in Kingston, Jamaica, Norman Girvan has been Senior Research Fellow at the United Nations African Institute for Economic Development and Planning and a Ford Foundation Fellow.

In 1966 he received his Ph.D. in economics from the University of London and then served on the faculty of the University of the West Indies until 1973. He has been an advisor and consultant to several governments and is the author of Copper in Chile (1973) and other works.